THE EGYPTIAN PATH OF LOVE

Katy Noura Butler

T0302995

First published by O Books, 2007
O Books is an imprint of John Hunt Publishing Ltd.,
The Bothy, Deershot Lodge, Park Lane, Ropley, Hants, SO24 0BE, UK
office1@o-books.net
www.o-books.net

Distribution in:

UK and Europe
Orca Book Services
orders@orcabookservices.co.uk
Tel: 01202 665432 Fax: 01202 666219 Int. code (44)

USA and Canada
NBN
custserv@nbnbooks.com
Tel: 1 800 462 6420 Fax: 1 800 338 4550

Australia and New Zealand
Brumby Books
sales@brumbybooks.com.au
Tel: 61 3 9761 5535 Fax: 61 3 9761 7095

Far East (offices in Singapore, Thailand, Hong Kong, Taiwan)
Pansing Distribution Pte Ltd
kemal@pansing.com
Tel: 65 6319 9939 Fax: 65 6462 5761

South Africa
Alternative Books
altbook@peterhyde.co.za
Tel: 021 447 5300 Fax: 021 447 1430

Text copyright Katy Noura Butler 2007

Design: Stuart Davies

ISBN: 978 1 84694 064 4

A CIP catalogue record for this book is available from the British Library.

Printed in the US by Maple Vail

THE EGYPTIAN PATH OF LOVE

Katy Noura Butler

BOOKS

Winchester, UK
Washington, USA

For Josie
Peter
And Janet

CONTENTS

INTRODUCTION   1

CHAPTER ONE   ANUBIS: THE OPENER OF WAYS   72

CHAPTER TWO   SEKHMET: THE ILLUMINED
                   LIONESS   91

CHAPTER THREE   HORUS: RADIANT CHILD OF THE
                   SUN THE THIRD LEVEL   107

CHAPTER FOUR   HATHOR: THE LADY OF LOVE
                   AND BEAUTY   122

CHAPTER FIVE   THE SACRED MARRIAGE
                   OF HORUS AND HATHOR   143

CHAPTER SIX   PTAH: DIVINE ARCHITECT   160

CHAPTER SEVEN   THE SACRED MARRIAGE
                   OF SEKHMET AND PTAH   178

CHAPTER EIGHT   ISIS: QUEEN OF HEALING
                   AND MAGIC   195

CHAPTER NINE   NEPHTHYS: THE DARK SISTER   215

CHAPTER TEN   OSIRIS: LORD OF THE LIVING
                   AND THE RIGHTEOUS DEAD   223

CHAPTER ELEVEN   THE SACRED MARRIAGE
                   OF ISIS AND OSIRIS   245

CHAPTER TWELVE   SET   263

INTRODUCTION

I had been developing and teaching a method of the Egyptian alchemical mysteries of sacred marriage for eight years, when I awoke in my bed at the Pyramids with a dawning wonder. Six-year-old Hasan lay sprawled, fully clad outside the covers, at my side. From the bottom of the bed, blinking cats eyed me hopefully, thinking of breakfast. Horses neighed outside, and the cries of the camel men calling to each other mingled with birdsong and the plaintive crying of baby goats on my neighbour's roof. They were the same sounds I heard every morning on waking, but this morning, they had a completely new meaning and a deeper, yet fresher beauty. Hisham was not in the bed. Last night was his time with his other wife; my night for the harem children and the cats – and important dreams.

I had awoken from dreaming a powerful experience of my mother's love. I closed my eyes again, trying to catch a glimpse of her, but she was not there. This time she had not even been there. I realised that I had not been visited by her; she had not been there at all. My mother, my dearest friend and sweetest companion, whom I'd always called Josie, had not been in my dream as *she,* but I had most certainly felt and been blessed by her love in a strength and intensity I'd never felt before, not during her life nor in the seventeen years since her death. The curious thing was that it was most definitely my mother's love I had experienced, her own essential loving-beingness, which somehow included her personality and etheric aspect, her definite 'Josieness'. But that personality, the appearance of her, had gone. It seemed as though at last it must have become integrated into her soul.

My father had died less than two months before. It was a clear and graceful passing for both my father and me. We had been greatly challenged in the months before his death, but had found the courage and clarity to acknowledge and forgive each other at the end. I had felt his soul fly straight home, and had had no independent dreams or visions of him since. I wondered if their two souls had integrated, and perhaps that was why I had no sense or experience of 'Josie' any more.

I also considered the work I had been doing recently with the Egyptian mysteries. During the period since my father's death, I had had to work arduously with students who seemed more difficult than usual. This had disappointed me at first as they were all from Glastonbury, with the expected spiritual background knowledge to properly understand and benefit from the work on Egyptian consciousness. I can bless them for this now, but at the time, I was pulled to my utmost to explain and inculcate the teachings. They constantly quarreled amongst themselves, seeming to seek self-gratification rather than self-knowledge. It was a real trial of strength and commitment to continue, let alone finish the course. However, finish it we did. On the morning of my dream, I had just recovered from a five-day period of exhausted depletion after their departure. On reflection of the past two months, I realised that the difficult students had given me the great chance truly to put the Egyptian mysteries to the test. The main ethos of Egyptian spiritual teaching is the integration of all levels of consciousness. Working so hard to explain these principles had surely instilled them more deeply into my own consciousness. Perhaps the integration of my mother's personality was part of my own integration. Perhaps the hard work and challenges of the past year, my father's death, crowned with the task of teaching unusually difficult students, had given me the opportunity to integrate my parents love into my own being.

The great love I felt in my dream has stayed with me ever since. That morning I began to see my life through the eyes of my mother's love for me, and I realised that all the powerful work I had been doing for the past eight years had brought me to this point of simple understanding. I began to see how the teachings I had been giving on the sacred marriage of Egyptian alchemy could be readily translated into an accessible path to loving and being loved.

Another contributory factor to my epiphany was that the night before I had given a session to a friend and Tarot student who had recently fallen in love with a war journalist. With his base in Cairo, he would spend four to six weeks at a time incommunicado in Iraq, in the heart of very real and present danger. It was the eve of his return and she was expecting him with a mixture of joy, relief and dread of her feelings spilling over and spoiling their relationship. At one point in the session, she said:

'He doesn't want me to love him.'

I said:

'Of course he does.'

She began to weep. I said:

'Nobody minds being loved. That's ridiculous'

She said:

'He'll leave me if I say I love him'

I said:

'Love is never a problem nor a burden. False expectations can smother love, that's all.'

This snippet came back to me as I lay in bed, looking at Hasan and the cats, and listening to the morning sounds. I felt a wash of loving tenderness for Hasan. He had been with me since he was four. We did not like him much when he first came here, but we love him now. He has become integrated into our family as a valuable and valued member of it. He came to live with us from a bad situation, to be with his mother and baby brother whom we had taken in from birth and all adored, and it was very difficult for everyone when he arrived. Then Hasan grew to be himself and we all like that person very much. He is happy and spontaneous and appreciative. I began to think about Hasan, and my Tarot friend with the war journalist, and my mother, and my father, and the difficult time I'd had with the Glastonbury students, and I saw a glorious connection. I saw how the teachings that were given to me, worked through me, and I saw how I could write them down for everyone. This time it would not be an esoteric manual on the Egyptian mysteries, but a plain and simple workbook on how to stay on the path of love.

Integration of Personality with Soul: The Ba Ka process

Since I experienced my mother's love as an integration of her personality and soul, and thus an integrated part of myself, I began to understand that love *is* self. As I experienced her personality, or 'Josieness' integrating with her soul, I understood that when this process occurs, after life, or even during it, the individual self becomes love-in-itself. This allows us to look through the eyes of love, and love is not just ours, we are its.

The effects on me after the experience were profound but subtle. I noticed it markedly when I first got on my horse, Habiba. She is a spirited Arab, who requires concentration and strength of will to ride properly, but the first time I rode her in the desert after that morning, she and I became one. We melted into each other, heart and will. It was like driving a Mercedes after a Beetle, and yet it was the same Habiba. She felt the difference at once. Her personality no longer got in the way of our ride together. She had integrated too.

Our personality, which is made up of our individual ideas of whom we are, changes from life to life, and indeed often changes within the one same life, but our soul-body, or love nature, is immortal. The personality itself does not love, but seeks to be loved. It acts as a mirror and a barrier, a magnetic force-field and a protective repellent. We may love other people's personalities, but their personalities do not love us. We need to learn to love our own personalities, because we ourselves, the immortal soul part of ourselves, have created them. The more conscious we are of our immortal soul the more true our personality will be. We will 'ring true'. Our personality will mirror and reflect our truest essential self, attracting our heart's desires to us and protecting us from danger.

Personality is created by thought. It is the thinking aspect of self, which forms it. Therefore, what we think, and who we think we are will be projected out into the world as our outward expression of being. Spiritual disciplines help to create real and positive thoughts of self, so that personality will be true to the soul. The more conscious of soul we become, our personality or 'ego self' will find itself yearning more towards, or more 'in love' with, soul, and can then 'marry' or commit to it in love. We need many lives, and therefore many personalities to realise ourselves through love, because our immortal soul seeks to understand how to love from every angle and perspective of individuality. This is what 'personality' means. In some circles, it has come to mean charm and vitality, but it means literally, 'individual person-ness'. It is ephemeral, and it can change. Personality can be the part of oneself that is remembered when we leave a place. It lingers for a while before it is integrated into the essential being, or disappears. False personality will disappear, but true personality will integrate. Ghosts are the disintegrated personalities of unconscious souls; they cannot love, but have no real power to harm.

The Egyptians called the personality the *ka* body. They understood it as being made of astral light, the etheric double of the *aufu* or physical body, which arrived from the soul's desire to individuate, and was kept strong and active by conscious thought. It was vital to be in control and command of the *ka,* to keep it aligned with the physical body by purity of thought and cleanliness of habit. When this was managed, the two bodies both physical and astral could then integrate with the soul or *ba* body, and a constant state of love-in-selfness could ensue. This process, known as the *ba ka* process, brought about the remarkable achievements in art and administration for which Egyptian culture is remembered and celebrated. Esotericists and alchemists termed this process of integration the 'sacred marriage'.

I have been working for many years with students and aspirants to help them arrive at this. When, shortly after my father's death, I experienced my mother's love within myself as this very *ba ka* process, it had many resonances and questions for me.

Is it possible to affect the integration process with a discarnate being? This question raised powerful and exciting ideas. Josie, who possessed a very strong and loveable personality in life, had been present to me *as* a personality at intervals during the seventeen-year period since her death. During the first ten years, she had been more or less a constant, helpful presence in my mind and astral state. Her death had been sudden and unforeseen, but its effects brought enormous change to my life and consciousness. It undoubtedly created a bridge for me to the unseen worlds from which I have since been able to bring spiritual comfort and guidance to others

During the subsequent seven years, after I came to Egypt to take up my work on the sacred marriage, I focused on understanding and releasing Josie. I felt love for her in my heart, but no need for her support or help. I rarely had 'visits' or dreams of her, but when I did, it was her words and personality that I remembered. I loved her, and knew that she loved me, but I never did actually *feel* her love. I did not need her and presumed that she did not need me. This free, independent loving mirrored itself in my relationships within the Egyptian village culture that I found myself in, and with all the students who came to work with me there. I was also learning to control and modulate my own personality in circumspection to the ethos of the village, and to take on the heart-centred value system, which prevails here.

The spiritual system which I found, combined with the strong beliefs of the culture that surrounded me, provided me with the understanding and abilities to be a real support to my father in his last year, which we enjoyed tremendously together, and helped me to be a positive presence at his passing. I felt blessed that with my remaining parent there had been time to prepare for our farewell. During this period, I had no particular sense of Josie. I did not feel that she was waiting eagerly on 'the other side' to welcome him, or that my father was in any way in communication with her. In any case, he had re-married a younger woman, a Soviet Russian atheist who was in denial of his mortality, and his conjugal energies were exhausted in reassuring and comforting her.

When he died I returned to Egypt to take up my work again. I was tired but at peace. So that when, after the challenging time with the Glastonbury people, in which we managed with tears and toil to effect the sacred marriage, I then actually experienced it as having taken place within Josie's consciousness, I was, although somewhat surprised, in a clear enough state of mind to assess it.

Immersed as I am in the Egyptian mysteries of life and death, it is not beyond my comprehension or experience to allow that 'consciousness' work can be done from beyond the grave. Where there is love and connection between the worlds, there is no reason at all why there cannot be a two-way traffic of work and ideas. The ancients themselves taught that heaven and earth, as the god-forces Nut and Geb, are in married love with each other, and rely each upon the other for growth and continuance. The idea was not new, but I had hitherto cautiously translated it in my teaching as the divine spark of spiritual energy (heaven) within each of us, descending to earthly consciousness to learn from its limitations. I had not properly considered that energetic work done with love from the earthly plane could have an effect on the evolution of the spiritual dimensions. I know that the Catholic Church teaches that prayer has a helpful effect on the souls in Purgatory, but had dismissed this idea as mediaeval and controlling. I now needed to revise it.

If my work with my father and the Glastonbury people had been the last hard slog needed in me to connect with what I understood to be the soul-level link between my mother and myself, could it also have been a determining factor in her growth and evolution as a discarnate entity? Was it arrogance to think that my work could have affected her being? Alternatively, was it narrow-mindedness to believe that when we were 'ready' we could receive spontaneous teaching from 'them', but they could not receive help and healing from us? Are we not all part of a harmonious cosmic pattern that supports itself and self- evolves? Is it not true that everything that is separate from us is also part of us?

After considering these questions, I decided to allow the idea of Josie's integration or *ba ka* process as a separate entity from myself, to be real.

This then raised another question.

Does work on spiritual integration, undertaken from the earth plane, help those on the higher levels?
I supposed that it must. Those who are no longer of the earth, but continue

to guide and instruct its children, must require some sort of feedback from time to time. As positive consciousness accelerates through the cosmos, it is met and matched on the earth-plane by its negative opposite. This is a sad fact of the dual nature of the density of matter. Since the onset of the so-called New Age, insights into the cosmic laws are getting clearer for so many of us, but so much is murkier, too. Fear and greed for diminishing resources are wracking this planet, and there is surely a subsequently heightened awareness of the perils of material existence from our guides and teachers on the higher planes. As personality seems to be gaining precedence in society over soul, those of us who are committed to integration with our higher natures can perhaps give ourselves an extra boost by realising that our work, which is a gift from the subtler realms of being, was given to us in part to help them too. An analogy here could be the Higher Mathematics graduate who takes a post-graduate certificate in education to teach in a primary school, and finds himself outclassed by the infants' skill with computer games. If he can transmute that skill, by wise and imaginative teaching, to application of the laws of mathematics, everybody will have gained. Our integrated consciousness could actually be helping to bring love through, from us to them and from them to us, to maintain the continuum cycle for consciousness to evolve. In an increasingly troubled and confused world order, evolved consciousness must be the way to prevent disaster and extinction.

Given that we have free will, the higher or 'inner planes' of consciousness that guide and direct our spiritual progress have no direct control over our behaviour on the earth plane. What we create here is dependent on our own values and desires. Inner plane guides and masters, 'the gods' of ancient Egypt, can influence our decisions, but only if we are prepared to take the time and effort to communicate with them. This cannot be done unless we work from the heart, or in Egyptian terms, go through the *ba ka* process, and we cannot trust the heart or soul-body properly unless we marry it in love to the personality. When personality works alone, alienated from heart, we make dreadful mistakes.

So that, as spiritual energy descends through our centres, making us more aware of our true individuality, and thus of the alienations of being incarnate beings, perhaps we have something to give to the spiritual realms. Something, which they do not have, something that will help them in their teaching to us. Feedback.

I concluded that it was probably more important than ever to commit to the work of integration, and it was safe and positive to allow for the idea of our earth-bound lessons and spiritual work as being helpful to the 'gods'. This compounded my decision to release my work on the sacred marriage to the world.

Sacred marriage

The idea of spiritual integration as sacred marriage is very powerful and positive. Nearly all of the Egyptian gods are happily married, or combined in committed loving-consciousness with their polarised others. They are all in love. The Egyptian gods symbolise archetypal levels within our own consciousness. When we can recognise these levels in ourselves, we can work to vivify our inner gods by use of the qualities and virtues allotted to them by the ancient teachings. We can also 'marry' them to their respective partners, thus keeping a constant relationship and dialogue going between our higher and lower selves. This way our highest purpose becomes aligned with our deepest desire; all that we are finds harmony with all that we are not, so that male and female, light and shadow, life and death, even heaven and earth become balanced within us. This balance, as in any marriage, springs from love and commitment, but in sacred marriage, the first commitment is to love-in-self. Love-in-self allows us to love everywhere, all the time, whatever we do. Then the world becomes a safer, more meaningful place for others, the inner gods, and us. Sacred marriage is not only marriage between the inner gods themselves, but also a marriage between them and us.

Marriage is dependent on love, understanding and recognition of the space that lies between the two partners. The credo of the alchemists was '*solve et coagula*'. This means 'separate in order to unify'. It is loving acknowledgement of the differences between partners that gives meaning and power to relationship. Loving this difference is the true task and crown of the sacred mystery of marriage. When we become aware that we love and are loved by each other, the gods and the Creator, we ourselves become conscious of our role in the divine plan of the cosmos, and can work to affect it through everything we think or do. This is what the Egyptians called 'magic'. Magic, or *heka*, was understood to be the divine thread that linked everything together. It could only operate through the true knowledge, which lived in the heart of the 'magician'. True knowledge is self-knowledge, because when we come to truly know ourselves from a heart (or soul) level, we can relate to everything else from the perspective of love. Then the difficulties we encounter become learning experiences and whatever or whomever we are relating to becomes blessed. When we integrate soul with personality, both our deepest feelings and our thoughts and ideas of self begin to love and trust one another. Then we are ready to release our magic into the world.

One cannot, however, just choose to operate from the heart without first encountering and strengthening the personality. Submerged or subsumed personality leads to resentment or even pathology. In marriage, there must be a clear sense of two individual personalities, and healthy respect for their differences. In sacred marriage there must be understanding and recognition of the definition between personality and heart; mind and soul; or *ka* and *ba*. Awareness of the *ka* is experienced in the solar plexus centre, and the *ba ka* process takes place in the heart. When personality is strong and true it will want to commit to soul, but not before. Soul is always committed to personality, but cannot be reached by it if it is not true. This dynamic between soul and personality is mirrored in love story and legend where the personality is illustrated as the heroic warrior or prince who must face adventure and peril to find the lovely imprisoned woman, or soul, waiting for him to free her.

There are three different levels to this love story, which was illustrated by the Egyptians in three different sacred marriages. This story or process becomes more intense and magical as it deepens and grows.

1. The sacred marriage of **Horus and Hathor**
   Conscious union of personality with soul. The *ba ka* process
   Solar plexus chakra marries heart chakra
2. The sacred marriage of **Sekhmet and Ptah**
   Conscious union of primal power with higher design.
   Aufu links with *ba*
   Body marries soul
   Sacral chakra marries throat chakra
3. The sacred marriage of **Isis and Osiris**
   Conscious connection of soul consciousness with divine spirit.
   Ba connects with *khu*
   Brow chakra marries crown chakra

All three of these marriages can co-exist in the psychic and spiritual system of the individual, but the first, the marriage of Horus and Hathor, as an integration of the solar plexus with the heart or the personality with the soul, is integral and the most important.

Before this marriage can be celebrated, a certain amount of background work and training must be undertaken. If we want our marriage to succeed, we do not approach the sacrament of marriage as innocent children, but as conscious and prepared adults. The integration of solar plexus and heart can only happen if the lower chakras are strong, active and free. On committing ourselves to the sacred marriage, we begin to follow the path of love along our own chakric system.

We can start by recognising the delineations between our separate 'bodies', as the Egyptians knew them. Then we can, by respecting their differences, integrate, or marry them to each other in love.

The ancient Egyptians perceived life as having five levels or planes, which they termed the 'five bodies'.

They are defined as:

1. The shadow, *khaibit*
2. The earthly or physical body, *aufu*
3. The astral, mental and personality level, *ka*
4. The heart-soul body, *ba*
5. The spiritual and magical body, *khu*

These levels existed within each individual as five 'bodies', each one differing in subtlety from the next. It was the task of the Egyptian initiates to be fully conscious of each of these five 'bodies' in themselves, so that the will of heaven, as *khu*, descending through the powerhouse of the emotional nature or *ba*, became thoughts, ideas and visions as personality or *ka*, and thus manifested into their actual physical being as *aufu*.

Throughout the entire on-going process of integration, consciousness needed to be maintained of the *khaibit*, or shadow body. This process is implicit in the spiritual practice of mummification, and of course, in the timeless presence of the Pyramids. Embalming was undertaken not to retain consciousness *from* the body after death, as sensationalist drama delights in portraying, but to retain consciousness of the *aufu*, from the more subtle realms, so that divine inspiration could flow back to earth, and earthly consciousness back to spirit. The Pyramids are a living testament to the practice of integrating celestial and earthly levels. Scientists are still puzzling over the secrets of their construction, positing theories upon *how*, without really considering *why* they were built. Contemplation on the perfection of their form and experience of the majesty of their presence brings deeper understanding. It is wonderful enough that they are here. Perhaps they are here to demonstrate that manifestation of the most spiritual ideal is possible on the earth plane. If the ancients knew the secrets of moving matter, they could only achieve it to the glory of God, and for the future inspiration of humankind. They could manifest the time-defying perfection of the Pyramids in simple stone because it was in the natural order of the cosmos that they should. Centuries have passed, and they are still living monuments to the inspiration of Egyptian consciousness, and the practice of integration. *We* cannot move thirty-ton blocks of granite without iron tools or the wheel. We can take inspiration from these man-made constructions – which point to the heavens with their four corners securely based on earth – to integrate our spirits, souls, personalities, bodies and shadows, so that we may accomplish miracles in our own personal ways and inspire others to do the same.

Definition of the five levels of human consciousness is still practiced today in Cabalistic schools. Here it is taught as divine energy descending through spheres of consciousness via five Worlds, namely **Aziluth** (*khu* or the spirit), **Briah** (*ba* or the soul), **Yetzirah** (*ka* or the personality), **Assiah** (*aufu* or the body), and the shadow sphere of **Daath** *(khaibit* or the shadow).

The integrative journey that we will be taking along the path of love awakens seven god- and goddess-forces in their spheres, or chakras, in a linear, upwardly aspiring direction from our physical *aufu* and its accompanying *khaibit*, to consciousness of our spiritual *khu*, integrating all levels and five bodies en route.

KHAIBIT
Fears and Shadows

The Shadow Self. The largely unacknowledged part of consciousness, which nevertheless has the power of 'locomotion and omnipresence'
Muata Ashby

As we embark on a spiritual quest, it is important to be both clear and cautious. There is great validity in the aphorism, 'the brighter the light, the darker the shadow'. In earthly life, there is always a shadow. When we are cast from the one-ness of God as a fragment of divinity encased in flesh, we are given the free will to ultimately return to that one-ness with full consciousness of earthly life and experience. We can err, sin, blaspheme and lose all consciousness of God, but the way is always there for us to return, as return we ultimately will. There are many paths and disciplines to expedite this process. Whatever path we choose, we always need to be aware, when aspiring to heightened levels of awareness and spirituality, that we are mere mortals with natural fears and failings. If we were not, we would not be here. As humans we have psychological mechanisms that, in order to maintain equilibrium in survival, will tend to blot out or change that which we do not enjoy thinking about. Consequently, these very human fears and failings are not usually conscious. If we do not actively seek them out, they misguide us into believing they are less than dangerous, or even not there at all. It is quite natural to 'project' them on to other people. These fears and failings, which are particular to our individual natures, can be thought of as forming themselves into a shape or 'body' of their own, into a dark picture of self, which we can call our shadow body, or *khaibit*. Although it is shadowy, it is very real indeed, and very powerful. This shadow body has its own independent power. It is subject to the physical laws, but because of its insubstantial, amorphous nature, can also travel with us to the higher realms. If we are not conscious of its constant presence, it causes us at the very least, to fail. However, the good thing is that we can learn a great deal about our higher potential from acquaintance with it. We can recognise our resistances to growth and we can find the love in or own hearts to defeat them. For fears, although they are always with us as we live in flesh, are there to be overcome by love. Finding the love to transform our darkness is the primary building block of spiritual development.

We are solely responsible for ourselves and our destinies; therefore, we need to be sharply perceptive of any inner motivations that are based on fear. As power is released into our consciousness through psycho-spiritual techniques and magical knowledge, it is critical that we duly recognise and lay claim to the darker aspects of our natures, for the more powerful we become, the more honest we need to be. The dual nature of earthly existence dictates that the more light we shed, the greater will be the darkness that surrounds it. Light defeats darkness every time as the light of knowledge overcomes fear, but true self-knowledge and self-love proceed from recognition of this darkness.

The Egyptians fully recognised the power of the shadow body, or the **khaibit**. The journey through the *dwaat*, or subconscious realm, was beset by trials and terrors, which the prepared aspirant had to learn the proper passwords and spells to overcome. This is analogous to the recognition of inner fears and the practice of spiritual disciplines which, with self-knowledge and faith, allows us to understand and thus overcome them.

On the path of love, we gain acquaintance with our *khaibit* body in the first sphere – the root chakra, the energy vortex of earthly survival issues, guarded and protected by the dog-god **Anubis**.

Fears, lies and shadows are the province of Anubis. He knows all the magic formulae to take us through the darker aspects of self-discovery, and once awakened and integrated, he will trot faithfully at our heels throughout the journey. His instincts are sharply attuned to any insincerity of purpose. He is there to encourage our training, witness our self-examinations, and help us find and re-member our truest spiritual essence at eventual and everlasting Paradise.

AUFU
The Physical Body on the Physical Plane

The presence of the living conscious physical body, known to the Egyptians as the *Aufu*, does not require detailed definition. It is enough to recognise that our physicality has its own intelligence, which derives from the physical brain and cortex. It is important, however, to acknowledge that a healthy physical system depends upon a sense of natural integrity where primal nature can be expressed with freedom and dignity. The Egyptians, who did not isolate the *aufu* from the more subtle levels, recognised that it could not operate to advantage if it was not in harmony with them. Physical well-being occurs when the self is happy in its body, or when the mind, the emotions and the flesh are all operating in harmony together. The body is happy when the more subtle levels are happy with it, and vice-versa. Low self-image of a physical nature often leads to self-destructive behaviour, such as eating disorders which are fairly endemic amongst younger women in Western culture, or self-mutilations which are, thankfully, less so. These problems often spring from childhood repressions and a lack of intrinsic sexual identity. Many fatal diseases are blithely described as 'stress-related' without any real guidance as to how to relieve the stress, often the result of the unconscious anguish of internalised anger and repressed joy. Regular expression of passion can do much to prevent these disorders. A raging torrent of tears, a good-belly-laugh, an occasional righteous explosion of wrath and, most especially, ecstatic sacred sex, releases all those powerful primal pent-up energies, which can turn in upon the patient, causing their physical systems to self-destruct.

This system places recognition of the *Aufu* in the **sacral** chakra, the seat of our primal passions. This sphere is the domain of the illumined, ferocious lioness goddess, **Sekhmet**. An elemental force for destruction, Sekhmet rules the joy and the power of healthy animal physicality. Queen of the beasts – beautiful, free and exalted – she represents the wildest most savage aspect of our inner feminine, or earthly nature. Destroyer of plagues and pestilence, she awakens the self to the power and wonder of the conscious maintenance of well-being. Knowledge and experience of her bring order and harmony to the realm of the body.

KA

The Astral Double and Mental Body: The Personality

Become the Ka of Horus and the Neters

Egyptian Proverb

The Egyptians perceived the *ka* in two ways. Firstly, it was understood to be the subtle auric emanation of the self, known as the *etheric double*. This is the astral body of the individual, which has descended from the spiritual realms. It is formed by the thoughts and ideas of universal consciousness in its desire to become an individual entity before it densifies into its material body or *aufu*.

The *ka* body has the exact shape and form as the *aufu*, but is of a more refined substance. We only glimpse it in other people or connect with it in trance, dreams or astral/shamanic journeys.

The other aspect of the *ka* body is the individual personality, the living part of self that communicates and expresses itself. We can think of it as the abstract personality, the body from which we express our individuality. This is the aspect of a person, which comes to mind when we think of them. Our *ka* body is made up of our thoughts and ideas of ourselves. It defines our ego, or concept of self. It holds our visions and our aspirations. It is the body of the conscious mind.

It is the part of self that is left behind when we leave a place, and subsequently the part that is remembered when we are gone. The Egyptians made offerings to the *ka* of the dead, which they depicted on their tombs in the knowledge that this was a sure way of communication with those who had moved on.

It is a very powerful protective force. The Egyptians depicted the *ka* as two raised arms connected at the base. This is understood to symbolise the protective nature of the personality. It is through control of this level that we can 'shed a glamour' to make ourselves noticed or make ourselves seem 'invisible' if we so desire.

A helpful way to connect to the *ka* body is to visualise yourself wearing it as a multi-coloured, shimmering, you-shaped cloak, which you can swirl about you to dazzle and attract, or allow to hang serenely in shining folds when you want to be quiet.

It is important to be on good terms with your *ka* and to keep it aligned with your *aufu*. Once you have visualised it, it is simple to recall it again with inner vision. If it looks out of line, you can make it return into place by making yourself 'see' it shimmering around you in perfect alignment with your physical body. If it seems dull or patchy in places, you can redress this by polishing it up. When the *ka* and the *aufu* are consciously integrated, we gain the faculty of control over our personality and the serenity of a healthy self-image.

As our journey proceeds, we become conscious of the *ka* body from the **solar plexus** chakra. This chakra, which connects us to our higher mind and individuality, is the power point in our psychic system of the god-force **Horus**.

Horus, as divine protector of humanity and the god-force of vision, intelligence and purpose, is a shining exemplar of *ka* qualities. With Horus on our minds, we can only prevail. Our personalities will shine and our sense of individual purpose sharpens with the clarity of assured victory.

BA

The Soul with Wings

The fourth body or level of being that we integrate into our consciousness is our higher emotional level, or heart-soul body. The Egyptians called this aspect of self the ***ba***. The *ba*, which was immortal and transcendent, connected to the *ka* body through the heart.

Fashioned by divine longings for self-realisation and unity, the individual *ba* descends as a fragment of the ***universal ba*** or cosmic soul consciousness, to which it returns when we finally become enlightened. Then the *ba* body has no more use for its *ka* and its *aufu*, and it discards them. When enlightenment occurs, the individual heart is judged as being as 'light as the feather of Maat.' This means we have reached the state of being in perfect harmony with universal principles of rightness and order. At this stage, the *ba,* having no more need to fragment into individual consciousness, can return to *universal ba*, fully conscious of the lessons of earth. During the process of reincarnation, when this sublime state has yet to be realised, it is our *ba* that decides how its next *aufu* and *ka* will manifest on earth.

The *ba* aspect of self is the first transpersonal body of which we become aware. When we connect to our *ba* we learn that it longs to direct both our personality and our physical levels to the highest good. It operates solely through love. It may be conversed with, because it proceeds from *universal ba*, but only if it is integrated with the *ka*.

The *ba* body of the individual *was* depicted by the Egyptians as a beautiful bird with the physical face of its bearer. Your *ba* can be experienced as an angelic part of you, which can enfold you in wings of love and fly you to dizzying heights of consciousness, once you have integrated and understood it.

This system places consciousness of the *ba* body in the sphere and home of the god **Ptah** on awakening of the **throat** chakra. Before expanding on this, we should look further at the process of integrating the *ka* and the *ba,* which has an intermediately level of its own, called ***ba ka***.

Ba Ka

Ba ka is a process that takes place in the heart. The heart – which was considered the seat of true self-knowledge by the Egyptians – in this sense can be thought of as our individual and personal conscience. In our hearts lie the deepest secrets of who we really are, and what we really want. However, we do need to *ask*. When we ask we are given knowledge of what is unequivocally true and right for us, but we need to open ourselves to the heart in order to question it. We can dialogue with our heart through regular meditation, prayer, and clear, loving self-examination. This will form a natural loving link between our *ka* and *ba b*odies which will help us to celebrate the sacred marriage of **Horus and Hathor**. The Egyptians called this process ***ba ka*** and regarded it as an 'impregnation' of the etheric levels by the spiritual will.

In the system laid out in these pages the *ba ka* process takes place as we rise to the **heart** chakra, and awaken ourselves to the beauty and love of the goddess **Hathor**.

Hathor, as principle goddess-force in the Egyptian pantheon of love-in-relationship and the generosity of the artist, helps us to understand the ineffable beauty of soul consciousness. With her love and commitment for her husband, Horus, divine protector and lord of the *ka,* she links our soul to our personality/mind levels through an open and loving heart.

Universal Ba

Connecting and integrating our *ba* body into consciousness, and gaining knowledge and understanding of our individual heart-soul, allows us a dialogue with **universal ba**. This means that we can gain access to higher levels of teaching available to us from universal or cosmic levels. As we rise to the throat chakra and the sphere of Ptah, we come into new awareness of a greater source of love and wisdom, which we know, has always been there. The essence of Ptah, as the divine Architect of the cosmos, can then become alive and active within us, designing and directing our lives to their truest potential in conscious harmony with the cosmic plan. Both the powerful hierophant within and the gentle teacher of the Word of God can be expressed by us into the world through an open flowing throat chakra, proceeding from our widest and most loving perspective.

From this perspective, we may connect back with love to the *aufu*, which our *ba* body has designed and loved. We can now celebrate the conscious link between throat and sacrum as our second sacred marriage. This part of the process is celebrated as the sacred marriage of Sekhmet and Ptah.

KHU

Indwelling Divinity. The Enlightening Part of the Spirit

The most subtle and magical of the five bodies is known as the ***khu***. We can think of it as our immortal in-dwelling divinity, or spiritual will, which is omniscient and omnipresent. It is the divine spark of magic and creativity that connects us to our highest purpose – and our highest purpose *is* to connect with it. It is the enlightening part of the spirit.

The *khu* body was defined by the Egyptians as being the spiritual-soul, as opposed to the heart-soul of the *ba*, but it was linked in love, or 'married' to the *ba*, and could only be accessed through the *ba*. This meant that it was always latent in individual consciousness, only to be awakened in those who reached full understanding of, and dialogue with, their *ba* bodies. Only when all the other levels were integrated could *khu* manifest into consciousness. When this happened, the person lived and interacted with spiritual beings, even the gods. This was the ultimate aim and purpose of the Egyptian initiate.

In this system, we may awaken to a sense of our *khu* body when we reach the **crown** chakra, the sphere of the Risen Lord, **Osiris.** When we reach this level, we are ready to celebrate the sacred marriage of Isis and Osiris. Before we do this however, we undergo an intermediately process of preparation and revelation called ***khu ba***, which takes place as we activate our **brow** chakra, and receive its revelations from the sphere of the goddess **Isis**.

Khu Ba

The sacred marriage of Isis and Osiris has a direct enactable psycho-spiritual theme. It is a marriage of such passion and intensity that it supercedes every love story ever written. Its theme is joy in union, agony in separation, dedication to love itself, and the search for meaning which eventually re-unites the lovers in spiritual understanding and truth, from whence they cast a loving light upon the world.

Osiris, who represents the light of the *khu* body in humanity, is 'dismembered' or dis-integrated from earthly consciousness. It is the task of Isis, rising from the higher emotional heart-soul of the *ba* with all the power of her magic, her grief and her commitment, to re-member him. On the path of love, the process of ***khu ba*** can be approached as a dedication to the sacred marriage of Isis and Osiris, when we finally open to the crown chakra, and gain consciousness of Osiris as resurrected and risen Lord.

As we rise to the brow chakra and the higher wisdom of Isis, we undergo a sense of 'dedication' as we prepare ourselves for our ultimate integration: the awakening to the *khu* body, and the crown chakra. This is a serious undertaking, which requires a special ceremony. As part of the process, a dedication vow is provided to honour the procedure and to help to focus on integration of the *khu ba* bodies.

The sacred marriage of Isis and Osiris is a celebration of our connection to our *khu* body. When this happens the light of spiritual essence motivates our whole consciousness, and we may 'walk with the gods', or learn to attain the highest qualities that they 'came to teach us'. On attaining the qualities of this sacred marriage, we can gain a sense of union with the Divine, which is constant and everlasting.

Diagram **Showing** the Seven God-forces with Chakras and Levels

KHU LEVEL
Osiris===Crown Chakra

KHU BA LEVEL
Isis ===Brow Chakra

BA LEVEL
Ptah=== Throat Chakra

BA KA LEVEL
Hathor===Heart Chakra

KA LEVEL
Horus===Solar Plexus Chakra

AUFU LEVEL
Sekhmet===Sacral Chakra

KHAIBIT LEVEL
Anubis===Root Chakra

The Seven God and Goddess-forces and the Seven Chakras

There are seven aspects of the divine on the path of love. Each one can be met within one of our seven chakras. There are three masculine and three feminine god- and goddess-forces, which form into their respective sacred marriages, and one unmarried guide or witness.

All principles, apart from Anubis who acts as the witness, have their masculine or feminine marriage partner whom they can reach for in love and commitment, once they are awakened and understood. As knowledge and power of the gods within are integrated *en route*, our vital energy and consciousness is 'raised' or released upwards through a seven-fold chakric awakening process during which these three aspects of sacred marriage can be celebrated within the self. By working to raise our energy levels and transform them through our chakras, we are also gaining recognition of the five bodies and how to integrate them.

The names and titles of the gods and goddesses in their chakric placements are:

1. Root Chakra
Anubis: The Witness. God of Embalming. Lord of the Shadow (unmarried)
2. Sacrum
Sekhmet*:* The Passionate Lioness (married to **Ptah***)*
3. Solar Plexus
Horus: Radiant Child of the Sun (married to **Hathor**)
4. Heart Chakra
Hathor: Lady of Love and Beauty (married to **Horus)**
5. Throat Chakra
Ptah: Architect of the Cosmos (married to **Sekhmet**)
6. Brow Chakra
Isis: Queen of Healing and Magic (married to **Osiris**)
7. Crown Chakra
Osiris: Lord of the Living and the Righteous Dead (married to **Isis)**

The process of encountering, awakening and integrating these seven sacred principles within ourselves perfectly matches the process known in Hindu science as 'raising the Kundalini.' This is a systematic activation of the **seven chakras**, or energy centres, within the human psychic-system. In this way, the god-forces themselves are experienced on seven separate 'levels', each one more subtle in energy, but increasing in love than the one preceding it. Thus, if we give each god- or goddess-level a corresponding chakra, attuning them to our chakric system's subtly graduating series of awakenings, we raise and refine our consciousness to the appropriate energetic level for each of our seven encounters with the gods. We can think of our chakras as being the respective 'spheres' or 'homes' of the gods within.

In this way both the seven god-forces and our seven chakras become activated and awakened together. Understanding and love of the different divine forces within us strengthens and grows accordingly.

As we learn to know and love these aspects of our indwelling divinity, and realise, through the myths and magic of the Egyptians, with whom they are intimately connected by 'parentage' and marriage, we are able to understand how these powerful inner forces arrive into consciousness. We also learn to celebrate how they relate to each other within us. We can apply the dynamics of their relationships to ourselves and our lives in order to stay on the path of love.

The three sacred marriages of the god- and goddess-forces, which occur during the seven stages of the journey, teach us how to love on three levels. Horus and Hathor teach us how to love ourselves and each other; Sekhmet and Ptah teach us how to love the world; and Isis and Osiris teach us how to love Love itself.

As we approach the final stages of the journey, and the third sacred marriage, we become aware that the whole process has been closely interwoven with the mythic journey of the passion, loss and reunion of Isis and Osiris, taking us though our own personal experience of the mysteries of 'dismemberment' and 're-memberment.' We undergo the whole process of love so that we might return in consciousness to our divine essence.

Starting at the **root** chakra, we awaken firstly to our divine essence as the god-force Anubis. This 'opens' and prepares us for the greater influxes of power and love we shall be receiving and releasing along the path. It also gives us recognition of our perfectly normal failings and weaknesses, which we shall need to hold awareness of during the journey. Anubis acts as our witness, and is the lord of the *khaibit*, or shadow body. He stays with us all along the way. Without recognition of our shadow, we cannot be reliable self- witnesses.

The next stage, taking us to the second chakra, or **sacrum**, awakens us to the primal passions of the goddess Sekhmet, where we become conscious of the power and dignity of our animal nature. Sekhmet is the lady of the *aufu*, or physical body; her issues teach us to recognise and love our physical integrity and respect boundaries.

When we rise to the **solar plexus** centre, we become aware of ourselves as the god-force Horus. This is the level of the *ka*, or personality, with its individual purpose, pain and challenges.

The lower three chakras are now activated and alive. We have gained recognition of the shadow, learned how to love and respect the physical nature, and have begun to acknowledge and strengthen the true personality. At this stage, we can prepare for the first sacred marriage. This happens after we have arrived at the fourth level, the **heart** chakra, and its corresponding sphere of Hathor, the beloved wife of Horus.

Hathor, the goddess of love and beauty, brings us to the *ba ka* process. From now on, we can trust the heart and all its workings. Everything we do will be blessed by love.

The fifth level brings us to the sphere of Ptah, the divine Architect and Creator god of Memphis who designed and 'named everything'. At this stage, we raise our consciousness up to the **throat** chakra. We have completed the *ba ka* process, and have integrated our soul consciousness into our living reality. We have prepared ourselves to make contact with *universal ba*, which has designed our other disparate levels. Now, from the throat chakra, and the light of Ptah, we must connect back to the **sacrum** to celebrate the second sacred marriage, that of Sekhmet and Ptah. This sacral-cranial link brings our primal desires in alignment with the higher design of our lives. *Aufu* makes a loving link with *ba*; soul consciousness can operate in the material world through our physical presence. Proceeding from heart-centred self-knowledge we can now begin to manifest our magic.

We do this to release our love into the world.

At the next stage, we raise consciousness to the **brow** chakra, the home of the Lady Isis, the goddess-force of revelation, intuition and higher wisdom. Isis represents the fragmentation of our *ba* body away from *universal ba*. The supreme gifts she offers to the world and the terrible losses she sustains illustrate the quest of individual *ba* to realise itself through love in the harsh density of material existence. When we both awaken the sixth chakra and realise the qualities of Isis into our being we are ready to receive our own revelations, or be in dialogue with *universal ba*.

Once we have integrated this level into our being we may complete the journey by connecting to Isis' husband, Osiris, in the seventh or **crown** chakra, and our indwelling spark of divine essence or *khu*. Integrating with our *khu* gives us knowledge and recognition of our truest spiritual self and constant communion with it. We achieve self- sovereignty. The upward reaching of Isis for Osiris, or brow for crown exists as a process known as *khu ba*. It represents the flow of light between spirituality and intuition, which facilitates true revelation. It is illustrated in the story of Isis as her supreme commitment to Osiris' re-memberment, and her constant communication with him, after she has 'found' his 'body', or integrated all the other levels.

We may at last celebrate the marriage of these two divine principles as a union between the brightest and most spiritual polarities within us. Our crown and brow chakras will then commit to and love each other continuously as the sacred marriage of Isis and Osiris. Divine essence will flow into our consciousness as intuition and wholeness: intuition and wholeness will constantly love and seek to be guided by the light of God. Spiritual guidance will be ours. Our love will be complete and everlasting on all levels. Like Isis and Osiris, we shall be able to rule our lives 'from Paradise'.

This sacred marriage gives us the ability to love and be loved by the higher dimensions – the gods, the angels and the ascended masters.

So we can see that this ten-stage journey of awakening the god-forces and celebrating their marriages brings a graduating self-awareness from the organic roots of our becoming to the spiritual power of our integrated self-sovereignty. As knowledge, power and love of our inner gods is integrated *en route*, energy and consciousness flow upwards from root to crown chakras, giving us understanding of our separate levels, and the desire to unite them in love. In this, we undergo the entire spectrum of psycho-spiritual experience from recognition of the shadow, through needs and passions, self-worth and sense of purpose, relationships, power-issues, losses and search, to eventual wholeness.

The chakra correspondences for the seven god-forces are as follows:

1. Anubis: Root Chakra.

2. Sekhmet: Sacral Chakra

3. Horus: Solar Plexus Chakra

4. Hathor: Heart Chakra

5. Ptah: Throat Chakra

6. Isis: Brow Chakra

7. Osiris: Crown Chakra

The Functions of the God-forces through the Chakras

As each chakra is activated and its residing god-force awakened and under-stood, consciousness of divinity within the self becomes alive. This gives us the space and intention for our most spiritual qualities to unfold and be released into the world. Meeting the gods in this way provides a workable and realisable structure for understanding, and, more importantly, manifesting their most powerful attributes into our lives. When we know how to manifest our most divine aspects of being, then our lives, like those of the Egyptians, will most certainly be lived in the constant awareness of magic and beauty – or love. All unconscious, unsatisfied yearnings, which cause disillusionment and despair, can be released and focused into a proper commitment towards unity.

Each god-force whom we meet on our pathway along the seven-fold system of the chakras has been 'placed' there by nature of its appropriateness to the 'energy-field' and level of self-awareness released by each developing chakra.

1. **Anubis: (Root)** *Guide and Witness. Guardian of the Threshold*
2. **Sekhmet: (Sacrum***) Protectress and Destroyer. Awakener of Primal Power*
3. **Horus: (Solar Plexus***) Avenger and Divine Child. Provides Understanding of Self and Purpose. Protector of Humanity*
4. **Hathor: (Heart)** *Provider of Love and Abundance. Giver of Beauty and Grace*
5. **Ptah: (Throat)** *Divine Architect. Releaser of Creative Power into Form*
6. **Isis: (Brow)** *Magician and Healer. Revealer of the Divine Plan*
7. **Osiris: (Crown)** *Sovereign Ruler. Resurrected and Risen Lord. Gives Re-memberment of Spiritual Self*

THREE SACRED MARRIAGES
Anubis. The Witness
Root (first chakra)
Horus and Hathor
Solar Plexus and Heart (third and fourth chakras)
Sekhmet and Ptah
Throat and Sacrum (fifth and second chakras)
Isis and Osiris
Brow and Crown (sixth and seventh chakras)

We can see that energy released from the third and fourth chakras, namely solar plexus and heart (as **Horus a**nd **Hathor**), can be said to be potentially linked or 'married' within us. The same can be said for the second and fifth chakras, sacrum and throat (as **Sekhmet** and **Ptah**), and the sixth and seventh, brow and crown (as **Isis** and **Osiris**). Anubis in the root chakra is unmarried; he conducts the journey and witnesses the commitments and celebrations.

Sacred Marriage as Levels of Initiation

Each sacred marriage marks a stage in our spiritual development where we become aware of more sensitive and powerful levels of our consciousness emerging and synthesising. The path of love, however, requires commitment and dedication. It is through the application and use of virtue that we keep ourselves upon it. Spiritual exercises, guided meditations and magical techniques are provided within these pages as preparation and support, but it is the qualities of the god-forces themselves that we need to emulate in order to live in love and grace.

Each god- or goddess-force in its corresponding chakra has itself seven chakric levels – to each of which this book ascribes an essential gift or virtue, which we can find within ourselves. To put it simply, there are seven god-forces and each god-force has seven internal chakras. Each of those internal chakras has a special quality or virtue particular and appropriate to the god-force that emanates from it. In order to attain recognition and knowledge of our inner gods, all we have to do is to follow the system by realising and expressing those qualities and virtues. Then the gods become real to us, for us, and we become them in ourselves. We assume the divine qualities and attributes of each god-force on every level of our selves from our most primal security needs at the root, to our transcendent spiritual understanding at the crown.

When we arrive at the levels where the sacred marriages take place, we are then prepared to combine the chakric qualities of the 'bride' and 'groom' into the spiritual 'wedding gifts', or gifts of the higher consciousness, which transform our lives and the lives of those we connect with.

THE CHAKRAS

The word 'chakra' is actually a Sanskrit word, meaning 'wheel'. We can imagine these seven 'wheels' as integral cogs in the machinery of our psychic system, or outwardly spinning 'wheels of light'. They are vortices, which connect us through our actual physical bodies to the divine rays of the cosmos. In Egyptian thought, these divine rays were the gods, whom they termed *neters*. We can understand each chakra or 'wheel' to mean a subtle vehicle within ourselves, which conveys us home to the power and beauty of the immanent god-forces. The Egyptians, with their highly symbolic hieroglyphic language, called the chakras the 'seven unalterable or ineffable' powers', meaning that, like the stars and the gods, they were fixed and immutable. Like any other vehicle, the chakras do not work on their own. They need to be motivated. Their 'fuel' is our own consciousness.

In the human body, they are located at seven intervals along the spine, facilitating the passage of a two-way flow of vital force, of both earth-power from 'below' and spiritual energy from 'above'. Hindu science refers to this as force as *prana* and Chinese philosophy as *chi*. The Egyptians had different names for this power as it passed through the chakras, linking consciousness to the different divine forces. In the lower centres it was known as *sekhem* or 'dynamic personal power'. When it issued as communicative magic from the throat, it was referred to as *sa* or 'breath of life'. The power of *sekhem* correlates to the Hindu *Kundalini,* or Shakti power, which is visualised as a coiled ser pent asleep in the sacral chakra of the unawakened individual. Through seriously applied meditational techniques, *sekhem* power could be awakened, raised and integrated with the *sa* to manifest power and goodness in the world. This process is clearly symbolised by the sacred marriage of Sekhmet and Ptah. The *uraeus* crown, with its erect serpent's head, worn by the ancient Egyptian initiates, demonstrated that its wearer had 'raised' and transformed their awakened Kundalini power, or raw sexual energy, and had control over it for the common good.

The ancients visualised the chakras as seven closed flower buds; the rose, or more usually the lotus-flower, which through loving motivation, unfurled to release their sacred essences through the system of the individual into the cosmos.

Each chakra has its own particular function, colour, body part, perfume and level of consciousness that correspond to the god-forces who 'reside' there. Auric colours, which can be seen clairvoyantly or 'felt' by sensitives, are emanations produced by activated, 'open' chakras. When a person emanates particular colours, it is usually an indication of the levels of consciousness they are proceeding from at that time. The brighter and clearer the hues, the more conscious of those levels the individual is, and thus the more active in application of their corresponding gifts and qualities. Dull muddy hues without much 'light' behind them indicate that they have unconscious or 'uncommitted' relationships to the levels and functions of their chakras.

Root Chakra

Consciousness:	sense of being an organism
Issues:	survival, security and growth
Colour:	red
Perfume:	amber
Physical placement:	between the legs.
God-force:	Anubis

Sacral Chakra

Consciousness:	sense of being a male or female animal
Issues:	primal creativity, sexuality
Colour:	orange
Perfume:	musk, patchouli
Physical placement:	spleen, lower belly
God-force:	Sekhmet

Solar Plexus Chakra:

Consciousness:	sense of being a human individual
Issues:	intelligence, courage, sense of self

Colour:	golden-yellow
Perfume:	jasmine; neroli
Physical placement:	centre of the body
God-force:	Horus

Heart Chakra

Consciousness:	sense of being part of humanity
Issues:	love, sharing
Colour:	green, rose-pink
Perfume:	rose
Physical placement:	the heart
God-force:	Hathor

Throat Chakra:

Consciousness:	sense of being part of the divine plan
Issues:	communication, self-expression
Colour:	clear blue
Perfume:	lavender
Physical placement:	throat
God-force:	Ptah

Brow Chakra:

Consciousness:	sense of spiritual self
Issues:	intuition, higher wisdom
Colour:	violet
Perfume:	sandalwood, violet
Physical placement:	middle of the brow, 'third eye'
God-force:	Isis

Crown Chakra:

Consciousness:	sense of being part of the Oneness of God

Issues:	spiritual connection, integration
Colour:	diamond white, spectrum
Perfume:	lotus flower
Physical placement:	top of the head
God-force:	Osiris

The Seven Power Points. The Spheres of the Gods

It was an integral practice of the Egyptians to consecrate different parts and areas of the body to their different *neters*. There were in fact god-forces and spiritual attributes for every part of the living body. The limbs, vital organs, eyes, tongue, head, bones, belly, and especially the heart, were all perceived to have their own animating principles. Much can be found in the '*Book of the Dead*' and the *Pyramid Texts* to support this. Jeremy Naydlor in his excellent book *Temple of the Cosmos* posits that 'it is now necessary to go further, and seriously consider that psychic attributes were experienced [by them] as 'situated' in various parts of the body'.

This belief gave rise to understanding of seven energy fields or 'spheres' within the physical/psychic system where it is possible to locate and experience the separate god-forces named in this book, namely the 'seven ineffable powers' or chakras of the Egyptians. By experiencing the different god-forces on a chakric path, each sacred experience becomes a preparation for the next, until, at the crown and pinnacle of our journey we are able to achieve the Crown of Osiris, and 're-member' our truest and most spiritual selves.

The Seven Ineffable Powers

One…Sefekht	Root Chakra
Two…Te	Sacrum
Three…Ab	Solar Plexus
Four…Heper	Heart
Five…Sekhem	Throat
Six…Mer	Brow

Seven...Ikh   Crown

Root Chakra

The first chakra, *Sefert* to the Egyptians, is referred to as the **root** or base chakra. This first energy centre is situated in the body at the absolute base of the spine. In the human organic system, it can be experienced as lying between the rectum and the sexual organs. As the chakra closest to the ground, it is the vortex for connection to earth-power, and is therefore the centre where we experience consciousness of ourselves as living growing organisms on the surface of the Earth. If we feel insecure – 'ungrounded' – or lose awareness of our physicality it is probably because our root chakra has become sluggish or dormant.

Its colour is a bright ruby-red, the colour of flowing blood. The essential oils and perfumes, which help to awaken the root chakra, are the warming and 'grounding' *amber* and the richly organic smelling *vetivert.*

Issues which emerge for us when we undertake work on the root chakra are those of *security, survival* and *growth*. We can help to activate our root chakra by concentrating on the mighty powers of earth below us, and claiming them for our own. Visualising glowing red light flowing up from the centre of Earth through our feet and legs into our root, nourishing and warming it, will help to make us feel safe and connected. We are all children of Earth and creatures of form. As organic beings, we have an inalienable right to energetic nourishment from its source to empower our presence on its surface where we belong. A strong, well-activated root chakra promotes the physical vigour that brings security and confidence of survival.

Because our physical organic system is apparently ephemeral and transitory, the root chakra is also the domain of darker aspects of blood and survival. If energy is blocked in its flow upwards towards the higher centres, it can cause mindless greed and the tyranny of unrestrained growth. Nature, we are told is 'red in tooth and claw', but awareness of the bright ruby-red of our root chakra, consciously activated, will allow us to draw upon those violent forces of nature to sustain our growth, in constant mindfulness of the shadow of death.

The god-force whom we encounter when we activate the root chakra is the dog-god **Anubis**. The Egyptians honoured him as the god of embalming, the guardian of thresholds and the conductor of souls on the journey towards Paradise. He is the bastard son of Osiris and Nephthys. Conceived by an adulterous deception on the part of his mother Nephthys, the dark sister of Isis, he nevertheless grows to become a great support to both his mother and his aunt in their trials and agonising quest to find the missing parts of Osiris which have been dismembered and scattered by the agents of Set, his foster-father and real uncle. When they eventually re-member Osiris, who represents the disconnected parts of the spiritual self on earth, the gods confer upon Anubis the title of God of Embalming. He presides at the mummification of Osiris, being instrumental in the order that Osirian consciousness always be maintained on earth *(see the story of Anubis p72)*.

Containing both the brightness of his true father Osiris, and the darkness and deception of his mother Nephthys within him, Anubis personifies both the light and the shadow principles of the psyche. His half- animal, half-god nature allows him free passage between the worlds, and, as such, he represents that aspect of our self, which can travel from one level of consciousness to the next.

Anubis represents our shadow self, our divine animal nature, or 'instinct', and can therefore be our guide and protector on the journey of awakening the chakras towards full integration of self or Osiris consciousness.

The priesthood of Anubis was primarily concerned with the processes of mummification and embalming; these arts were held to preserve the physical body from decay and dissolution, so that the spirit might still retain consciousness of it from the unseen realms. Their other main function was to perform the ritual known as the 'opening of the mouth', which released the '*ka*' or etheric body from the dead person in order that it might begin its journey through the perils of the *dwaat* or underworld, until it reached Osiris in Paradise. Anubis conducts us throughout our entire journey from its inception in the deepest, most organic aspect of our being to the 'light of paradise' at its crown. His dual aspect of light and shadow gives him the impartiality to witness the weighing of the Heart in the 'halls of judgment', or give us truthful self-assessment on our inner journeyings. And as the lord of death and mummification, he 'rules' our organic consciousness which is situated in the root chakra.

Sacral Chakra

The second chakra or **sacrum** was known to the Egyptians as *Tekh*. This centre, situated in the belly just above the reproductive organs, is the seat of pro-regenerative power and sexuality. Sometimes referred to as the 'spleen', it is the vortex that links us to primal creative forces such as passion, joy and wrath. The sacrum is the vehicle for our animal nature to express itself naturally and freely, and is considered to be the chakra where the first 'division' or sorting out process occurs. It is here that we derive consciousness of ourselves as either male or female mammals.

A well-activated sacrum gives us all the animal vitality, including a healthy sex-drive, which we need in order to draw upon our natural creative/destructive energies with freedom and lack of inhibition. We can recognise this centre as the source of both anger and joy, and thus be able to release both appropriately without repression or fear of reprisals. As a 'lower' or more primal centre, its concerns are with the more primitive aspects of our being, which are primary motivating factors behind any real 'magical' work or valuable creative achievement. The sacrum is the seat of the intrinsic power and majesty of the individual.

If we feel depressed, apathetic or preoccupied with self-doubt, and have a correspondingly low sex-drive, this can very often be the result of a blocked or sluggish sacrum.

Its colour is a brilliant flame-orange. We can help to activate the sacral chakra by visualising ourselves in flame-coloured light drawn up from the very crucible of Earth. Then we can experience the slumbering powers of our dormant animal nature opening to its warmth. As energy rises from root to sacrum, our consciousness rises from the organic to the animal nature, and the ruby-red light of the root chakra, flowing upwards into the sacrum, will brighten, refining itself into a clear bright orange colour which heats the belly and 'fires' us to action. Concentrating the body on basic rhythm in drumming and dancing will help to awaken us to the power of the sacrum. Egyptian belly dancing in particular is an excellent technique, or the joyously controlled Sufic whirling, which admittedly takes a little more practice.

As animals, we are born with basic territorial and boundary needs, and it is from the sacrum that the instinctual boundaries of the individual are formed. Sexual choice, self-respect and freedom of primal self-expression are the most important reasons for these boundaries; knowledge and preservation of them one of the functions of the awakened sacrum.

The essential oil that helps to animate the sacrum is the aphrodisiac *musk.* This is a powerful 'animal' perfume, which has a direct effect on blocked sexual energies or repressed anger. I find it interesting that it is used in many Sufi shrines in Egypt where love and passion for God are expressed through dance and music. If *musk* is not available, a very small amount of *patchouli* will serve instead.

The goddess-force, whom we meet when we activate the second chakra or sacrum, is the savage and illumined Lioness **Sekhmet**.

Sekhmet, as the most primary, unrefined aspect of the feminine principle in the Egyptian pantheon, is the guardian of all our sacral issues such as territoriality, primal passion, self-respect and raw power. As queen of the beasts, she represents the untamed forces of vitality and sexuality, which exist in our animal nature. Moreover, as roamer and ruler of the desert wastelands, she is also a formidable enemy and an unrivalled mistress of destruction. She is, however, the un-transformed aspect of Hathor, the goddess of love-in-relationship: it is important to honour her as the Egyptians did, and understand that fully awakened Sekhmet consciousness is integral to the maintenance of strong healthy relationships (*see the story of Sekhmet p.76*).

One of Sekhmet's titles is 'Flaming One', which attributes her power to the fiery sacral colour. Two others are 'Ruler of Serpents and Dragons' and 'Great Serpent on the Head of her Father', both allusions to the Kundalini energy, which uncoils in the sacrum, eventually reaching transformation at the brow.

Her magic was considered very powerful by the ancients. Married to Ptah, one of the major Creator gods, she can be thought of as the raw 'earth magic' upon which he draws to form his creations and oversee their construction and maintenance. She was also named Protectress of the Divine Order, which gives her the sacral aspects of 'sorting out' the menacing from the benign and guarding and defending the boundaries of the self.

Robert Masters who has written extensively on the mysteries of Sekhmet in his book *The Goddess Sekhmet* says:

A Goddess of Wrath, Sekhmet retaliates with total savagery whenever she or her allies are attacked or provoked in some way. However, although She may seem to welcome the opportunity to respond to aggression, there is no evidence of Her ever initiating or provoking conflict. Her great power is dedicated to righteous ends, and it is because of Her power that morally correct but destructive tasks are made Hers.

However, she is also recognised as an ecstatic force, a bringer of joys and jubilation. Not only an exponent of righteous wrath, but of its equal opposite, mindless exultation or rapture, which is another primal quality of the sacrum, and as another inalienable human right, the pinnacle of our sexual experience.

Sekhmet is as such the presiding goddess of the sacrum. When she wakes up in our second chakra, she brings the majesty of the lioness to our primal concerns of passion, power and self-protectiveness. Illuminating and empowering, she enflames with dignity, liberating our repressions so that we may find the self-respect to express them in truth and consciousness.

Solar Plexus Chakra

The third chakra or **solar plexus** lies in the centre of the body. The Egyptian name for it was '*ab*', which translates as 'heart' in the sense of 'absolute centre'. The solar plexus energy vortex is the site for our connection to our human individuality. It is our true 'place of the Sun'. It is from here that we realise who we really are, and why we are who we are. It is the seat of our higher mind, our sense of self and special purpose in the world. As such, it is the centre of consciousness of ourselves as intelligent human beings with a role in the world, particular gifts and attributes to offer, and spiritual goals to accomplish. In psychological terms, it is the home of the ego where the 'I am' is discovered and expressed. Energy rising from the sacrum to the solar plexus shifts awareness from the sense of 'I am a *woman*' to 'I am *me*, Katy', and gives rise to the intelligent curiosity which then wishes to know '*why* am I Katy?' and '*how* can I realise Katy into her truest potential?' An open, activated solar plexus promotes courage and confidence in expression of all the 'solar' qualities of self; the 'will to be', the recognition of true purpose and the intelligence of will to focus on achievement of it.

Its colour is a radiant gold, the colour of sunlight. The solar plexus chakra is traditionally the centre of the divine child within us; the spontaneous, natural, honest part of our being who 'shines' without false modesty or cowardice. In societies such as Great Britain where most people have been taught as children not to 'show off' nor draw attention to themselves, it is not uncommon to find many problems resulting from blocked solar plexus centres. One of these is alcoholism, where alcohol, which releases social inhibition, has been constantly abused to give a false sense of self-confidence and courage. Programmes for substance abusers which encourage them to 'open up' and offer their personal experiences 'on stage' to an audience, owe much of their success to releasing blockages in solar plexus chakras. Public speaking, which many people find absolutely terrifying, requires and derives from a strong and active solar plexus. Being the seat of both courage and intelligence, it is the centre from where we find the integrity to acknowledge our personal gifts and qualities, and like the Sun, naturally radiate them out, so that everything is warmed and blessed by our presence.

It is from the solar plexus that we radiate our light or 'stardom'. The Sun is, after all, a star, and a central force to the consciousness of our planet.

A helpful exercise to activate solar plexus light is to visualise a luminous golden ray of sunlight shining down, encompassing you with warmth and life-giving power. At the same time, you can draw up the mighty power of earth in the same way as for the lower chakras, but this time connecting to it as proceeding from the innermost Sun at the core of Earth. As this energy passes up from the red of the root chakra, glowing into a translucent flame-orange in the sacrum, you can cause it to flow up into your solar plexus, refining it into a radiant gold that warms, encourages and sheds its light.

Through the experience of the root and sacral chakras, we become wholly conscious of ourselves firstly as organic and subsequently as mammalian beings. As awareness of self-rises to the solar plexus level, we recognise ourselves as human. It is therefore at this stage that we become conscious of our individual self, and our issues of immortality. This brings into focus a sense of our own purpose and thrust, our pain and loneliness, our nourishment and our enemy.

The essential oil to help stimulate this chakra is *neroli,* the essence of orange blossom. This is the traditional essence to inspire self-confidence and feelings of youthfulness, which promote full engagement with life's challenges.

The god-force whom we meet and awaken when rising to the solar plexus centre is the divine child and victorious warrior of the Egyptian pantheon, **Horus**.

Horus, the posthumous son of the much-loved murdered Osiris, is conceived by an act of great magic. His mother Isis transforms herself into a sparrow hawk, and raises enough life to receive the seed of her dead lord *(see the birth of Horus p.75)*. As a child, he is under constant threat from extinction, but he grows to avenge the wrongs of the world, symbolised by the murder and dismemberment of his father. Whilst aspiring to his ultimate victory he marries the lady of love and beauty, Hathor.

Horus, like Sekhmet, is a powerful solar force, which protects righteousness and defeats ill intent. However, as Horus this force becomes more personal, as consciousness begins to perceive itself as Self from the solar plexus centre. The god-force of Horus expresses its individuality within the universe with the grace and discipline of the spiritual warrior, the honest spontaneity of the divine child and the all-seeing vision of the *wadjet eye,* the divine protector of humanity.

In Egyptian theology, Horus is afforded three solar titles or roles, all aspects of the Sun from the perspective of human physical eyesight. These three aspects denote the journey of his kinsman Ra, who symbolises the cosmic idea of the Sun, across the heavens in the course of one day. In his three roles Horus describes the different powers of the rising, noonday and setting Sun. As rising sun, he is the divine child, open and glowing; at high noon, he is the radiant yet merciless warrior; and at the glory of sunset, he is aware of himself as the protector of the righteous who leads the initiate to the shores of Paradise. He is usually depicted as a falcon or a hawk, sometimes with the sun-disc of Ra upon his head.

As the final god in the Egyptian pantheon to incarnate, Horus represents the returning ego of the individual to earth. This is the part of our being which feels as if it has returned to the physical realms to 'avenge' or redress the wrongs of its past.

The life of Horus provides a shining example of how, as humans, we may achieve a sense of immortality from the earthly level. On reaching youthful maturity, he decides to meet his adversary (Set). He then consciously clarifies this decision into a determination to defeat him. He recognises the adversary within himself and then undertakes to 'learn the arts of warfare from his dead father in the *dwaat*', receiving guidance and instruction in dreams or unconscious levels. He engages in a personal war against wrongdoing – and he wins.

As prevailing victor in the war against the forces of darkness, Horus represents the spiritual intelligence and courage of the individual, with all its personal goals, gifts and purpose. When we rise to meet and realise the god Horus within ourselves in the solar-plexus centre, we experience both the pain of the dis-memberment of the inner father, which often prevents our true expressions of courage and creativity, and the radiant resolve of the healed and triumphant divine child. Horus is that part of the human self, experienced in the solar plexus centre, which recognises itself as a child of, and thus a developing part, of God.

Horus then, as divine exponent of the solar plexus, is the embodiment of all the glorious 'solar' qualities of our humanity. His whole life, against many odds, is focused on to the purposes of vindication and victory. He is both a loving and obedient son, and a mighty force for truth and justice. Every Pharaoh, to deserve and accomplish the responsibilities of rulership, had to strive to realise those qualities as a ruler on earth. With a fully awakened and active solar plexus, we can begin to do the same.

Heart Chakra

The fourth chakra is known as the **heart**. The Egyptian name for it was *Heper,* which was firmly held to be the seat of all knowledge. If any knowledge is held 'by heart', it is completely integrated into consciousness and cannot be forgotten. This is why many magical traditions, such as the Druidic colleges and the Homeric schools, forbade the use of written language – so that the sacred scripts could not be adulterated, dissipated or lost, but expressed from living memory. The Egyptians however, valued the heart more as the organ of self-knowledge and thus, self-judgment.

Perfect judgment requires 'mercy' or compassion. As Shakespeare knew, 'it droppeth as the gentle rain from Heaven upon the place beneath' and is 'twice blessed'. When energy rises to the heart chakra, consciousness becomes aware of itself as a two-way flow of universal energy, both offering and receiving. It perceives others in relation to itself and itself in relation to others, and thus begins to become aware of itself as part of something greater and more wonderful than itself, which nonetheless includes itself. Consciousness flowing from the heart chakra operates from the power of love.

When energy flows through an open, activated heart chakra, it can be experienced as a stream of light flowing across the breast and shoulders, down the arms and out through the two hands, allowing the giving and receiving of universal energy to flow naturally to and from the individual.

The heart is the sacred alchemical vessel where the two-way flow of earth power and spiritual consciousness meets and mingles. As cosmic energy flows down from above through activation of the higher three chakras, and earth power is drawn up from below through activation of the three lower chakras, the two different forces of nature both earthly and spiritual combine in the heart. This underlines its absolute importance and value in any magical or power-raising disciplines. The heart is where two aspects of true self, both spiritual and earthly are experienced, and thus from here, the self can be truly *known*.

The function of the heart chakra is to love, to honour and to share. A closed-up, or 'cold' heart leads to pathological disorder, even mayhem and tyranny. One can always 'trust ones heart' if one has understanding and knowledge of it is as the centre of ones own truth. The Egyptians understood this completely. The strength of their whole civilisation stemmed from a firm belief in the principle of justice or *Maat,* meaning 'order'. For divine 'order' to be supremely effective in life, it needed to be in perfect harmony with the heart, as illustrated by the temple paintings of the *'weighing of the heart'.*

The colours related to the heart chakra are rose pink and the clear green of the Earth in springtime.

Rose-pink, 'the breath of God' is a useful colour to work with if the heart feels 'heavy', neglected or sore. Wearing garments or crystals of rose-pink around the heart area, or visualising oneself surrounded by a cloud of rosy light, soothes and uplifts, promoting qualities of gentleness and affection which allow energy to flow more readily through the heart centre.

Spring green is a more powerful colour to promote activation of the heart chakra. A good exercise for using the vibrational ray of green (which is of course a blend of yellow and blue) is to imagine the golden light of the solar plexus radiating up into the heart where it meets the clear, blue light of descending throat chakra energy. Then it is necessary to visualise the blending process as these two colours merge and alchemise into the vibrant green of a spring meadow. This green light flows through the heart, promoting feelings of happiness, beneficence and a love for nature; the green earth with all its creations and creatures including oneself.

The essential oil or fragrance that helps to stimulate the heart is *rose.* This is a great favourite in Egypt today. In the villages, it is diluted with water and sprinkled over nuptial beds in honour of its properties. Red roses are a traditional lover's gift all over the world. The perfume of the rose helps to release blocked heart energy, when we become self-absorbed and afraid to love.

The heart chakra is the vortex that connects us to cosmic powers of love-in-relationship or marriage. Like the solar plexus, its concerns are with immortality, but in this case, not so much the immortality of the individual, but the immortality of love. True love is constant and eternal. When two people join together in open, flowing, conscious heart chakra energy, they actually *create* consciousness, and once created it can never die. Earth energy and spiritual essence blended together in the sacred vessel of the heart, and focused on the function of love itself, can make manifest that which only exists as potential in the higher and lower levels of consciousness.

It is when we reach the level of the heart that we can consider ourselves ready for marriage.

The goddess-force whom we awaken and encounter when our consciousness ascends to the heart chakra is the lady of love and beauty, **Hathor**. Not only the civilised and humanised aspect of Sekhmet, Hathor is also the earthly representation of the transcendent sky goddess Nut, the mother of Isis and Osiris. Hathor is the goddess as woman, the 'bridge' between the primal and stellar aspects of the divine feminine. She represents the two-way flow of cosmic energy, from spirit to earth, and from earth to spirit. In this case, she can be understood as absolute ruling deity of the heart chakra.

In her functions of goddess of art, music and nature, Hathor rules the outpouring of transformed earth power through the consciousness of the individual as the giving and receiving of universal love. Music, art and nature – all powerful 'keys' to opening the heart centre – are created manifestations of both human and divine love which raise awareness to higher levels. In addition, as the goddess of beauty, Hathor is that divine aspect of the self, which not only celebrates aesthetic beauty, but sees and recognises beauty in everything, especially differences. This equips her for her title of Lady of Love, meaning romantic or sexual love, a necessary component for the art of marriage.

Married to Horus, the closest principle to the human psychological condition, she herself is the most accessible aspect of the goddess to human understanding. The first sacred marriage occurs in the heart of Hathor. It can be construed as a conscious loving link between the two central chakras, the solar plexus and heart, or personal consciousness and universal outpourings of love. It brings the ability to know oneself 'by heart', and thereafter to trust the workings of ones heart implicitly forever.

Throat Chakra

The fifth or **throat** chakra is situated in the human body at the base of the throat, in the little hollow where the clavicle bones meet. Its Egyptian name was '*sekhem*' meaning centre of 'dynamic power'. It is interesting to note that this word is the same as the word used for the magical power that issues from the *Tekh* or sacrum, pointing to the fact that the Egyptians recognised the powerful energetic connection or sacred marriage between these two chakric points.

To the Egyptians, the throat chakra was the seat of magic, or '*heka*', which they understood to be the magical force behind utterance, which linked everything together in divinity. If a magician uttered the *heka*, his words would then be given independent power from conscious activation of '*sekhem*', the dynamic force which issued from his sacrum and was released by his throat chakra.

Traditionally, the throat chakra is the vortex that connects us to the 'Word' or *vibration* of God. It is the generating centre for releasing our 'magical utterance' or animated creativity. This means our empowered and conscious expressions of self, having their *own life*, can create change in the world. As energy rises from the torso to the neck, consciousness rises from personal to transpersonal levels. Through an activated throat chakra, this can be released by the 'true voice' of the individual as part of the loving design of the spiritual realms.

The throat chakra, one of the three 'higher' chakras, is nonetheless the centre from which we express and communicate our personal creativity. But if we desire it to be 'magical,' meaning we want it to make a difference in the world, we release energy from the throat, proceeding from our own true knowledge, which lives in the heart. The great god Ptah says in the ancient texts that his 'tongue is the agent of his heart'.

Activation of the throat chakra allows energy to flow down from the higher mind of the individual to be released as inspired language. Conversely, as awareness proceeds upwards from the heart, where earthly and spiritual consciousness have met and 'married', and self- knowledge has duly been acquired, it becomes a simple matter to express that knowledge from an open and activated throat.

When we experience blockages of creative force, such as 'writer's block' or the horrible immobilisation caused by 'student fatigue' and terrors of impending examinations, it is often due to an obstructed throat chakra. This can even impede smooth relationships with others, allowing situations where we feel unable to express ourselves with simplicity and truth.

The colour for the throat chakra is a clear translucent blue, the azure of the Egyptian sky. A useful meditational exercise to release and activate energy from the throat chakra is to imagine oneself encircled by a beam of sparkling blue light, shining down from the highest levels of universal consciousness. Allowing oneself to be bathed and imbued with this light brings feelings of tranquility and spiritual inspiration. In my capacity as a channel and Tarot reader, I have employed this simple exercise without exception before every session I have ever conducted, and it has never failed me. A clear, sky-blue colour is an excellent shade for walls and furnishings in areas set aside for inspirational work. Lapis-lazuli or turquoise necklaces are also very helpful in opening and releasing energy from the throat.

The essential oil, which helps open this chakra, is the purifying and relaxing *lavender.*

The Egyptian god-force whom we meet when our consciousness ascends to the throat chakra is the great Architect of the cosmos, the creator god, **Ptah**.

Ptah, one of the primary creator gods of the old Memphite kingdoms of Egypt, created the world and established all order upon it by the power of his utterances, by 'naming' everything. This precurses the Biblical statement, also upheld in Western Mystery traditions, '*in the beginning was the Word*', or 'all matter is vibration'. Although worshipped as the Great Architect of the cosmos, Ptah is always depicted as a simple craftsman – gentle, humble and approachable. When we aspire to the god-force Ptah by releasing our creative powers from an awakened and relaxed throat chakra, we are connecting to the aspect of self that recognises itself as part of the divine plan or 'architecture' of the universe. We realise that we are a force, which vibrates in harmony with God, and thus we can consciously 'approach' or attune ourselves to it. We can become the voice of God.

When we rise to release the voice of Ptah in the throat, we are connecting with our own role in the great harmonious design of the cosmos, and we can then consciously express ourselves to that purpose

Ptah is husband to the primal lioness goddess Sekhmet, whom we meet in the awakened sacrum. As we activate the throat, we can be considered ready to celebrate the second sacred marriage, combining throat and sacral energies in love as a union of primal power with higher design. This commitment prepares us to practice and effect *heka* or 'magic'. Magic is traditionally defined as 'the ability to cause change by the power of will'.

When we can lovingly integrate our primal will to the higher design of the cosmos, our 'words' will then carry the weight and power to perpetrate positive change in the world and our lives thereafter begin to unfold in miraculous ways.

Brow Chakra
The sixth chakra is called the **brow** chakra, often referred to as the third eye as it is situated between the eyes in the middle of the forehead. The Egyptian name for it was *Mer.* The brow chakra is the energy vortex for connection to the higher, more subtle levels of consciousness, where the meanings behind apparent reality can be discerned. It is the centre from which the spiritual 'sight' or insight and intuition of the individual can function. Issues that arise from activation and energising of the brow chakra relate to higher wisdom, revelation and a sense of spirituality.

A well-activated brow chakra enables the higher intuition, or ability to recognise patterns of universal energy as they flow down from the tides of the cosmos into individual consciousness, and most importantly, to comprehend their meanings. As one of the higher chakras, situated in the head, the issues of the brow chakra are of a more spiritual nature than the lower ones. But if energetic links with the lower chakras of the individual are not harmoniously conjoined with it, there is no conscious control over this powerful connector to the unseen realms. This can lead to sudden flashes of clairvoyant insight, which have little or no positive effect in the world, or even in severe cases, to madness or 'schizophrenia'. Certain 'mind-altering' drugs can chemically open the brow chakra, but if these are abused or taken without the necessary spiritual disciplines to support the experience, the entire psychic mechanism of the individual can 'burn out'.

Quite often, new students and aspirants have brought the private worry to me that they have no 'clairvoyant ability', that they do not 'see' things in the way that others whom they work with seem to be able to. Usually, interestingly, these very people are operating from well-awakened and integrated brow chakras. Instead of receiving astounding and dynamic visions in their meditations, which, being highly personal, require interpretation, they are often operating from developed intuition, or *inner knowing*, which is ultimately much more valuable to themselves and others. I do not at all mean to imply here that clairvoyant vision is a trivial or negative faculty, only to make the point that the brow chakra is both a sensitive and a powerful point of connection to higher, more subtle levels of existence, and that it cannot work effectively or safely on its own. Before any work may be undertaken on awakening the brow chakra, it is both wise and enjoyable to prepare for it by firstly connecting with all the lower centres.

The colour of the brow chakra is violet, a deep amethyst shade often seen at moonrise on the sea and in the desert sky.

To awaken a chakra it is helpful to make sure you are sitting comfortably with feet on the ground, or lying down on the floor. You can then attempt to veil your physical presence in violet-coloured light, concentrating on allowing this violet light to cloak you, making you seem invisible.

Then, to undergo a chakra raising exercise from the root upwards, you should concentrate on forming the different colours of the lower chakras, from red through orange and gold until you reach the green at your heart. As these colours emerge from you at their chakric placements along your body, your violet-coloured cloak becomes transparent, allowing them to shine through.

As your consciousness moves upwards into a clear blue colour at your throat, you can experience its blue deepening into violet as it flows upwards into your head, gradually attaining its proper depth at your brow.

At this stage, you will be ready to receive a 'revelation'. It may or may not occur as actual instruction or bright vision, but it will imbue you with a sense of quiet spirituality and inner knowing.

The essential oils and fragrances that help to activate the brow chakra are *violet,* and *sandalwood.* Violet, the essence of the beautiful 'shy' or hidden woodland flower, helps contact with the unseen aspects of nature. It is also used to heal the unconscious pains of childhood, which is why it is often used to scent baby powder. Sandalwood's powerful and subtle aroma connects us to the more mystical qualities of the brow chakra, the opening of intuition and wisdom.

The goddess-force that we awaken on activating the brow chakra is the goddess of healing and magic **Isis**.

Isis, the bright queen of the gods, is the principle who, through the paramount force of love, searches for and finds all the dismembered parts of her slain husband, the bright lord Osiris. We can think of Osiris as representing the principle of divinity from which all humanity feels 'cut off' in life. When we encounter the light of Isis from the brow chakra, we feel that we have ascended to understanding of our highest feminine qualities or the 'bright queen' within us, which has been assiduously searching for our lost, forgotten selves, gathering different life experiences to a place of wholeness. This new understanding brings revelations to us, as Isis in the brow chakra becomes 'unveiled'.

In the ancient texts, Isis claims that she 'brings islands up out of the depths and into the light'. This is a beautiful illustration of the function of the brow chakra. On activating this centre we can be aware of the 'depths' of power that issue from our lower centres, and how to manifest it in the world, or 'bring islands up' into the light of our own intuition. This light of Isis connects us to the divine purpose of spiritual wholeness, for Isis is queen of both heaven and earth. One of the most powerful magicians in the pantheon, her entire life is devoted to the maintenance of rightness and order. Notwithstanding terrible losses and separation, she sorrows and searches until, with the enormous power of her love, she re-members and she resurrects Osiris.

At the brow chakra, the penultimate stage of our journey, we not only receive revelation, but we stand revealed to our true selves, with all our human aspects integrated. Insight and integration provide the spiritual wisdom that renders us ready to approach the journey's apotheosis where we consciously connect with spiritual essence at our crown. Here, Isis, integrated with her dark sister Nephthys, stands in perpetuity at the throne of her beloved husband Osiris in Paradise.

Crown Chakra

The seventh chakra or **crown** is situated in the physical body at the crown of the head. It is on the exact spot, called the *fontanel* on babies, where our cranial bones close up at the stage when our personality begins to form, bringing new consciousness of ourselves as separate individual beings. Before the fontanel closes, we have a direct physical link to universal light through the crown chakra.

The crown chakra is the vehicle for receiving experience of divine essence. It is from the crown chakra that we become aware that spiritual and stellar energy is pouring down into earth through our human consciousness. It can be thought of as the supreme gateway in our psychic system, which, acting as a bridge between our subtle and grosser levels, provides us with the conscious undertaking to marry heaven to earth, for ourselves, each other, and for the cosmos.

Awareness of the function of the crown chakra brings both a sense of the majesty and glory of divinity and intimations of the coalescence of universal life. The Egyptian name for it was *Ikh*. Egyptian culture, which is the first known culture to have been ruled by kingship over a unified nation, thrived on benign and peaceful hierarchy. The double crown of Upper and Lower Egypt worn by Osiris and all the Pharaohs was a powerful symbol for this integrated rulership within the individual. The Pharaoh himself, once crowned, was a living symbol of divinity-in-humanity. It is from the open crown chakra that we receive consciousness of ourselves as a spark of the divine essence of God. In addition, it is also from the crown that we release all our individuality into the coalescence of the universe. When all the chakras are integrated within the individual, and comingled cosmic and earthly energy flows through an open, spinning crown, the integration of all levels of consciousness is complete, and the crown of self-rulership may be adopted.

The colour of the crown chakra is the sparkling many-hued iridescence of a diamond, as it produces all the colours of the spectrum before they separate and devolve into material consciousness.

To awaken and stimulate your crown chakra, become aware of a spinning vortex of diamond-brilliant light, flashing with rainbow colours, flowing down from the great One-ness beyond the stars, and pouring into the crown of your head. Experience it as a beneficent ray of power and love, sent for you individually from the Godhead Itself. It links you to the universal power of God, and yet it is especially for you. It brings you your essential individuality and your unity. It brings awareness of both your responsibility and your prize.

It is critical to remember that no attempt to close down this last most important chakra should be attempted in any healing work. As our consciousness rises to the crown, we become aware that it has been open and active all the time, shedding the light of God upon us, and through us, that we might be both separate and united.

Perfumes and essential oils, which help to activate the crown chakra, are *Lotus* and *Spikenard*.

Lotus, which can be obtained in Egypt, brings remembrance of heaven from a perspective of earth, just as the lotus flower living on the surface of the waters, lifts its face to the sky, drawing nourishment from deep roots embedded in the mud.

Spikenard is a very holy oil, mentioned in the Bible as the precious oil the Magdalene poured upon the feet of Jesus. It helps to bring us to a true sense of worship. As we attain our divine Kingship at the crown, we release our personal will into our highest will, which is of course, the will of God. This is the meaning of redemption.

The crown is the chakra of the god **Osiris**, the ruling, risen and re-membered Lord. Consciousness of Osiris – the Lord of the Righteous Dead – in the crown, takes us to the self-sovereignty of re-memberment. Linking us to our spiritual home, beginnings and future, Osiris is a three-fold principle. As bright king, he 'rules' our lives with love; as scarified god, he teaches us the value of separation; and as risen lord, he gives us the conscious and willing return to the world of spirit.

As we approach the crown chakra, the seventh and final stage on our pathway from the level of Isis at the awakened brow chakra, we are ready to commit to the third sacred marriage. This union of brow and crown as Isis and Osiris, brings together nascent powers of self-sovereignty and wholeness, and here we can unite the two highest aspects of our consciousness in order to rule ourselves and our lives with perfect love.

Virtues, Qualities and Wedding Gifts

After considering our inner gods in their chakras and making the conscious commitment to meet and marry them to each other, we need to think about how we are going to achieve this. If these marriages are going to be productive, we need to know exactly what we are committing to and how to realise that commitment. We do not want to have a glorious wedding feast and honeymoon, only to become disillusioned and bored when it's time to do the laundry or feed the babies. We need to remind ourselves that when we travel the path of love we need never feel lonely or preoccupied. We will find ourselves stretched and challenged, certainly. Sometimes we will look outside and wonder if we could have done better for ourselves elsewhere, but if we allow for the true freedom of commitment and the real responsibility of choice, we will find the path of love in our own hearts and the inner peace that ensues from dedication to it.

The most important tools we possess for a stable and happy eternal sacred marriage lie right within our own selves. We only need to know their names and where they are kept in order to learn to use them with skill. When we apply them to ourselves and our lives, we can create wonders in the name of love. After all, we are contemplating marriage with the divine! As the divine principles marry each other within us, we are marrying ourselves to the gods.

The tools we require are the divine attributes of the god-forces themselves as they proceed through our own chakric system. They are all realisable, workable and readily available. They are our human gifts and virtues.

The concept of virtue is not fashionable. It carries with it overtones of hypocrisy and sterile condescension which is the furthest possible view of it from its true meaning. Virtue is vibrancy, a freedom and a joy. Virtue makes the heart sing. Virtue is a pleasure.

As we learn about the inner gods and their relationships, we will be working with their particular gifts and qualities to promote virtue in ourselves. These gifts and qualities are by no means dull or boring. Expression and realisation of them does not require us to live like Puritans nor deny ourselves the pleasures of life. In fact, the reverse is true. However, realisation of virtue does require consciousness and commitment to love.

I have attributed to each of the seven god-forces mentioned above seven internal chakras of their own. Each of these internal chakras emanates a particular **gift or quality**. Work on the path of love requires knowledge and understanding of these qualities and the commitment to find and use them on the path. This is how we can really realise the divine principles within us; by finding these special gifts and qualities and expressing them. Where the sacred marriages occur, each one of the seven special separate qualities of the marriage partner combines in love with each of the seven of its beloved Other to produce **Wedding Gifts**. These are precious gifts of the higher consciousness with which we can really work to transform ourselves and the world. As we marry each level of our various levels to each other in love, we not only integrate and are integrated, but we are able to produce wonderful 'offspring', these precious fruits of the spirit that inspire, nourish and delight all the worlds.

Affirmations

Affirmations are very helpful in the realisation of virtue. Each god-force on the path of love has, as well as its seven special chakric qualities, personal affirmations, which need to be spoken aloud. One of the main beliefs in the actualisation of Egyptian magic or *heka* is that the spoken word has the power to manifest, if it proceeds from true heart knowledge. By repeating the affirmations, *from the heart,* several times in different ways and with different emphases, they become real. Some of the provided affirmations will already be real and easy to repeat; some will be new. In this case, they need to be learned by the personality, but they are all true of the soul. This is the value of repeating them like prayers or mantras until they are 'known by heart'. In fact, the heart already knows them, but the personality must accept them as true for them to become completely real.

Invocations and Guided Meditations

The act of 'invocation' literally means a 'calling up', or a prayer spoken with intent to invoke a presence from *within.* The invocations to the various god-forces or *neters* provided in this work are designed to awaken our imagination and inner knowledge to the powers of love in our unconscious levels. They should be spoken simply and clearly without declamation, but, in the same way that the affirmations work best, they do need to be spoken aloud to be effective. A heart-felt delivery is best. It is also very productive to visualise the images provided in each invocation whilst it is being spoken, and to try to experience each invoked *neter* on the emotional level, to *feel* the inner presence of the god-force rising within and entering our space. The words 'Hail Anubis! (or whichever god). Hail and welcome!' which end each invocation, allow time and space to focus entirely on that particular aspect of our being during the guided meditation, which follows. When the guided meditation is finished the words 'Hail and Farewell' will denote that the intensity of experience is over, and it is time to 'close down' and integrate our new knowledge.

The guided meditation on each *neter*, which follows the invocation, can be read from the page. It is, of course much more effective once it is learned. For solitary work, recording it on tape beforehand and playing it to oneself allows more focus. The guided meditations have been channeled as a way of 'entering the spheres of the gods'. It is important to try and stay with their images and feelings and not go wandering off. Spaces for individual experiences have been allowed. If you fall asleep or find yourself somewhere else, then the experience has not been wholly successful, and you will need to try it again later.

If you have not had the opportunity to develop your creative imagination in this way, and you find it difficult to form images and find feelings on demand, then it is merely a question of practice. The great occultist Dion Fortune always affirmed that she herself was not a 'natural' but a *trained* psychic and magician. She states in her writings that it was the difficulties she sustained in her early work which gave her the necessary disciplines for adept hood. In addition, she was duly thankful for them. If you practice forming the images as they occur during guided meditations, they will start to become alive for you. The discipline this training gives you is a necessary foundation for occult work. Magic is a serious discipline. Egyptian temple trainings took many years; and a Druidic education took nineteen. Attune your capabilities to your will, open your heart, and trust that you will receive your revelations and visions exactly when you are ready to understand them.

The Myths

All of the work in these pages springs from the sacred mythology of the Egyptians. One definition of a myth is a 'living truth which is told as a story'. These myths belong to everyone. Their tales illustrate our deepest spiritual mysteries and psychological processes. They bring life and understanding to complex psycho-spiritual ideas in the most ready and simple ways. It is important to know them. Then the principles of love and order, as characters in the stories, become very real for us as we identify with their struggles and their becoming. Every character is a part of our developing consciousness. Their struggles and sorrows teach us how to understand the difficulties of being alive; their victories give us knowledge of how to attain peace and spiritual grace.

By understanding of their myths, the Egyptians were able to produce a uniquely sophisticated and subtle culture, rich in wonders, and harmonious from within. If these tales can live for us as they did for the Egyptians, could we not, too, promote those very values, and aspire to those very heights of excellence in our own world? Every principle in the whole body of the Egyptian mythology is a part of our being. We *are* Anubis, Sekhmet, Horus, Hathor, Ptah, Isis and Osiris. We are also Set and Nephthys. These darker gods are necessary parts of our being, and as such, I have included them in the work. Without them, the ongoing work of evolution could not happen.

These myths are alive. For many years, they slept in our consciousness, discounted by the world as superstitious fairy tales; now they are being received with amazed discovery at their wisdom. Perhaps we have grown to perceive their truth; perhaps they have grown with us. Certainly, there is much more they can teach us. I have included potted versions of the relevant mythology for this work. It is recommended that they be read several times, until their message becomes alive, and their principles loved. Then, hopefully the tales can be told again as they are meant to be, in the nursery, the tavern and market place; not merely skimmed over as part of an esoteric manual or a scientific analysis.

Preparation

In preparation for the work of sacred marriage, we need to become properly aware of its structure so that we can pace ourselves accordingly. As mentioned before, this work is a seven-fold process that allows for three 'initiations' or powerful statements of love to take place along its pathway. It therefore operates in ten stages. We can recognise these stages as the seven god-forces or *neters* in their chakric placements, and their three sacred marriages.

Our task is to awaken each of the seven gods-forces in their relevant chakras, integrating each god-force into our consciousness as we go, so that we become more aware of our subtle bodies and can draw upon their powerful reservoirs of love.

We can celebrate the three sacred marriages along the pathway of the chakras as degrees of commitment to, and attainment of, spiritual integration.

In order to achieve this we are prepared to learn about the divine principles existing within ourselves as the *neters,* realise their qualities and claim their gifts.

Meditational exercises, personal affirmations and guided meditations are provided for each god-force/chakra awakening.

Ritual procedures and ceremonies are included to give focus to the work.

MAGICAL DIARY:

It is most important to keep a written record of our experiences during the whole process.

The first *neter* whom we meet on the path is Anubis, our guide and witness. When we have realised and integrated his qualities, we find the objectivity to be clear and impartial self-witnesses along the further levels. Keeping a 'magical diary' really serves to maintain this essential attribute. The diary becomes invaluable as we later understand how to plot our progress, and see how we were able to 'ground' our inner visions by writing them down. It is advisable to keep the magical diary by the bed so that any elusive dreams can be remembered and interpreted.

THE SIGN OF THE PENTAGRAM

The pentagram is a five-pointed star with one point at each of the four directions and one above.

Symbolising the integration of spirit (the topmost point) with matter (the four directions and elements of manifestation), it is a very powerful and protective sign. Drawing the pentagram 'opens the veil' to the subtle levels and creates a protective force field against psychic intrusion. It is important to know how to make the sign of the pentagram in energetic and magical work. The sign of the pentagram is made as a continuous movement of five lines.

1. Using your right forefinger, trace a line in the air from the lower left corner to the apex of the star.

Fig 1:

2. Then take the line down to the lower right point

Fig 2:

3. From the lower right point, take the line diagonally across to the upper left point

Fig 3:

4. From the upper left point, trace the line horizontally across the star to the upper right point.

Fig 4:

5. From the upper right point, trace the line diagonally down to the first point at the lower left. This completes and closes the star.

Fig 5:

A short practice will ensure that the sign of the pentagram can be done easily without thinking.

APPENDICES

In order to know our brighter, higher levels of self as Isis and Osiris, we also need to be acquainted with their dark twins, Nephthys and Set. They are as necessary to each other as night and day. I have therefore included work on them as appendices. This work can be done separately, after the course is completed, or as polarities for Isis and Osiris during the work. There is an appropriate stage of self-assessment to explore, once the level of Isis is reached.

The first thing to do, is to familiarise oneself with the myths.

THE STORY OF NUT AND GEB

After the Beginning, when the shining One-ness of Atum needed to create force and form, two wonderful lion-headed Gods of Air appeared into being from His limitless light. They were husband and wife, and brother and sister, and they were named Shu and Tefnut. Shu emerged as a Force of dry air, or Breath and Sound, and Tefnut, his wife and sister, appeared as a moist Form of colour and perfume. Their love was so great, it opened the gateway to Manifestation, so that Shu as Sound might descend into Consciousness, and Tefnut as moist colour devolve into Matter. The divine harmony of their union ensured that all things that formed from their embrace would contain both individuality and the divine spark of God within them.

Eventually their love produced two beautiful, magnificent children. These were Geb, the potent, greening Earth God, and Nut, the transcendently beautiful Sky Goddess.

Nut and Geb were married, they adored each other, and they lay in the ecstasy of their divine embrace for axons.

However, their father Shu had plans for them.

'You have been formed so that Consciousness might evolve and grow,' he informed them. 'You cannot lie together like this any longer. You must serve the Cause of Evolution. The spiritual energy of your love must descend to Earth. I'm sorry, but I must separate you.'

Therefore, as Breath of Life, he stood between them, and he held them apart forever. After this, their yearning love was so powerful that it caused all the polarisations that cause energy to crystallize into matter, spring up in the aching distance that spread between them.

Nut arched her beautiful body over Geb, the greening Earth, and shed her celestial light over him in protection. Geb released his seed from the powerful depths of his loneliness into the womb of the distant Sky.

Consequently, Nut gave birth to two luminous sons. One was Ra, who was a radiant, raging, creative Solar force, and the other was Thoth, the contemplative Lunar Lord and Wise Measurer. Ra, deciding to make the Cosmic Year, divided the distance between his parents into three hundred and sixty degrees of Days, and then, from the mighty power of his Will and hand, masturbated his energy onto the Earth, so all the people were born and irradiated with his consciousness. Thoth sorted out the stellar laws of the Heavens and reflected their Light on to his brother as newly formed creations.

Ra loved his subjects so well that he himself adopted the shape and form of mankind that he might rule them with compassion and order. And for many axons there was a Golden Age in the Land of Egypt, when the Solar order of the Sun and the reflective wisdom of the Moon prevailed with harmony and peace.

But because Ra had taken upon himself the limitations of the Material Plane, he eventually began to age, and his powers to diminish.

THE EPAGOMENAL DAYS

Five more children formed in the womb of Nut. Ra was furious.

'I am the Sun,' he raged. 'I am a sole solar force. I have created the Year. No usurper will come on any day of my Year. I don't want any siblings, and what's more I will not allow it.'

And the five siblings grew larger and stronger in the womb of the Sky, but they could not be born. Nut groaned in fruitless agony.

Thoth, in pity for his mother, hit upon a plan.

'Ra,' he said, 'I'm rather bored. I feel like a game. I challenge you to a game of dice, and if I win, which I very much doubt as you're so much better than I at games, I'll name my prize!'

Ra could not resist the challenge. He lost. Thoth's prize was to add five more days to the Year. On these days, the great Sky Goddess Nut gave birth to her children, who had come to rule the land of Egypt in Ra's place. The eldest she named Horus or Horus-the-Elder and she set him up in the sky with her, to protect Mankind. Then she produced two Bright children as husband and wife, these were named Isis and Osiris, and two Dark children, Set and Nephthys. These four children were to rule the people and the Two Lands of Egypt.

The Bright pair, Isis and Osiris were given the Black Lands of Khem, the fertile delta of Lower Egypt where they could teach their people agriculture and ecology, arts, crafts, and the laws of love and order. Set and Nephthys were to rule the Red Lands of the Sinai and the barren waste of Upper Egypt where all the rich mineral deposits and gold lay buried under the sand. There, Nephthys practiced her sorcery, and Set rampaged about the country, hunting, and drinking and brooding on rebellion.

THE STORY OF ANUBIS

Nephthys became restless and concerned. She was beautiful, powerful and fertile, and her husband, Set, did not pay her much attention. He had homosexual proclivities, and, besides, her magical knowledge was such that she knew about his secret sterility. She came on a visit to Khem.

While Osiris was asleep, she borrowed her sister's perfumes, and loosening her hair, she rubbed the essence of violet and lotus into its shining tresses. She crept into Osiris' bed, and he, half-asleep, mistaking her for Isis, embraced her passionately. In this way, she was able to conceive her only son, the Dog God, Anubis.

She returned to her husband the next day. Very soon, she informed him that he was to become a father. Her secret was never divulged. When Anubis was born she taught him all her arts, and he was always closer in his heart to his real father, Osiris, and to his aunt, Isis, than to his foster-father, Set.

THE DEATH OF OSIRIS

Isis and Osiris ruled happily and wisely in the Land of Khem. Perfectly suited for their role and function, they became more and more powerful, and more and more beloved. Isis ordained that women should be loved by men, she devised marriage contracts and ordered business in the sea. She was easily able to depose Ra, by the power of her magic, and together with her husband she set up a system of equality and righteousness that made the people of Egypt sing her praises every day at their work. Osiris was so beloved in the hearts of his people, that they longed for his messages of wisdom and peace, and followed his teachings with joy.

As far as the barren wastelands of Upper Egypt, the name of Osiris was carried on the winds with love and blessings. Set became obsessed with envy. Life was unbearable to him. He began to hate Osiris with all his heart, and, gathering his seventy-two conspirators about him, tried to plot his downfall. But he could not stir up rebellion against his bright brother.

Everybody loved him too much, it was impossible. Being a brilliant strategist, Set put his mind to work, and devised a plan. Waiting until a time when he knew that Isis was away travelling, he sent Osiris a letter.

'My dear Brother' he wrote, 'I long for reconciliation with you. Could you forgive my stupidity in allowing this rift to occur between us? Please accept my apology, and come to a banquet that I want to hold in honour of our brotherhood and our love'

This was irresistible to Osiris. Naturally, he accepted. In preparation for the banquet, Set sent a spy to Khem to determine the exact measurements of his brother's body. He then had fashioned from all the finest gold and silver and electrum in his Kingdom the most exquisitely wrought casket, made to fit Osiris. It was encrusted with gems, with turquoise and faience, and carnelian. It was breathtaking.

The day arrived and Osiris came to Set's palace. The banquet was sumptuous. Course after course of the most delicious food and wine were served with generosity and good humour.

Set kept filling Osiris' wine-cup, making him drink toast after toast to their reconciliation, in praise of his brother's nobility and forgiveness until Osiris was quite drunk. Then Set sat back upon his couch and said:

'Bring out the Casket.'

When it appeared, everybody gasped in awe. It was truly magnificent.

Set opened his arms.

'You know what?' he said. 'I am so happy that I am reconciled with my dear brother, even this magnificent artifact has lost its meaning for me. As a commemoration of this joyful occasion, I am prepared to give it away. Whoever fits it, can have it.' And he shrugged his shoulders, and turned away to embrace Osiris one more time.

One by one the assembled men, for there were never any women at Set's banquets, climbed into the jeweled casket. But they were all the wrong size.

Until Osiris rose, slightly unsteady on his feet, and lay down, laughing, inside the box.

It fitted him perfectly. Immediately, the lid was slammed shut. The seventy-two conspirators rushed forward and sealed up the coffin of Osiris, and cast it into the sea. It floated away to Byblos in Syria where the people embedded it in a tree and worshipped it.

THE ANGUISH OF ISIS

When Isis returned to find her beloved lord dead and dispatched, she went insane with grief. The once proud and powerful Queen was transformed into a wailing, keening madwoman. The people were awe-stricken at the immensity of her woe. Smeared with ashes, with her hair torn out, she ranged and raved amongst them sorrowing and searching for her sanity and her Love. But eventually she calmed down and found her resolve.

She left Egypt on a long quest to find the sacred body of Osiris. She had many adventures and faced many perils. And at last, she came to Byblos. Taking a job as a nursemaid to the Queen of Syria, she discovered the Casket in its tree, and she stole it in the night, and brought it back to Egypt.

Finding the most secret, magical place in the Delta, she took the body of Osiris to a hiding place, and there she began to work her magic.

With all the mighty force of her love, her infinite yearning sorrow and her considerable knowledge and gifts of High Magic, she transformed herself into a sparrow-hawk, cruelest of all the birds in the sky, and seven times she called the name of Osiris, as she hovered over his dead body in passionate waiting. At last, in a moment of terrible stillness and with a tremendous leap of love and power, from the depths of Earth and from the firmament of Heaven, life entered the body of Osiris as she hovered there. For one wonderful heart-stopping moment life poured through the sacred phallus of Osiris, as the seed of Osiris entered her intensely waiting body, and with a fierce cry of mingled anguish and joy, she conceived the Divine Child.

Osiris' spirit went to the Dwaat, the astral realms, where he remained in communion with her. And Isis hid herself, and the body of her lord, deep in the marshes to await the birth of her son, whom she named Horus, after her brother in the sky.

THE BIRTH OF HORUS

The infant Horus was born in the sleeping green richness of the fertile wetlands, where Isis nourished and hid him, lavishing him with love and tenderness.

But the spies and agents of Set discovered their whereabouts. They killed Horus with a scorpion's bite. But Thoth came to the rescue, and stopped time so that Isis could revivify him. She summoned the Scorpion Goddess Selket to watch over him, and keep him safe. But a worse outrage was soon to occur.

THE DISMEMBERMENT OF OSIRIS

Set maintained an effective network of spies. Inevitably, they discovered where body of Osiris lay in the dreaming marshes. On one terrible day, they seized it, and chopped it into forty-two pieces, which they scattered over the length and breadth of the two lands. Osiris now was dismembered, fragmented, and as Set hoped, soon to be forgotten. All the Gods wept. It was a day of mourning in Heaven. Nephthys and Anubis abandoned Set forever, and came hotfoot to Khem to the aid and support of Isis.

THE SEARCH OF ISIS

Isis was not deterred. She left Horus with Selket, and embarked on a marathon quest to find and sanctify all the missing limbs and members of Osiris. She determined to set up temples of worship in the places where she found them, where she would teach all the people of his love and Laws. And this she did. In this way, the Laws of Osiris were disseminated over the Two Lands, which eventually became united under them. Nephthys and Anubis went with her, and they returned from time to time to check on Horus and monitor his progress. It took many years to find all the missing members.

THE TRAINING OF HORUS

During that time under the care of attendant goddesses, Horus grew to youthful manhood. One night, on one of his mother's visits, he came into her chamber. She was lying on her couch as though asleep. However, she was veiled in a deep and powerful trance. On her face was a look of bliss as her lips spoke the name of Osiris. Horus was angry and jealous to find her in such deep loving communion with his dead father and he left the chamber feeling hurt and rejected. He spent a long night trying to understand what had happened.

In the morning, he had reached a realisation.

He determined to reach Osiris himself, and ask him for guidance. And this he did.

He received training in the arts of warfare from his father from the astral realms, and he found the courage and resolution to defeat his father's murderer, to rid the world of the malice and chaos of Set.

While Isis and Nepthys searched and gathered, Horus practiced hard. He was young but he was strong, noble and completely resolved. At last, he was ready to engage in the first of a long series of skirmishes and battles with his uncle. Horus' name was heard in the songs of the people as they began to live in hope again. He gathered about him a growing band of followers. These were called The Companions of Horus. Under his direction they formed into a disciplined and shining army. At length there was one final battle to go, and one last missing member to find. The sacred phallus of Osiris could not be found.

THE PENULTIMATE BATTLE

Horus gathered his army and went to confront Set at Edfu. It was a fierce and bloody encounter where many of Horus' Companions were slain. The God of Wisdom, Thoth, came to Edfu to offer counsel and encouragement to Horus. Although they were greatly outnumbered, the followers of Horus fought on bravely, until Horus found himself in hand-to-hand combat with his uncle Set. Set fighting without honour, gouged out one of Horus eyes, whereupon Thoth set it up in the sky to protect the righteous. The beautiful goddess Hathor, from her Temple at Dendera, across the Nile, noticed it, immediately fell in love with the young heroic warrior, and promptly *married him.*

THE FINAL BATTLE

At last, Horus defeated Set and took him prisoner. Horus had defeated the powers of malice and chaos, avenged his father, and prevailed for the good of Mankind. Isis pleaded for mercy for her brother and so Horus did not kill Set. He merely castrated him because Isis told him that there was a need for evil to exist in the world, as long as it was made powerless. Afterwards Set was assigned the task of blowing the wind that propelled the Boat of Isis, to keep him out of trouble.

THE RE-MEMBERMENT OF OSIRIS

Although Set had been defeated, Isis and Nephthys were still searching for the lost Phallus of Osiris. Their lamentations were so great that Anubis came to help them.

And with his help they found it.

The body of Osiris was now complete. Temples of his worship were ensconced throughout the Two Lands. Horus, married to the goddess Hathor, the Lady of Love, was ready to rule over a united and ordered Kingdom.

The sacred body of Osiris was mummified and preserved for perpetuity by Anubis, who became the god of Embalming; he also had bestowed upon him the role of guide, or Psychopomp of Souls, as a just reward for his loyalty and devotion. From thenceforth it is Anubis who assesses the Scales and witnesses the weighing of the Heart in the Halls of Judgment and it is he who brings enlightened individuals to the shores of Paradise.

Isis and Nephthys were allowed to enter Paradise to assist Osiris, who now rules over both the Living and the Righteous Dead.

THE STORY OF SEKHMET

When Ra ruled in the Land of Egypt during the Golden Age, there were many axons of peace and order. Ra ruled with great power and structure, the harmony of his laws and the mighty force of his being instilled into all the people a marvelous sense of stability and prosperous growth. But Ra, having assumed the a shape and body of a man, in order to rule Mankind with justice and understanding, eventually became subject to one of the limitations of mortality, and he grew old. Consequently he grew rather tired, and his powers began to diminish.

When this happened, the people no longer experienced the warm safety of living under a strong and trusted sovereign. Fear crept into their hearts. And it manifested amongst them as greed, and envy, and arrogance. They began to fight amongst themselves, and very soon, for the first time, evil appeared in the Land of Egypt.

Ra was devastated. He was almost at a loss what to do. So he summoned a council of all the Gods at Heliopolis. He called his father, Geb, the great Earth God, and his mother, Nut, the transcendently lovely Goddess of the Stars. His grandparents Shu and Tefnut, the beautiful lion-headed Gods of Air and Moisture were called and his brother Thoth, the wise Measurer and Lord of the Moon. When they were all assembled he asked them:

'What can I do? I could not foresee this. Shall I destroy them? I have a good mind to send my burning glance over all the land and annihilate them.'

But Thoth spoke up:

'I wouldn't do that, Ra,' he said calmly. 'It would be such a waste. All of Egypt would become a barren desert. No, I think the people need a retributive force. Why not create something like that? Something that will teach them a lesson? Your work would become easier then. We're all here, and we will help you create the Very Thing.'

So Ra summoned up the collective force of all the assembled Gods, and went deep into a long and powerful Meditation. He sent his Will down into the very core of Earth, and he rose to the very heights of Heaven. Eventually he opened his eyes, released his throat and pronounced the name **'Sekhmet!'**

Before their eyes the most beautiful, the most radiant and glorious

Lioness Goddess sprang into being.

'Welcome, Beautiful Daughter,' said Ra. 'Now go off and do your work.'

And with an exultant roar, Sekhmet leapt into her joyous task of killing, and rampaging and bloodletting.

Before long, she was a byword in the land. The people very quickly recognised that there was a powerful force for retribution amongst them.

'Sekhmet!' they whispered in hurried whispers in the market places and temples

'Sekhmet is Out There'. And they began to be kinder to one another, banding together for protection. They forgot to be greedy and malicious and envious and arrogant. They learned their lesson very quickly.

But Sekhmet could not stop. Having started on her course of bloodletting and destruction she only developed a thirst for more. It was her function and her purpose, and she loved it.

So Ra had to call all his stewards and his servants. He set them, day and night, to making enormous vats of barley beer. Whilst they were doing this, he sent hundreds of messengers down to the First Cataract where, on the banks of the Nile, there can be found the red ochre peculiar to that place. When the messengers returned with the red ochre, he instructed everybody to mix it into the vats of beer. Then, on enormous sleds, they took the great vats to the place in the marshes where Sekhmet lay, sleeping off her blood lust of the night before.

Whilst she lay dreaming, they poured all the beer on to the marshes, and they crept away.

Night fell; the Moon rose, and Sekhmet awoke. She sighed and stretched, and as she opened her beautiful golden eyes, she beheld, gleaming in the moonlight, the liquid, red as blood. With a roar of delight , imagining it to be blood she had shed the night before, she fell upon it thirstily, lapping it up, and gulping it down, immersing herself in it completely.

High noon arrived, and Sekhmet came, staggering drunkenly, down the Avenue at Heliopolis.

Ra and all the assembled company were waiting.

And Ra held out his arms to her.

'My lovely Daughter, you come in peace!' he smiled. 'A whole night has passed, and you have not shed one single drop of blood. It is surely time to confer upon you a new name and a new power, even more terrible than the last. From this day you shall be known as Hathor, the Lady of Love and Beauty, and Mankind shall know a new pain and a new terror.'

THE MANIFESTATION OF PTAH

The great shining force that is Atum was known as the Lake of Flame. This was such a mighty force of Universal Love that it emerged, fully formed as Atum from the Primordial Waters of Nun, so that it might pour out through Him, and create the world.

When He first emerged from the Primordial Waters Atum was glorious beyond splendour. Powerfully conscious of both His Force and his Form, He looked around Him.

His love was a mighty deluge of blazing light, and He longed to pour it forth into His Creation, but He made himself rest a while upon the waters of Nun to consider what to do.

Drawing upon the deep still powers of darkness and inertia below him, He realised that He must create that which always had its Other, for without it, it would have nowhere to put its love. He knew that in order to do this He must divide Himself, for He must give himself a World to love.

While He was thinking in this way, He became aware of His Heart. It was from the very Heart of Atum that the knowledge came of who He was, and what He wanted to do. In his Heart he longed to create a World peopled by gods, a lush and fertile World filled with abundance and glory.

And then He became aware of his Tongue. He knew that when he spoke the names of his creations, they would live forever, and He would live forever within them.

As Atum pondered upon his Heart and his Tongue, He became conscious that they derived from the Absolute Spirit, which had dictated that He should emerge from the Waters as Himself. And he realised that the Absolute

Spirit within his Heart and Tongue gave him both the knowledge and the power to create that which He longed to live in, and with forever.

And He knew that the Absolute Spirit was named **Ptah.**

So Atum pronounced the name of Ptah. And He became Him.

Now we are ready to proceed.

CHAPTER ONE

ANUBIS: THE OPENER OF WAYS

THE FIRST LEVEL
THE ROOT CHAKRA.
THE KHAIBIT BODY

The first *neter* we encounter on the path of love is **Anubis**, the dog-headed lord of shadow. Opener of ways, our guiding principle and witness to self-judgment, he is a beautiful energy with which to begin. Anubis exemplifies all that is best in the canine soul – protectiveness, responsibility, charm and forgiveness – and yet, as lord of the gates of death, he is also an enigmatic and deeply arcane force.

Interpretation of the mythological life of Anubis offers profound psychological and spiritual insight into the workings of the human heart. The betrayal by his mother Nephthys of both her sister and her husband bears a sweet fruit. Anubis, half god, half animal, is fully competent to assess the balance between light and shadow in the self-knowledge (heart) of humanity. He is able to travel freely between the worlds, wholly belonging to neither, and yet the denizen of both. He is unmarried, illegitimate and brought up, as so many of us are, in a family situation of lies and collusions, yet his animal instincts are employed for the highest good and in the service of healing and light. He exemplifies the highest and most noble qualities of the dog, being loyal, instinctive, protective, completely trustworthy and perfectly at peace with his lower nature.

As the god of embalming and mummification he is the one god-force who is given the responsibility to hold and maintain Heaven's link with the physical plane. As a god of the **root** chakra he links us to the blood-red beginnings of our organic self. As opener of the ways, and guardian of the threshold, he can provide us with the training and opportunity to meet and explore completely new dimensions of self. Anubis is the god of the neophyte or 'spiritual beginner'; it is he who asks for the passwords that give access to the untrodden paths of the secret worlds. This then is our god-force to guide and protect us on our journey of evolving consciousness. He is our companion, our shadow, our spiritual potential and our root. As the lord of death, he delivers us over the threshold to a new life.

Anubis' consciousness gives us a happy connection with the lower nature, and promotes the highest qualities of the canine within us – loyalty, humour, protectiveness, guardianship and the gift of training. Also the arts of discretion and impartiality, for Anubis guards secrets and mysteries as well as doorways. These are all the qualities necessary for the neophyte, and no matter how knowledgeable or advanced we feel we have become on the road to self-realisation we need to be constantly aware of the shadow trotting at our heels, reminding us that we are always only beginning.

Illegitimacy and the Single State:
Both the root chakra and the *khaibit* body give awareness of security and survival. As we embark upon the journey along the path of love, the issues that we confront are, quite naturally, those of 'not belonging'. We feel that we are neither secure nor beloved. It is important to acknowledge and respect these feelings. The story of Anubis was told to show us how to deal with and change them. The shadow aspect of self will always feel them; whilst we are alive they will always be a part of us. In fact it is these very feelings of loneliness and separateness which promote us to grow and gather strength. Anubis has a 'shameful' past; so do we. The lies and secrets that surround his parentage and beginnings, reflect the hidden guilt and shame which we all carry, and which, if we do not understand and forgive, lead us to act out destructive behaviour and unkindness to others. Consideration of Anubis' life and purpose gives us the understanding and the ability to feel safe, and to belong. Consider how dogs need to 'belong'. It is a primary motivation for them. When they have no sense of purpose or person to serve they become savage and destructive, but when they do, they astound with

their intelligence and resourcefulness. They are humanity's 'best friend'. When we can recognise it, our shadow body is our best friend. Dogs forgive readily and seek forgiveness; it is one of their most endearing qualities. We need to find that constant state of forgiveness for others and ourselves, for we all suffer from alienation and are none of us perfect. We need to remember that we 'are all assholes'. I use this term advisedly because it always makes my students laugh in recognition of their human failings, and feel the readiness to give that recognition to everyone else.

Dogs have powerful instincts, tenacity, willingness to work and learn and supreme loyalty to their chosen masters. They can also love beyond their own survival needs. These qualities are god-given and, as such, we can find them in ourselves as we look for the Lord Anubis within, and awaken to him in the root chakra.

We can now think of our root chakra and the lord Anubis as having seven chakras of their own. Each of these internal chakras has an appropriate gift or quality, which we can realise on our quest for understanding our *khaibit* body and how to use it along the path of love. Whilst considering these qualities and gifts it is important to try to actualise them by first feeling where they 'live' in their chakric placement, and then claiming them. When they are placed and named they are readily accessible. As a spiritual prepa-ration for the ritual awakening of Anubis, spend at least five minutes contemplating each quality, locating their progress on your own chakric path.

GIFTS OF ANUBIS THROUGH THE CHAKRAS

ROOT:	*Instinct*
SACRUM:	*Preservation*
SOLAR PLEXUS:	*Training*
HEART:	*Loyalty*
THROAT	*Learning*
BROW:	*Impartiality*
CROWN:	*Freedom*

INSTINCT: THE ROOT OF ANUBIS

The gift of **instinct** lies at our root of roots, and is the natural god-given survival force of our divine animal nature. It is of fundamental importance to be aware of our instincts and trust them, for they cannot lie. They are primal and basic, particular to each of us; they cannot be explained but are there to promote our continuance. We experience them physically as 'hunches' or 'gut reactions', unexplained goose bumps, spine shivers, or tingles of excitement. They lead us away from dangers and into exciting new dimensions of experience. They are physical clues to the uncovering of mysteries. The very first task we undertake on the path of love lies in the root chakra of Anubis. We need to re-discover our instinct and respect it.

PRESERVATION: THE SACRUM OF ANUBIS

As we take our energy up from the root to the sacrum of Anubis, our instinctual survival needs will form into a primal desire to 'preserve' that which is valid and helpful for our continuance. Anubis, as god of embalming, represents this quality for us. The priests of Anubis kept the physical body of the Pharaoh from decay so that the land of Egypt would continue in power and prosperity, in the belief that the preservation of his material form would help to ensure that his good works would also be preserved.

Preservation does not mean 'hoarding', or holding on to that which is outmoded or irrelevant; it derives from the sacral ability to 'sort out' what is valuable from what is not, and then protect it from harm. Anubis is a good guard and he brings this special gift to us from the sacrum. This is the place to consider what is truly valuable to you, what you desire to preserve, and to determine to do so.

TRAINING: THE SOLAR PLEXUS OF ANUBIS

We experience Anubis in the solar plexus by connecting to our **training**. It is Anubis who knows the secret formulae and passwords that will give us access to higher, brighter realms, and as such he represents our training: the inculcated disciplines that we carry with us so that we need never lose touch with our animal nature, which, as creatures of earth, is our inheritance and our joy. Training gives us a constant sense of working towards and reaching for our highest potential. We keep ourselves in training in readiness for life's challenges. Training ensures that we are alert and ready. Training comes in many forms, but it is never lost. It is a golden quality and, like gold, it is hard earned and valued beyond price. Spiritual training brings the intelligence to recognise our shadow body and the ability to hear our own excuses.

As our energy rises from 'preservation' in the sacrum, we can focus it at solar plexus level to direct or 'train' what we need to preserve into our life-task.

At this point we can find the clarity and intelligence to respect the training we have been given and the commitment to continue on our own.

LOYALTY: THE HEART OF ANUBIS

On rising to the heart of Anubis, we find there the divine canine gift of **loyalty**. Loyalty combines 'support' and 'protection'. Having trained our energies, we can now use them to offer support to our loved ones, beliefs and 'masters'. We find commitment to our higher calling, and the love to support and protect it. We can also find the self-belief to receive support and protection, knowing in our heart that while our belief is strong, we too are supported and protected. Anubis is always there. Our shadow body travels with us wherever we go. We are not alone. We can begin to understand ourselves from a place of trust and self-belief, without equivocation or denial. Loyalty is a fixed quality of the heart; once we find it, it never leaves us. It is the heart of the root. When it takes root in our heart we experience the glow of knowing that we can be 'called upon' to fulfill our tasks in the name of love, and we will always be ready.

At this point we can find love for our loyalty.

LEARNING: THE THROAT OF ANUBIS

Learning is the gift of Anubis in the throat. From the commitment of loyalty in the heart, we find the openness to learn and the freedom to release our learning. As we learn who we are, light and shadow become one. We never stop learning. It is the gift of growth from the throat of the root. While we learn we feel truly alive and flourishing. Learning is the very breath of love. To keep learning is to be in love with life; to have a constant dialogue with life, to allow surprises and to be surprising. The more we learn of our shadow body, the more it will surprise us. All that we ever learned can only bring us to the place of being able to learn. We can express learning from the throat as 'learnedness', but in so doing we only learn more. Learning, like love and breath, is inexhaustible.

Here, we can allow our learning function to flow from the throat as an expression of love for ourselves and the world.

IMPARTIALITY: THE BROW OF ANUBIS

When 'learning' rises to the brow of Anubis we attain the gift of **impartiality**. Anubis witnesses the weighing of the heart in the Halls of Judgment, adjusting the balance to make sure the calibration is correct. At the brow level of the root chakra, we reach the wisdom necessary to assess the workings of our own heart. We can recognise our brightness and our shadow, and balance them with judgment and discretion. By realising all the previous gifts on the ray and level of Anubis, we are ready for clear self-assessment and self-witnessing. The shadow holds no terrors for us; we have come to see it as our friend.

At this part of the exercise, we can assess our impartiality, thus allowing it to become real.

FREEDOM: THE CROWN OF ANUBIS

At the crown of Anubis we receive the gift of **freedom**. In awakening the root chakra to find our inner security, we travel from 'instinct' to 'preservation.' This provides us with an *organic* sense of security, which we focus into 'training' at the solar plexus, and 'loyalty' in the heart. These last two gifts provide the *moral* security of discipline and commitment. From there we reach for the constant sense of learning and the wisdom of impartiality, which gives us spiritual security. All of these gifts are needed to take us to freedom. In recognition of the shadow, we claim our freedom from uncertainty. Like Anubis, we can travel freely between the worlds in celebration of the freedom of our own choice. When we arrive at freedom, we know how to love.

Here, at the end of the exercise, we can claim our freedom.

PERSONAL AFFIRMATIONS ON THE GOD-FORCE ANUBIS

This next stage is to repeat **aloud** the following personal affirmations many times, until they all feel easy to repeat with clarity and confidence.

I am ready to learn and guard the higher mysteries of Life

I emerge from the darkness of my past to the clear light of my present

I am an imperfect being, and I am not equipped to judge others

As I belong to Earth I am welcome in Heaven

To whosoever seeks my helpful guidance, I will gladly offer it

RITUAL PROCEDURE
Once the gifts of Anubis have been claimed, and his affirmations truthfully announced, we can consider ourselves ready to proceed with the ritual awakening of the god-force Anubis. Ritual creates a focus of concentration, which permits access to the more magical and spiritual levels of self from the earthly plane. By applying all the appropriate colours, perfumes, images and so on, which traditionally correspond to the 'sphere' of each god-force, we create clarity of space and intention to awaken to its presence. We 'sanctify' this space by imbuing it with love and truth. There is no point in

performing a ritual without positive thoughts of self and others. Ritual is an honouring of each shining aspect of self we wish to invoke. It does not have to be a solemn or gloomy procedure. Lightness of heart and natural laughter during any part of the process are signs of proper self-preparation and balance. Before starting, make sure that you have allowed yourself a good two hours when you will not be disturbed or called away. The hours of dusk, or 'dawn twilight', are appropriate times to work with Anubis. Cleanse your mind of any preoccupying thoughts in order to focus your whole attention on the procedure. If you have a prevailing problem that needs to be addressed, you can 'place' it correctly if you take responsibility for it, regarding it as part of your shadow body. Consider yourself a temple neophyte who is preparing to meet a god. Actively connect with the idea that, as well as meeting the god, you are preparing to awaken and activate your root chakra and gain knowledge of your *khaibit* body. The following correspondences are offered to bring power and focus to the awakening of the energy of the god-force Anubis in ritual conditions.

RITUAL CORRESPONDENCES ON THE PRINCIPLE OF ANUBIS

COLOUR:	***Red, black***
PERFUME:	***Amber***
INCENSE:	***Myrhh***
ANIMAL:	***Dog***
CHAKRA:	***Root***
BODY:	***Khaibit***
TIME OF DAY:	***Dusk***
SACRED SYMBOL:	***A Sarcophagus***
TAROT CARD:	***'The Fool,' 'The Star'***

SPACE PREPARATION

The ritual space should be uncluttered, with just a small table for a shrine or altar. Before starting, burn some **myrhh** on a piece of charcoal to purify the space with its smoke, leaving the incense burning on the altar. Place an unlit candle or a tea-light in a saucer on the floor at each of the four directions. If you have Tibetan bells or a gong, chime them a few times to clear old psychic vibrations. See that the space is pleasing to your eyes with nothing there to distract you. If you like, you can play some soothing music on a tape or C.D, but not the television or radio.

PREPARING THE ALTAR

Your altar should be in front of you as you face the East. Cover it with a **black** or **red** cloth, and place a cup containing spring water, a small dish of salt and a representation of Anubis upon it. If you do not have a statue or picture of Anubis, you could use a photograph of a loved and trusted dog, or a representation of a sarcophagus. You could place the Tarot cards of 'The Fool' and 'The Star' on each side of it. There should be a black or a red unlit candle in front of Anubis. Anything you wish to consecrate, such as a crystal, Tarot pack or a piece of jewelry, can also be placed on the altar.

PURIFICATION, ANOINTING AND ROBING

Bathe or shower. Dip your finger in amber or myrhh oil and anoint your root chakra with the sign of a pentagram. Put on a clean garment; ideally it should be a simple white robe or gown that you only wear for rituals. Keep your feet bare and if your hair is long, loosen it.

DELINEATION OF THE SACRED SPACE

This next stage is very important. You are preparing both an inner and outer space in which to awaken a powerful archetypal force, and they both need to be protected and sanctified. The following exercise has been adapted from a more complicated magical procedure known as 'Calling the Quarters' it is a very effective protective and energising technique for any ritual work.

Standing to face your altar in the East, raise your arms. Imagine the rising sun, blessing you with the glory of its presence, its dawning rays flowing through your body and out through your hands.

'I call upon the Angels and Elements of Air, Guardians and Powers of the East, to sanctify this Temple and inspire my thoughts.'

Light your Eastern candle.

Turn to your right. Imagine the fierce power of the midday sun from the south radiating from your centre, empowering your will.

'I call upon the Angels and Elements of Fire, Guardians and Powers of the South to sanctify this Temple and illumine my Will.'

Light your Southern candle.

Turn to your right again to face the west, and imagine the glory of the setting Sun, filling your heart with beauty and true sadness.

'I call upon the Angels and Elements of Water, Guardians and Powers of the West to sanctify this Temple and open my Heart.'

Light your Western candle.

Turn to your right again, and imagine in the north, the dark stillness of the night descending upon you like a soft blanket of peace.

'I call upon the Angels and Elements of Earth, Guardians and Powers of the North to sanctify this Temple and protect me from harm.'

Light your Northern candle. Turn to your right once more to stand in front of the altar.

Placing your hands over the salt, bless it with the sign of the pentagram.

'I bless this salt in the name of the God who made me.'

Do likewise with the water.

'I bless this water in the name of Goddess who gives me Life.'

Pour the salt into the water, and sprinkle it around the ritual space in a clockwise circle.

'I conjure Thee O Circle of Power that Thou should create a safe boundary between the Worlds, wherein only Truth is spoken, and only Truth is heard.

So mote it be.'

Bring your focus to the god-force Anubis and light the altar candle.

'I dedicate this Altar to the Lord Anubis that I might proceed with

him to the Shores of Paradise.'

VISUALISATION OF CHAKRIC COLOUR

Seat yourself comfortably in the centre of your sacred space. Surround yourself with a blood-red light. Imagine a dull metal chalice, filled to the brim with sparkling rubies, hovering over your head. The light from these rubies drenches you in life-giving energy, which, as you breathe, sparkles through your veins imbuing you with vital nourishment. At the same time, imagine yourself drawing upon the deep powers of the Earth below you. Experience them flowing up into your root chakra, strengthening you, sustaining you, and warming your blood.

Acknowledge the chakric qualities of the lord Anubis in yourself, locating them in your chakra points. Give yourself time to make them real.

> **'I give thanks for my instinct.**
> **I give thanks for my preservation.**
> **I give thanks for my training.**
> **I give thanks for my loyalty.**
> **I give thanks for my learning.**
> **I give thanks for my impartiality.**
> **I give thanks for my freedom.'**

When you feel ready, stand before the altar for your invocation to Anubis. Again, this should be spoken aloud. It need not be theatrically declaimed; a truthful heart-felt delivery is best. Magical 'workings' are only effective if they proceed from the emotional centre. The stronger the emotion behind them, the more successful they prove to be. But the emotion must be honest and controlled.

INVOCATION TO ANUBIS

> *Hail Anubis, God of the Gates of Death and Life, enthroned in the*
> *Halls of Judgment and the Desert shadows of the Underworld.*
> *In Thy right hand the Feather of Truth,*

In Thy left, the soft cloak of Protective Love.
Thou art crowned with the sharp ears of the desert Dog
And thy nose scents the danger of insincerity and lies.
Waiting eternally at the Threshold of the Worlds
That there shall be a sweet welcome for Life which passes into Death
And a light swift welcome for Death, as it passes into Life.
Embracer and Protector of the journey of the Ka,
Lord of the Khaibit,
Soft-footed Guardian of the Twilight realm,
Awaken our senses to the sharp clearness of our own Inner Truth.
Stay with us in our Shadow place
That we may meet our strength and purpose in the Light.
Whenever Sleep follows Waking and Waking follows Sleep
Wherever Life passes from flesh to earth, to seed, to flower, to flesh
It is Thy Pathway that is trod; Thy step that is danced.
By the brevity and the eternity of Life
By the pulse of Light and Shadow
By the seed hidden under the sand
By the shed skin of the Serpent
And the shining light of the Dog-Star
We call upon Thee to be with us now
In Body and in Spirit.

HAIL ANUBIS!
Hail and Welcome.

As you welcome the god-force Anubis into your space, you could visualise his presence as a beautiful black dog, protecting and guarding your meditation.

You may now attempt the following meditation, which is a preamble to the *Sphere of Anubis*, and allows you to experience yourself as a creature of both heaven and earth.

EARTH AND HEAVEN MEDITATION

Seat yourself comfortably with your back supported and your feet firmly placed. Be aware of the firm, safe floor below you. The firm, safe floor that supports you perfectly upon the surface of the earth where you belong. Acknowledge your body, and fill your body with your self. Feel your self harmoniously distributed within your body.

Contact your centre, and the power of your will. Acknowledge that you have chosen this time and space of your own free will to attempt this exercise. Congratulate yourself for giving this time and experience to yourself.

With the power of your will and your imagination, send your own personal energy from your centre down to your feet. Feel the gravitational pull of the Earth in your feet, making them tingle.

Now send your personal energy down through the floor to the ground.

Make energetic contact with the living Earth below.

And now, send your energy deeper below the ground, into the rich fertile living soil.

Experience the quick light vibration of the insect kingdom corresponding to your own nervous system

And go deeper.

Feel the deep slow thrust of the Plant Kingdom, and root yourself in the living, breathing soil.

And go deeper.

Feel the magical vibrations of the crystals and sacred ores and minerals deeper below in the Earth. Feel them linking to the minerals and trace elements in your body.

And go deeper.

Feel the veins of fairy magic within the Earth dancing in your blood.

And go deeper.

Through the very mantle of Earth, to the Source of pulsating power at Earth centre. And plug yourself in.

Link in to the mighty powers of Earth, from your centre to Earth's centre.

From your solar plexus, to the innermost Sun at the Earth's core.

And draw that power up.

Draw it up from the living fire, through to the living rock, and up and up and up.

Draw it up to the living soil. And up through the ground, and through the bricks and mortar and wood of the building. Draw it up through the substance of the floor to your own two feet.

And draw that power up through your legs to the root of your being.

And up through your body, past your centre to your heart.

And in your heart transmute it into Love.

Naturally and easily, love the Earth.

Love its shining greenness. Love its sparkling waters. Love its multi-farious flowers and plants and trees.

Love its animals and its birds and its fishes and its dolphins and its people.

Let the mighty powers of Earth resting in your heart flow back to Source as the indestructible force of human Love.

Become aware of yourself sitting in a pool of crystalline, sparkling, fragrant, rainbow-coloured light. The light is beaming down upon you. It is pouring into your crown chakra. It flows into your head, clearing and energising your mind, and freeing you from any anxiety or tension.

It flows down your spine like delicious particles of iridescent healing stardust, making you feel supple and relaxed. It flows down your legs and into your two feet, and down your arms into your hands, making them tingle with delight.

Breathe the perfumed light into your body so that you sparkle and glow, every cell and molecule dancing like stars.

You are a very effulgent being. You are a living star.

Stretch your mind upwards. Pass through the ceiling beyond the roof to the clouds. Encircle the moon and the planets.

Continue on to the stars and the galaxies and the Firmament. Let your consciousness merge into the great Cosmic Tides of Life.

Attune your spirit to the Great Spirit. Harmonise your will to the Will of

Heaven. Feel yourself stretched across the green and beautiful Earth, your mind arched across the blue vault of Heaven. Know that you are connected by yourself to everything that lives and breathes.

Know that you are utterly safe. Know that you are free in that safety.

Lie down comfortably with your forearms crossed over your breast for the following guided meditation on the *Sphere of Anubis.*

GUIDED MEDITATION ON THE SPHERE OF ANUBIS

You are in a dark, still ageless silence. You are quite alone. Lying supine on cool stone, you are perfectly relaxed and composed. Your breathing is even and deep. You can see and hear nothing, but you are immeasurably calm, as though you hold within yourself the awareness of Eternity. You are completely within yourself. You hold yourself inside your body with ease and precision. The only thing that slightly impinges upon your senses is the faint smell of unguent, amber and myrrh. It brings the hint of angelic presence to your deep and deliberate solitude.

You cannot tell what you are lying in. It is of no significance. The cool, flat surfaces, which surround you, reflect only Yourself. The presence of Yourself, the well-known energy, the oldest, dearest and most familiar Youness of You. **Your-own-ness.** *You are perfectly safe. You experience yourself as tranquil Wholeness. Each breath is like the rising and falling of the World.*

The entire Cosmos waits upon each breath. You are wrapped in silence. Your form is an outward expression of your divinity. Each time you breathe, Life and Death hang upon a thread. Your life is the essence of Life Itself.

As you lie, suspended in space, your body holds you serenely, and the place in which you lie contains you securely. It is flat. It is quiet. It is dark. You are utterly alone.

You are breathing in the stars.

You now become aware of a delicious sensation. Sparkling energy is pouring down upon you. It is like a refreshing shower of healing etheric light. It is infiltrating your body, bathing your soul, like balm.

Your entire sense of self is beginning to feel lighter, brighter, newer, and more awake. You are clear and open.........transparent.

You open your eyes.

The stone sarcophagus is open. You are lying in a shaft of starry light.

You are being charged, suffused with the essence of Universal Light. Your Mind, Body, Soul and Spirit are being prepared for the next level of your life.

Your eyes begin to see through the sparkling iridescence to the Point of the Pyramid and beyond. You see the sky, the milky radiance of the night.

You see two kindly eyes glowing in the night sky. They are the eyes of Anubis, your Guide and Protector, the Patron of Travelers, and the Guardian between the Worlds.

You rise to a sitting position. Your shaft of light has been absorbed into the darkness, and the Chamber is now glimmering with a half-light, like dawn or twilight.

The glowing eyes of Anubis appear before you. You make out his shape; his two long Jackal-like ears, his beautiful dark furry body. You stand to greet him. Stepping out of the sarcophagus you follow him to a secret door set into the farther wall. Passing through into a long, low narrow shaft, you crouch on all fours to make your way down, down, down in the darkness.

Reaching the bottom at last, you find yourself in a tunnel. You know that Anubis is just ahead of you. You can stand up now, and you pass along the tunnel easily and without fear.

The opening glimmers ahead of you, moonlight on sand. The outline of Anubis against the light.

You approach the opening. Anubis is standing beyond it.

He asks you

'What is the name of the threshold?'

You answer.

He moves aside, and you walk through.

You are standing on soft sand. Anubis is some distance away from you, his shape casting a giant shadow on the moonlit desert. You are facing the Great Pyramid with a perfect perspective of its proportions. You see that the moonlight makes a perfect path upon the sand from your resting place to the secret door you have just emerged from – a silver ribbon of light, symbolising your emergence from preparedness to experience. The Path that leads to your Inner Goal.

Here in the pale desert light you may ask Anubis to help you see a symbol, which will symbolise that Goal for you.

Attune your senses to the shape and level of the Dog God, and wait for the image to appear.

It will come from the stars of the Egyptian sky, and you will see it, superimposed upon the side of the Great Pyramid

You sit and drink in the beauty of the night. The soft clearness of the air, thematic of the moon among the stars, the protective presence of the God. And an image appears for you on the facing side of the mighty Pyramid.

You give thanks and meditate upon the message you have received.

And now, the first pink streaks of light in the sky tell you that Ra is about to appear above the Eastern horizon.

You stand and shake the sand from your clothes. Anubis fades into the glimmering dawn.

Now you may let the desert and the Pyramids fade, and return to your full waking consciousness, relaxed, refreshed and ready to resume your life.

INTEGRATION AND GROUNDING

On completion of this guided meditation, take careful note of the experience you have had. Write down a synopsis of the feelings you underwent, and the images you received. Do not discount anything. It is all valid, even if some of it was distraction and resistance. This is valid too. Remember that you have been working with your shadow side, as well as your emergence. It is important to be aware of what your distractions and resistances are likely to be as you advance to the more subtle and powerful levels further along the path. If you practice with a divinatory tool, such as Tarot, Runes or '*I*

Ching', you could use it here to gain insight into your experiences.

Your questions could be:

In what way is my Shadow likely to manifest for me during this work?

How can I best work with the symbols and images I have received?

What is the nature of my relationship with the god-force Anubis*?*

How may I integrate this new knowledge into my life?

I have worked extensively with Tarot for most of my adult life, and I find it unparalleled for providing immediate insight and guidance. The best way to use it for 'grounding' a meditation is to shuffle the pack whilst the meditation is still fresh in your mind. Spread the whole pack out, face down in a fan shape, so that you can see every card. Ask your question aloud. The more specific the question, the better. It is imperative to phrase your question carefully and positively.

For example:

What particular energy do I need in this situation? or ***What is the most positive approach for me to adopt regarding it?***

In this way, you maintain responsibility.

Having asked your question, choose one card from the pack. If you find this difficult, close your eyes and run your fingertips over them. You will *feel* the right card. If you are not familiar with the Tarot as a system, use a pack with all the cards highly symbolised such as the Ryder-Waite pack.

Having drawn your card, look hard and deep at its message for you. If you have asked your question genuinely, the answer will be there in the picture. Trust your intuition, and do not shirk or recoil if you do not like the image. *There is no such thing as a bad card.*

Keep a record of the questions you ask and the cards you draw. If you have not completely understood their message, allow yourself time and process. Symbols within the Tarot speak directly to the unconscious. Until you are familiar with them you need time to integrate them into your awareness. A good thing to do in this case is to take the actual card with you when you go to bed, place it under your pillow and ask for its message to be revealed to you in your dreams.

Where you received a special image or a symbol of your higher goal from Anubis during the meditation, it is a very good idea to manifest it by creating a representation of it. You can make a sketch of it, and then fashion it later in clay or fabric, or any material that feels appropriate. This is a very effective magical technique, which allows a channel for manifestation to occur from the inner or astral realms. It also serves as a working reminder on the *aufu* level of your higher goal. The more often and readily you are reminded of it, the more conscious you become of it, and the more accessible it becomes.

CLOSING DOWN

Stand to face the altar, and say aloud:

'Lord Anubis, I thank you for Your Presence and bid You Hail and Farewell!'

You then blow out the candle and close yourself down with your forefinger. Lightly draw a pentagram on your root chakra, imagining it as a beautiful red rose with its petals closing into a fresh bud. Stamp your feet to finish and ground your ritual work. Blowing out all your candles, say:

'Guardians, Angels and Powers of all Directions I thank you for your Presence in this Temple. I bid you return to your lovely realms. Hail and Farewell. The Temple is Closed.'

Take note of your dreams and any unusual happenings that occur in the period following this work, before you commit to the next level.

CHAPTER TWO

SEKHMET: ILLUMINED LIONESS

THE SECOND LEVEL
THE SACRAL CHAKRA. THE AUFU BODY

We are now ready to awaken ourselves to the second *neter* on the path of love. This takes our energy up to the **sacral chakra** where we gain consciousness of our physicality as the *aufu*, in order to express the mighty power of the lioness goddess **Sekhmet**. Sekhmet is the most raw and primal aspect of the Egyptian goddess, appropriately placed in the chakra where the first division takes place. Here we become aware of ourselves as female or male animals. It is in the sacrum that the *Kundalini* or serpent power of untransformed sexuality is awakened. Sometimes referred to as the spleen, it is the seat of anger and passion.

A vengeful and destructive force, the Egyptians depicted Sekhmet as a beautiful and dignified lioness, crowned with the disc of the Sun and holding the *ankh*, or Egyptian key of life.

Daughter of Ra, she sprang into being when he pronounced her name, to avenge the forces of evil that emerged in the hearts and minds of men when his own powers to prevent them became diminished through old age. She is the wife of Ptah, the gentle Architect of the cosmos, patron of artisans and craftsmen, but she is also a raging sexual force The erect serpent or *uraeus* on the headdresses of the Egyptian initiates were worn to symbolize the fully awakened, controlled and conscious use of the serpent (*Kundalini)* power of Sekhmet.

Sekhmet is dangerous and ruthless. Her thirst for blood was so overpowering that it became necessary to trick her into drunkenness to prevent her ferocious rampaging from destroying the entire population. She was much loved, however, and the ancients texts refer to her as 'Queen of Intoxications', 'Slayer of Evil', 'Roamer of Deserts' and 'Illuminator of Men', among many others.(See Robert Masters *Sekhmet)* Ra eventually transformed her into Hathor, the Lady of Love, bestowing upon her the greater and more terrible powers of romantic love and relationship. It is interesting to note that the Egyptians perceived that Ra (the creative life force of the universe) having breathed life into creation, could only transform his creations, not destroy them. This means that nothing created by God could die, only change into another level of being.

The cosmic aspect of Sekhmet (and Hathor) *is* Nut, the mother of the gods, the ineffably beautiful transcendent star goddess who adores and protects her husband Geb, the Earth, with the arch of her body.

Sekhmet represents the primal beginnings of the tri-partite love goddess, *Nut-Hathor-Sekhmet.* She is the aspect of this triad relating to the primal passions drawn from Earth's pulsating volcanic core, which the Egyptian understood to be transformed into love-in-relationship and art (as *Hathor*), or transpersonal love-of-humanity (as *Nut).*

Sekhmet Consciousness relates to passion, power, righteous anger and boundary issues. Like the wild lioness of the desert, she is free and unconstrained, operating from a primary and natural creative instinct.

The Ancient Egyptians linked the *sekhem,* or dynamic powers of the animal nature, which reside in the sacrum, with the *SA,* or magical life force which issues from the throat. This is illustrated as the sacred marriage of Sekhmet with Ptah (the god of Memphis, the throat chakra of Egypt) who created the world by 'naming it'. The mighty roar of the lioness is powerful delineation of a boundary. Vocalising rage and passion always releases them into the outer world.

Everything that links with Sekhmet is intensified in its nature and fuelled with the flame of fervour. Sexual passion is after all the primary creative force in a healthy marriage, and vocalised righteous wrath an energising and cleansing impetus that can often do more than modern medication to offset the effects of ennui and depression.

Sekhmet energy connects us to the wild woman within. This confers on us the right to claim our intrinsic power with natural pride and unashamed self-expression. Sekhmet Consciousness provides us with honest lust and sexual integrity, physical dignity, raw creativity, and passionate engagement with life.

In the Tarot Sekhmet is shown as *Strength,* or as older packs have termed her, 'The Enchantress'. In the magical system of Cabala, this card's Hebrew name is *Teth,* which translates as 'serpent', or *Kundalini.* The *Strength* card shows two aspects of Sekhmet – primal lioness and beautiful star maiden – in perfect synergy. The Alaister Crowley pack refers to it as *Lust,* meaning lust for life, or passion, but the Strength card really teaches of love as a powerful and natural force – the most powerful force indeed in the whole of God's universe. Therefore, to prepare ourselves to awaken the goddess-force of Sekhmet, we need to expend some time and energy on honest reflection of how passionately we love; how engaged we are with our lives. When, for example did we last burst into spontaneous laughter or song? How ready are we to voice our indignation at invasion? How sexually confident do we feel? How comfortable are we with the handling of personal power? On attaining the level of Sekhmet we raise awareness from the *khaibit* or shadow body to the *aufu* or physical body. Thus we can consider how well and healthy we are and how much animal magnetism we own. And,

Taking into account that once we magnetise energy into our own personal space we then become responsible for it, we can also consider if indeed this is as much or as little as we desire.

We can begin with contemplation of the seven chakric gifts of Sekhmet and meditation upon her qualities as they proceed through our own chakric system. Although we are primarily concentrating on the sacral chakra we are also using it as a wheel of power to activate all the other chakras, so that Sekhmet energy or *Kundalini* moves through them.

It is possible to arrive at a subjective and personal sense of her vibrational force if this exercise is done on the energetic level. This means that you try to recall these qualities from your physical memory, not merely consider them as ideas. You may find it helpful to gradually visualise yourself etherically becoming as a lion as you move upwards through the chakras.

THE GIFTS OF SEKHMET THROUGH THE CHAKRAS

ROOT:	*Passion*
SACRUM:	*Righteous Wrath; Joy*
SOLAR PLEXUS:	*Dignity.*
HEART:	*Power*
THROAT:	*Enchantment*
BROW:	*Exaltation*
CROWN:	*Ecstasy*

PASSION: THE ROOT OF SEKHMET

Passion is a life force. It stems from the core of earth. The roots of earth draw it up from the earth god's primal power. It flows through our own roots filling us with the desire for life. Sekhmet's primal experience is passionate. We are told that she 'drinks thirstily', that she leaps into the lakes of 'blood' with exultant roars. She is so engaged with her work that she cannot stop. Passion gives us the unthinking *need* to be who we really are. Passion thrusts us into a deep and powerful engagement with life. When we know passion, we *are* life. Life answers to us.

Sekhmet is a royal lady: queen of the beasts. From our *aufu* level we too are royal; the ruling royalty of the entire animal kingdom. When we are honest to that royalty, we claim rulership of life from the physical level. We can claim ownership. Life belongs to us, our bodies belong to us. We can allow ourselves to be passionately engaged with life because we have control over that aspect of it. We can draw upon the very volcanic forces below the mantle of earth to flow through all of its layers into our roots, and we can give life all that we have. And we can take all that it has to offer.

Passion lies at the root of the sacrum; it is the very reason for the sacrum. To awaken the lady Sekhmet and your sacrum, you have to find the passion first!

JOY AND RIGHTEOUS WRATH: THE SACRUM OF SEKHMET

The sacrum of Sekhmet is the sacrum of sacrums. Her essential core qualities are expressed from here. Her reasons for being who she is. Ra created her from his righteous wrath when evil first appeared in his realm. She gave him joy; she gladdened his heart, he 'welcomed his beautiful daughter.' She is a positive force for destruction.

In the sacrum, where energies and nutriments are 'sorted,' Sekhmet's primal passions sort themselves into the twins of **righteous wrath** and **joy**.

Both of these gifts are completely motivating for physical well-being and health, being thoroughly good feelings. A burst of righteous indignation as a natural response never fails to clear the air and seldom promotes ill feeling; in fact, it brings respect. We give little respect to those that have unclear boundaries. Joy and righteous wrath are delineators of our primal boundaries. Joy cannot be defined in itself. It just comes by itself when the boundary is clear and the sacrum is open. The two qualities work together. One cannot be alive without the other. Righteous wrath at invasion allows the gift of joy to awaken and rise to our higher chakras as sublimated sexual energy, as creativity, magic and mystical ecstasy.

In order to find your righteous wrath and your joy, you need to sort out your boundaries.

This is one of the most important aspects of the sacrum and the goddess Sekhmet on the path of love. It is paramount to be comfortable and alive in one's body, emanating the power that that body is inviolate and inviolable. When primal boundaries are conscious, psychic space is clear and ones own individual magical essence can permeate it, as both an attraction for what we require, and a repellent for what we do not. Then we can join in love and essence with whomever we delight in.

DIGNITY: THE SOLAR PLEXUS OF SEKHMET

At the solar plexus level, where primal will gains consciousness of identity, the essence of Sekhmet becomes conscious of herself as a lioness. She is beautiful, radiant and naturally noble; she is untamed and uncomplicated; she is completely what she is. She makes no excuses. This gives her **dignity**. Animals and small children have great dignity.

We have dignity when we do not demean ourselves by insincerity; when we are clear who we are; when we do not apologise for ourselves; when we know we have the right to be here.

We all do have the right. When we lift our awareness from acknowledgement of our and everyone else's inner boundary, we find the right to be wherever we choose to go. We go there with dignity.

You can experience your dignity by just allowing your joy and righteous wrath to rise up and radiate out of your solar plexus as a natural expression of you.

POWER: THE HEART OF SEKHMET

The greatest power is love. It moves mountains. Mothers have been known to find the physical strength to lift ten-ton trucks off their trapped children. In the heart of Sekhmet we find and emanate our truest **power**. When we realise that power is a gift, which issues from the heart, we may know and love our power. Then we are not afraid of it. Fear of our own power gives power to fear. Love of our power makes it safe. The more we love our power, recognising it as the power of love, the more powerful we become. When we awaken the heart of the mighty lioness Sekhmet, ruling deity of the *aufu,* we learn to release that power into our own physical system so that 'all inconsequence flees before us', and if disease and sickness are not necessary to our growth and development, we can dispatch them before they strike.

Finding power in the heart gives us the real power to be 'lion-hearted', to be fiercely protective of our boundaries and our young, and of the kingdom of the body.

To experience and realise power, all we have to do is to love it.

ENCHANTMENT: THE THROAT OF SEKHMET

It is said by those who have heard it that there is no sound more enthralling than a lion roaring in the wild. It has a compelling physical effect, making every hair on the body stand on end. When acknowledged power rises from the heart of Sekhmet to the throat chakra, we receive the gift of **enchantment**. Our words have the power to hold and enthrall. We command attention: we are heard, we are taken seriously. We do not say anything unless we mean it. Having processed all the previous gifts from 'passion' to 'power' we have no need to speak anything but our own truth. We have gained the ability to hold our own ground, and can now freely express ourselves from there. This brings the power of enchantment. Nothing is more riveting than the truth.

EXALTATION: THE BROW OF SEKHMET

As human beings we are undeniably the most exalted species walking the earth. At the brow of Sekhmet we recognise this **exaltation.** We experience ourselves as noble creatures; we are able to 'raise' our consciousness. We can 'see' beyond the trivial and the unnecessary. We can exalt situations, ideas and other people.

This part of the exercise reminds me irresistibly of an occasion when I was walking on Wimbledon Common.

Three children, the eldest no more than ten years old, were standing together in a little tableau by the lake. I noticed them from across the other side because they had extraordinary nobility of presence. As I walked around the lake towards them, the powerful effect created by their immobility and dignity did not falter for an instant. My curiosity was aroused. I was intrigued. I had to find out who these remarkable children were.

I greeted them airily:

'Hello children!' I called.

Immediately the air of nobility melted away. We exchanged a few pleasantries. They were very polite and charming children, but nothing particularly magnificent. I began to wonder if I had been mistaken. Then the youngest little girl piped up:

'Do you mind if we go back to being lions again?'

Of course! That was it! Lions!

The children had found in their bodies and their auras, the exaltation of the lion.

We can find it too.

ECSTASY: THE CROWN OF SEKHMET

Sekhmet is the Queen of Intoxications. When we rise to the crown of the sacrum, where we begin to experience levels which are more subtle than the physical, we can release ourselves from the body – into a dizzying sense of the sublime. We can allow ourselves natural **ecstasy**.

Ecstasy occurs when we release earth power through our bodies. It is a physical phenomenon, which happens when our bodies have built up enough power to 'let go'. The more conscious we become, the longer our bodies can sustain the experience of ecstasy.

At this point, we can look at all the qualities and gifts of Sekhmet and realise that, as sacral gifts, they all relate to sacred sex.

Passion and joy (righteous wrath having delineated the proper boundary for the sexual experience to take place) begin the experience. Dignity and power continue it. We experience the enchantment of sounds uttered in moments of love, the exaltation of being the beloved partner, and finally, the ecstasy of sharing in bliss. The crown of Sekhmet indeed

Having considered and remembered the gifts of Sekhmet, we can now repeat the personal affirmations. Keep on repeating them until they make your heart sing.

PERSONAL AFFIRMATIONS ON THE GODDESS SEKHMET

I rejoice in the gift of my sexuality

Nothing and no-one else can destroy my human dignity

I need never be afraid to voice my Truth

The Rhythm of Life pulses in my blood

I exercise free will and choice in all that I do

Having duly recalled the gifts of Sekhmet within our physical system and spoken her affirmations with truth, we can consider ourselves prepared for the ritual awakening of the goddess, the sacral chakra and consciousness of the *aufu*.

RITUAL PROCEDURE FOR AWAKENING THE GOD-FORCE SEKHMET

This ritual is more powerful if it is conducted before noon when the solar force is rising. Eat lightly after rising; a heavy breakfast can be enjoyed after your work. Spend some time out of doors before beginning. A walk in the park, a bicycle ride or a jog will clear your head and energise your body. My students are fortunate enough to ride horses in the desert before their Sekhmet work. It is the ideal exercise for strengthening the will and experiencing the animal nature from the sacrum. During this process, keep your focus on your body, in particular the sacral area.

The following ritual correspondences are provided to help.

RITUAL CORRESPONDENCES ON THE GODDESS-FORCE SEKHMET
    COLOUR: *Scarlet, Flame-Orange*

INCENSE:	*Frankincense*
PERFUME	*Musk, Patchouli*
ANIMAL:	*Lion (ess)*
CHAKRA:	*Sacrum*
BODY	*Aufu*
TIME OF DAY:	*Morning*
SACRED SYMBOL:	*Ankh*
TAROT CARD:	*'Strength'*

PREPARATION OF THE SPACE

Remove any clutter, and set your altar table in the east. Place your four candles in their directions. Burn some **frankincense** and smudge the ritual area, leaving it burning on the altar.

PREPARATION OF THE ALTAR

Cover your altar table with an **orange** cloth. Place on the altar the usual spring water in a cup or chalice, a small dish of salt and a scarlet or an orange candle. Add a representation of Sekhmet, or an *ankh*, or a picture of a lioness as a suggestion. You can also put some beer on the altar to drink after the meditation. A further suggestion for the strong is to put a sterilised sewing needle on the altar for a ritual bloodletting. I have found it helpful, as in the past, I noticed that aspirants would sometimes get nosebleeds or suffer small accidents during their Sekhmet days. When I pricked my finger and squeezed a drop of my blood over the incense, this never happened.

PURIFICATION, ANOINTING AND ROBING

Having bathed or showered, anoint your sacral chakra with **musk** or **patchouli** in the sign of the pentagram, taking care with the musk oil as it stains. A helpful tip is to rub a drop of the appropriate essential oil under your nose for the rituals, so that you can use the fragrances in the future to stimulate your memory.

Wear a loose robe or gown that feels pleasant against your skin. Orange knickers are a good idea, also an orange scarf tied around your hips. Always work in bare feet with unbound hair.

DELINEATION OF THE SACRED SPACE
Call the Quarters as on page 95, and create your circle of power. Lighting your altar candle, say:

> **'I dedicate this altar to the goddess Sekhmet that I may empower my life with dignity.'**

With your imagination and will, direct a ring of fire around the ritual space to protect and cleanse it.

VISUALISATION OF CHAKRIC COLOUR
Seating yourself comfortably in the circle, surround yourself in flame-coloured light. Experience it drenching you in life-giving force. Feel it filling every cell of your body with warmth and vitality. Acknowledge the gifts of Sekhmet as they proceed along your chakric path:

> **'I give thanks for my passion.**
> **I give thanks for my joy and my righteous wrath.**
> **I give thanks for my dignity.**
> **I give thanks for my power**
> **I give thanks for my enchantment.**
> **I give thanks for my exaltation.**
> **I give thanks for my ecstasy.'**

The next part of the work is devoted to experiencing the *aufu* and recognising inner boundaries.

Choose and mark out an area of the floor with your eyes as being ***your territory.*** Pace around it several times until you have claimed it. Having then claimed and delineated your territory begin to imbue it deliberately with your own *personal magical essence.* Create an invisible wall around your space (in which you will experience and enjoy your personal magical essence). Lie down in the space and roll about. Become as a Great Cat, claiming its territory and glorying in its own scent.

Allow a sound to emerge from the depths of your body, which expresses your relationship to your magically imbued territory. It might be a possessive growl, or a purr of enjoyment, or a coo of pleasure, or even a blend of all three: whatever it is, it is very important and positive to *express the feeling vocally.* Make sure that you experience the energy inside this bounded space as **yours and yours alone,** then the special magical essential energy with which you have filled this space will give you a wonderful feeling, which you can vocalise freely and easily without inhibition.

Spend a few minutes doing this, and really glory in it. Stretch your limbs, and roll and rub the length of your body over the floor, imprinting it with your own special scent and energy, vibration and sound, all of which you absolutely adore. Learn the smell, sound and vibratory force of your own magical essence.

Then rise to a comfortable sitting position. Close your eyes and *internalise the space.* Ingest it. Breathe it in. Take it right down to the sacral centre, and *sit on it inside.* It is all yours. Feel yourself easily and naturally exuding a vibrant glowing orange light.

You may now proceed with the invocation. The following invocation is to be spoken aloud and from the heart. This particular goddess invocation works very well to the accompaniment of a *tabla,* or any small drum. Visualise the shining presence of a golden ankh hovering above your head. Light pours through its loop, descending into a beam of golden light, which encompasses you as you recite.

INVOCATION TO SEKHMET

Hail to Thee Sekhmet!

Lioness Lady of Light and Lust, Munificent Mother, and Maker of Men.

In Thy right hand the Ankh of Eternal Outpouring,
Thy left holds the bare claws of sure, sudden death.
Thy face as lovely as thy Father's, the Sun God
His disc shines golden on Thy radiant mane.
Queen of the desert, the roaming wasteland,
Great One of Magic, Goddess of Flame,
Thy dance makes the coupling of Earth and the Heavens.
Power sent forth in the cry of Thy Name
Luminous Lady of righteous anger
Slayer of evil and lover of good
Who pours Thy radiance on to the Earth?
That all inconsequence may flee before Thee, and
Wrongdoing shrivel under Thy gaze
Sublime Queen of Intoxication and Enchantment
Lead us to ecstasy in communion with Thy Being.
Thy devotion is boundless in force and ferocity
Thy protection and passion a joy beyond knowing.
By the purest fire of the desert sun
By the fiercest kiss of the Lion's tongue
By the truth of Love and the joy of Being
By the immeasurable power of the Mother's heart
By the steady flame of Spirit
And the sacred flow of the Blood of Life
By all that are Thine and all that is growing
We call upon Thee
To be with us now
In Body and in Spirit.
HAIL SEKHMET!
Hail and Welcome.

You are now ready to undertake the guided meditation on the *Sphere of Sekhmet*. Make sure that you are comfortable and relaxed, lying down, or sitting with your back supported. Bless and acknowledge your *aufu* body, and begin.

GUIDED MEDITATION ON THE SPHERE OF SEKHMET

It is morning in the Sahara Desert. As far as your keen eyes can see, and much further, this desert belong to you. You alone. You are strong and free. Your powerful muscles ripple under your thick skin. The hot sand stings your bare feet. The red eye of Ra glares down inciting you to action. Blood runs fiercely in your veins. Your hair hangs long and loose down your back. The air shimmers with the heat. You can see it all around you. A magical haze.

You run easily and gladly through the desert. You are thirsty. You know an oasis where there are cool shady date palms, and a clear pool of sweet fresh water where you can bathe and drink your fill, and rest until the cool of the evening. You enjoy running. You match your stride with the slow and easy pounding of your heart. The sky is a cloudless blue. Kites wheel and circle over the dunes. This land is your Kingdom. You know every ridge and hollow. The clean, spare brightness fills you with exhilaration, but you pace your stride. You know how to survive. The desert is wild and pure and beautiful, but it is pitiless if not respected.

It is just like you.

You roam these plains every day. You hunt for food. You consort with your lovers. Your lovers are wild and very brave. But when you do make love, it a tremendous happening. And usually the whole desert resounds to the cries of your passion.

Today you are not interested in lovers. Today you are marking out your territory. This must be done regularly and efficiently if you are to continue as absolute ruler of yourself.

You reach a hilltop. The distance is spread out before you. Rose-tawny in the aching clearness. You stop suddenly. Something halts you.

A terrible, overpowering feeling of suspicion immobilizes you on the ridge as you watch and listen, every hair on your body standing on end to the awesome possibility of intrusion. Every sense and instinct attuning to the dreadful possibility of desecration and abuse.

Your eyes range across the horizon steadily. You stand motionless, concentrating every nerve, scenting the situation with every faculty you possess. If your suspicions are founded, you are prepared to attack unto death.

In timeless focus, you alert your entire being to the possibility of combat. Hatred for the intrusion runs into your spine. A clear pure encompassing antipathy for the violation of your estate.

The loathing forms a rumbling in your belly. It grows and gathers, it collects and accumulates. Growing larger and louder inside you, gathering momentum.

Running directly and menacingly towards the vileness, you open your throat and you ROAR.

Halfway down the hill the trespasser turns and flees.

With enormous relief and a certain pride, you toss your head, and continue smoothly on your way. The sun is now high in the sky, and it is certain time for your rest in the shade.

Go to your oasis. Have your drink and your bathe. Lie down under the palm tree.

Rest comfortably on the soft sand. And dream of your power, your rage and your passion. And in your own good time return to your full waking consciousness, refreshed and alert and ready to continue your life.

INTEGRATION AND GROUNDING

Spend some time integrating the experiences you have just undergone. Write them down or, if you are working with others, share them with the group. **Were you a lion? Did you recognise your intruder? Did you manage to find your roar? Did you feel impersonal hatred? What was it like in your oasis?**

The answers to these questions will indicate how attuned you are to the principle of Sekhmet.

Then 'ground' your inner work with your preferred method such as discussion, questions and divination. Some pertinent areas for exploration are:

Sexual freedom and choice
Boundary issues
The release of anger/joy
Questions you can ask the Tarot:
What is the nature of my present relationship to the goddess Sekhmet?
What particular energy or quality can I employ to integrate the goddess Sekhmet into my life?
How may I find and release my (any of the) chakric qualities of the Goddess Sekhmet?

Then drink your beer, blow out the candles and thank the goddess Sekhmet for her presence in your midst, bidding her **Hail and Farewell**. Close down in the usual way.

Blessed Be.

In the immediate period following this work be aware that you will have activated some primal creative power in your psychic system. It is therefore advisable to take steps to release it, such as enjoyable physical exercise, especially dancing, and shouting. Practice shouting whenever you can. It is very releasing and also vital that you should be able to shout readily and effectively when you need to. Forget that you were probably taught that it was 'wrong' to shout. You are now a responsible adult, and you need to know where your ROAR is, and to be able to access it on demand. *Blessed Be.*

CHAPTER THREE

HORUS: RADIANT CHILD OF THE SUN
THE THIRD LEVEL

THE SOLAR PLEXUS CHAKRA. THE KA
BODY

We now approach the **solar plexus** chakra, recognition of the ka body and the confident radiance of our divine warrior, and healed inner child, the god-force **Horus**.

Horus is the son of Isis and Osiris and the husband of Hathor, the goddess of love and beauty. He has three aspects throughout the Egyptian dynasties in which he was separately celebrated as Horus-the-Elder, Horus-the-Younger and Horus-in-the-Horizon. All of these combine to make him a truly magnificent radiant solar force.

As Horus-the-Elder, he is primarily a sky god, the 'heart of Ptah', and one of his main functions is to conduct the initiate through the perils of the *dwaat,* or astral planes. His four sons, Imsety, Hapy, Duamutef and Qebhsenuf, are instrumental in bringing the initiate to the brink of paradise. In this capacity, he can be regarded as the cosmic Horus, the divine Son of Heaven, or the higher consciousness of the individual, which determines and drives us towards our spiritual goals

As Horus-the-Younger, or Horus-the-Child, he represents the principle of divine child; the beautiful, spontaneous, natural part of self that is constantly fresh and alive to the present. In this guise he was known to the Egyptians as Harpocrates, a god of healing. In this aspect he represents connection to our true gifts and the capacity to express them with creativity and focus.

Horus-in-the-Horizon is the blazing sun; the young king, the heroic warrior-god who avenges the forces of darkness and betrayal.

The life of Horus is well documented. It provides much food for thought about our own growth processes and psychology. He is both a triumphant and a healing child; he is a virile and intelligent warrior and a force for rightful retribution and protection. He is married to Hathor, the goddess of love and sexual relationship. He is the victorious hero in all of us.

Horus consciousness gives us courage, endurance and passion to meet life's vicissitudes with optimism and valour. Horus offers himself and his gifts in the cause of spiritual fulfillment and growth. Above all, Horus wins. As the sun rises every morning, the divine child within us is reborn every minute with all the golden qualities of the solar plexus – courage, beauty, intelligence and a clear, strong and ever-present sense of self.

Osiris needs to die in flesh to be re-born on earth as Horus. This is the mystery of reincarnation. Every new life is, in some ways, an act of retribution for the past. Life is ever renewing, and the returning ego always seeks to redress its past wrongs.

The magical symbol for Horus is the *wadjet,* or all-seeing Eye. This was used as a powerful protective and healing amulet, and in fact even today in Egypt, a blue glass eye is commonly worn to protect against the 'bad eye' or the forces of jealousy and envy.

Ho Osiris! I am your son Horus; and I have come to you that I may greet you my father Osiris.

Ho Osiris! I am your son Horus, and I have come having felled your enemies for you.

Ho Osiris! I am your son Horus; I have come that I may remove all evil, which is upon you.

Therefore, before we begin our work on the third chapter of the path of love we need to address issues in ourselves that concern our courage, intelligence and creativity of purpose. The solar plexus chakra is the centre of our sense of individuality, the part of being that holds the will-to-be, and the essence of our purpose in this life, the 'returning ego' that needs to 'avenge' or expiate its wrongs and grow towards the wholeness of its future. As we approach the golden light of our own inner radiance, we can ask ourselves truthfully:

'Am I honestly offering my most special gifts to the world?'
'Is fear of failure preventing full engagement with my purpose?'
'Do I feel old?'
'Can I find creative fulfillment in my actual present?'

If the answers to these questions seem to raise negative responses and self-doubts, do not be discouraged. This is natural. We are, all of us, in some ways diminished by the effects of our early conditioning, by in fact the 'dismemberment 'of our 'fathers'. The myth of Horus was told by the Egyptians to inform us of this fact, and to inspire us to conquer, as well as we may, the dark forces of fear and self-doubt which always lurk within. To overcome and disempower the Enemy within, we need firstly to face the fact of its presence, and the sad fruits of its past successes. The Final Battle is ongoing. Moreover, the radiant shining sun that sheds its light from our own solar centre rises triumphantly every morning

I will take the opportunity to make a gentle point now: aspirants usually find this level of work painful. After the arcane experience of Anubis, and the passionate empowerment of the self, which is experienced on awakening the goddess Sekhmet, we rise to the part of ourselves that brings us recognition of our psychological conditioning. This awareness, which is painful, happens when we become thoroughly conscious of and therefore responsible for ourselves as individual people with individual personalities, backgrounds and purpose. Having emerged from the world of spirit as infants we are all faced with an imperfect world and imperfect parents. Not to admit this to oneself is being less than honest. At the level of Horus, whose prime and central qualities are 'intelligence', 'courage' and 'perfect honesty,' we are faced with all the imperfections of our past, and we must find the intelligence to recognise them, the courage to deal with them, and the honesty to admit them. Thus we may defeat the fears that perpetuate them, and attain' vision' and 'glory'. As we activate our solar plexus chakra, and gain consciousness of our sense of self, of our *ka* body or true personality, we become aware naturally of the pain and loneliness we suffered in childhood. We also become aware of the strictures and frustrations of childhood that have helped to shape our personality, and the unconscious injuries done to the self, by the self to protect itself from harm. Childhood, as exemplified by the life of Horus, is by its very nature a perilous and painful state, from which we all suffer, although our human psychological mechanisms help to cast a rosy light over it. When we are truly conscious of ourselves and realise the pain we as individual children have all undergone from the 'dismemberment' from perfect spiritual wholeness from which every parent proceeds, we can then begin to heal the pain from the perspective and vision of spiritual maturity.

We can prepare for our work on awakening the divine Horus within us by contemplating his gifts as they open for us along our own chakric pathway. They are all qualities required by the spiritual warrior in ourselves. This time as we work with them, we need to visualise ourselves actualising them. We need to 'see' ourselves attaining them, and to think about how and where we can use them in our lives. Be aware that integrating the qualities of the god-force Horus brings knowledge of your *ka* body or your true personality – which you may subsequently integrate with or marry to your deepest dearest heart-soul.

THE GIFTS OF HORUS THROUGH THE CHAKRAS

ROOT:	*Obedience*
SACRUM:	*Determination*
SOLAR PLEXUS:	*Intelligence*
HEART:	*Courage*
THROAT:	*Perfect Honesty*
BROW:	*Vision*
CROWN:	*Glory*

OBEDIENCE: THE ROOT OF HORUS.

The first and most important gift of the spiritual warrior is the rooted quality of **obedience.** It is fundamental; it is instilled. Coming from the root of the solar plexus, it is a willing engagement to discipline the self and listen to its higher directives. Horus receives instructions from his father on the arts of warfare. So do we.

Speaking personally, I had no firm sense of obedience until I came to Egypt to take up my life in the village community where I have since become a loved and respected member. This would never have happened if I had not listened to the instructions of my husband. It went hard with me to start with. I was a liberated Western woman; since childhood, nobody had ever told me what to wear or how to conduct myself in public. I had been acculturated to laxity in moral and social behaviour. I thought my husband was being jealous and controlling. He explained everything to me with patience. Within Egyptian village culture it is important for any woman to conduct herself like a queen. If she does so, she is treated as such. If not, not only does *she* lose respect, but her entire household and family does too. I listened to him; I learned and I gained immeasurable riches. He brought me a *harem.* He brought me his beautiful young daughter, an 'adopted' sister with her two adorable little boys, and women servants who are just like daughters. They were willing to obey me. How could I rule them with consciousness if I did not follow the rules of their culture? I read the Koran carefully, and I understood and respected its teachings. I learned to rule my household and my *harem* with love. They brought joy and meaning to my life and they serve my vision with integrity and wholehearted devotion. I gained the rootedness of obedience. If you subscribe to a spiritual ethos, it is of primary importance, when awakening the solar plexus and strengthening the true personality, to obey its dictums.

DETERMINATION: THE SACRUM OF HORUS

In the sacrum of the solar plexus, the *ka* body begins to sort itself out. Our true sense of identity forms. It is from here that we begin to determine who we are, and what we have to do. In his adolescent years, Horus unexpectedly enters his mother's chamber to find her in communion with his father. He is 'enraged' with jealousy, but he rises above this primal quality of the sacrum, finding the **determination** to take on the forces of corruption and ultimately defeat them. Using his obedience under instruction from Osiris, then his determination to conquer the adversary, all the cosmic forces spring to his support. He then realises himself as himself. He actualises the meaning behind the cosmic plan.

Each of us has a sense of divine purpose. We are all valid and integral sparks of universal design. Every one of us has our part to play in the unfoldment of it. Consciousness of this is one of the functions of the solar plexus; acknowledgment of the *ka* body expedites it. From the sacrum of Horus, we determine to do so.

INTELLIGENCE: THE SOLAR PLEXUS OF HORUS

The most personal gift we receive on the ray of Horus is when the golden light of **intelligence** shines from the solar plexus of the solar plexus. Intelligence is our clarity of mind, our alertness, our recognition, our ability to be present. Intelligence gives us self-awareness and the subsequent ability to outwit the enemy. Intelligence gives us the power of positivity.

His Holiness the Dalai Lama is a shining example of intelligence. Both semi-divine religious leader and divine child, he is also a wily spiritual warrior for his nation. His teachings constantly state the power of positivity.

On the path of love, energies, which have been determined and sorted in the sacrum, rise to the solar plexus to radiate out in consciousness of self and purpose. When we find the intelligence to recognise our true person-ality, we will attract everything we need to actualise that purpose. Intelligence, as solar of all the solar gifts, is the life-giving recognition of our will to be.

COURAGE: THE HEART OF HORUS

In the heart of Horus, we find our **courage.** Courage invariably springs from intelligence. Acts of real courage come from the hearts of Heroes, but firstly from their ability to be present, and secondly from their recognition of *why* the courageous acts need to be done. We can always find courage when we know it lives in our hearts and can be approached from our intelligence. When a thing needs to be done, and we are the one to do it, we can readily rise to our courage. Once we have found it, we can love it. Love your courage because it will never fail you. We are all Heroes, but the real hero does not seek to be thanked for his courage; he gives thanks for it. Courage in others moves the heart, but our own courage gladdens it. In the heart of the solar plexus, we find the ability to love who we really are, and this makes the personality or *ka* body strong and vibrant. However, not without courage. Courage is the key. In our hearts we always know what is right and true for us; in our hearts we find the courage to stand up for ourselves to maintain it.

PERFECT HONESTY: THE THROAT OF HORUS

When courage rises to the throat of Horus it is expressed and communicated as **perfect honesty.** It is a quality of solar consciousness. Perfect honesty, as opposed to blunt candour releases the preceding gifts of Horus, in as much as it takes intelligence to find courage and courage to release perfect honesty. Perfect honesty certainly derives from intelligence. It does not require that we be blisteringly frank all the time. It is not necessary to tell the truth, the whole truth and nothing but the truth, except when under oath. It is perfectly honest to refrain from comment when we consider it prudent to do so, and to choose our words with care when we find ourselves in delicate situations. Perfect honesty, however, does require that we do not lie in thought, word or deed. Having found the courage to express ourselves truthfully, we need never lie to ourselves. This is very empowering, as we do not seek to excuse ourselves to others; we realise that we answer to ourselves alone. We find real trust and meaning in our own particular viewpoint.

VISION: THE BROW OF HORUS

As we learn to acknowledge and trust our own particular viewpoint, we develop the gift of **vision.** The all-seeing eye of Horus can shine from our own brow chakra. We 'see' where we have to go and what we need to do in order to prevail. We recognise our potential and how to serve it to its maximum advantage. We see how our particular gifts and talents can operate best in the world. This provides us with a vision of our own to fulfill as opposed to just 'having visions'. Having a true vision gives you a sense of always being in achievement of your higher purpose, because as you live out your own vision you can always see how to serve it. As you realise your vision it will strengthen and grow for you as it serves the world. It will become more of itself, as you do.

GLORY: THE BROW OF HORUS

Life is glorious. Victory is glorious. Victory over life's vicissitudes brings a sense of **glory.** In attaining our own victor's crown at the crown of Horus, we can release personal achievement into the greater glory of God. We become heirs to the light. We have earned the right to a sense of glory, but it does not make us proud or 'vainglorious'. It brings us to the 'shores of paradise'. We achieve a sense of cosmic Horus, or Horus-the-Elder. We become a protective force for good and our achievements are offered to the greater glory. Our moments of glory are not missed. They are part of the glorious pattern of universal intelligence; and we appreciate that we have been given the opportunity to realise them.

Having considered his gifts, the next part of the exercise is to repeat the Personal Affirmations for the god-force Horus. As previously suggested, repeat them aloud several times. If you find that you cannot honestly repeat them with meaning, go a little deeper into your true self until you can.

PERSONAL AFFIRMATIONS ON THE GOD HORUS

I recognise my gifts and I offer them in the service of Humanity
I can always find the courage to express myself truthfully

I love my parents

I am prepared to fight for peace and order

Having successfully repeated these affirmations with truth, we are now ready to begin the ritual procedure for awakening the god-force Horus, the *ka* body and the solar plexus chakra.

RITUAL PROCEDURE FOR AWAKENING HORUS

This ritual works best around noon when the sun is directly overhead. Aim to start it in the late morning so that it can be finished as the power of the sun begins to decline. Before starting, spend time thinking about yourself; where you think you are in your life, and where you truly think you would like to be. Think positively about what you need to achieve. Think about what you perceive to be your shortcomings to your objectives, and how you might overcome them. Think about your childhood, with consideration of how far you have overcome its dangers and difficulties.

RITUAL CORRESPONDENCES ON THE PRINCIPLE OF HORUS

COLOUR	*Gold*
PERFUME	*Neroli, Orange, Jasmine*
INCENSE	*Frankincense*
ANIMAL	*Falcon*
CHAKRA	*Solar Plexus*
BODY	*Ka Body*
TIME OF DAY	*Noon*
SACRED SYMBOL	*The All-Seeing Eye*
TAROT CARDS	*'The Chariot', 'The Tower'*

PREPARATION OF THE ALTAR/ANOINTING/ROBING

To prepare your Ritual Space you may dress the altar with a **yellow** or **gold** cloth, and after your ritual purification bath, dress yourself in golden or yellow colours, and anoint yourself on the solar plexus with **neroli, orange**, or **jasmine**. Place on your altar a gold or yellow candle, an incense burner with **frankincense** and, if possible, a representation of the god Horus. If you have a photograph of yourself as a happy child, you can add that too, and perhaps a picture or photograph of someone who is a heroic icon for you. Provide yourself with some drawing materials, paper and coloured pencils. Spend some time before you begin re-connecting with a part of your childhood when you felt freely creative. Think about a favourite game and what it meant to you then. Try to remember one of your childhood heroes or heroines and what they represented for you. Remember that you are about to raise your consciousness to the level of your *ka* body, and spend some time connecting with the idea of your personality and the protective force of your etheric double.

After performing your usual sacred space delineation, create a ring of golden light around your ritual space, approach the altar and say:

'I dedicate this altar to the god Horus that I might radiate my light into the World.'

Light your altar candle and seat yourself in the centre.

VISUALISATON OF CHAKRIC COLOUR

Surround yourself in golden light. Experience the warmth of this golden light gently blessing and healing your psychological pains. Begin to become aware of your etheric body, also blessed and healed by golden light. Feel its shimmering presence as a protective force, hovering over you in perfect alignment with your *aufu.*

You may now give thanks for the qualities of Horus as they rise through your chakras. As you do this, keep yourself in a golden glow. Feel the light radiating out from your centre. As it radiates out, it surrounds you in a warm golden glowing haze. Then it emanates *in.* Each time you do this, the glow will become warmer, stronger and more radiant. Remember that as you experience these qualities, you are expressing them, and strengthening them in yourself. They are *yours.*

'I give thanks for my obedience.
I give thanks for my determination.

I give thanks for my intelligence.
I give thanks for my courage.
I give thanks for my perfect honesty.
I give thanks for my vision.
I give thanks for my glory.'

Now you may perform the invocation. Stand up to face the east and recite from the heart. As you do so, visualise the presence of the god Horus as a warm, strong vital force ascending within you and descending from above you to fill your inner and outer space with protective, radiant light.

INVOCATION TO HORUS

Hail Horus! Lord of Light, Divine Child of the Eternal Sun
Master of the Battleground and the Court.
In Thy Right Hand the Sword of Vengeance, in Thy Left the Staff of Healing.
On Thy Head the Hawks head Helmet and Thy Chariot is of radiant gold.
Wondrous is Thy glory in the Sight of all who have courage and nobility to perceive Thee.
Be Thou with me O Golden Hawk; Let Thy strength ascend within me that I may honour my Life and the Gods who are my parents and Originals.
Pour out Thy Love, the zest, the vision, and the fierce gentleness of Thy Being.
Illumine and warm the Worlds with the holy joy of Creation's Right.
Wherever winds blow or stars glow or blood flows for Children of Earth to claim their heritage of eternal freedom
Thy Glance is on the World.
By the Arts of Life, by Dance and Joyful Journey
By the Gold of summer and the Fountain of Eternal Youth
By the Power of Right, and the Glory of Forgiving

We call upon Thee to be with us now
In Body and in Spirit.
HAIL HORUS!
Hail and Welcome.

The guided meditation for the *Sphere of Horus* follows. Lie down, or sit with your back supported and begin.

GUIDED MEDITATION ONTHE SPHERE OF HORUS

You are in a garden. It is noontime on a warm summery day. The garden has a high wall around it and there are orange trees. The air smells very sweetly of their blossoms and leaves. The sunlight warms your head and skin. You are a grown, mature person. Your body is strong and complete. Your passions are active and vital, but your will is clear and controlled. You have self-command. You are in your strength.

As you lie on the grass, smelling the orange-blossom and enjoying the warm sun, a magical process starts to occur.

You are becoming younger.

You can become a little less in command of yourself.

Less autonomous.

Your limbs start to feel a little lighter.

Your blood a little thinner.

Your muscles more elastic.

There is a clearer feeling in your brow.

You are more relaxed, but also more responsive. More open. Newer.

You wriggle your fingers and toes.

You can feel the fresh grass under your body like a soft bed. You feel yourself falling into a light slumber. It is the sleep of rejuvenation. When you next open your eyes to the garden you will be seven years old.

After a little while, a bee buzzes past your ear and you wake easily. You feel immediately alert and present in the garden. You are seven years old.

For a little while you may amuse yourself as you like. Some of your

favourite playthings are with you, and there are trees, flowers and plants.
(Five minutes)

You hear a strange sound. A sound that disturbs you. You have never heard it before properly. You are not at all sure that you like it. It is the sound of a grown man weeping harshly. You see him sitting in the garden, his head in his hands.

He is your father.

You go to stand in front of him, and after a while he lifts his face to look at you.

If you ask him what has hurt him, he will tell you.

Then the man disappears. You go back to your game.

Then you notice a beautiful fountain in the garden. The sparkling water falls into a marble basin of clear blue. You gaze into the swirling water and see your face reflected back.

You have become twelve years old.

In the blue water you can see your eyes. They are very bright, like the piercing eyes of a hawk. In your reflected eyes you can see pictures. You see your father. You see his problems; you see his pain. You see his sadness and his weakness. You begin to see a scene unfolding before you where these things are revealed to you.

When you have seen enough you close your eyes. You focus on your heart. Love for your father wells up in your heart, and bubbles up like the jet in the fountain. Tears fall from your eyes and spill over into the blue marble basin.

When you open them again they feel fresh and clear. In the water you can make out the shadowy specter of your father who smiles at you before he fades away.

You turn from the fountain. On the grass before you are spread out some writing and drawing implements, art materials, a musical instrument, some actor's props and costume, dancing shoes. Tools for creative self-expression.

You go to the things that appeal to you. You make a representation of the experience you have just undergone. As you make it, you feel free and light and focused on your task. You are easy and present and full of confidence in your ability.

When your task is finished you enjoy the product. You have grown to your present age.

Let the garden and the product fade, and return to your full waking consciousness, refreshed and renewed and ready to resume your life.

Having completed this, write down your experiences and make a drawing of the creative representation you made in the garden of Horus. Place this on your altar and leave it there until you are ready for the next level. You may then proceed with the integrative part of the experience with divination and discussion. Remember that everything that occurs for you in your guided meditations is real and should be taken seriously.

Questions you can ask here relate to the experiences and visions you obtained during your meditation, and any insights you require regarding your relationship with your father and/or your spiritual goals and aspirations.

What was in the garden when you first became aware of it? How did you occupy yourself? Did your father tell you what had hurt him? Did you see anything in the fountain? What creative tools did you choose to work with? What did you make with them? What does this mean to you?

Questions you can ask the Tarot:

What energy or aspect of myself can I express to bring me to a clear perspective of my seven-year-old self? My twelve-year-old self?

How do I really view my father? How can I improve upon this?

What, in myself, prevents me from attaining my spiritual goals?

How can I realise more readily my (any of the) chakric qualities of the god-force Horus?

What do I need to integrate the god-force Horus into my life?

A very helpful way to 'ground' this experience is to commit to a task or project that you have been deferring, and expedite it as soon as possible. You may now blow out your candles and close down, thanking the god Horus for his radiant presence, bidding him, and all his companion guardians and Powers,

HAIL AND FAREWELL

CHAPTER FOUR

HATHOR: THE LADY OF LOVE AND BEAUTY

THE FOURTH LEVEL THE HEART CHAKRA. THE BA/KA PROCESS

We now arrive at the fourth level along the path of love, which begins our process of integrating awareness of self as *ka,* with the heart-soul, or *ba* body. Here, on awakening the **heart chakra,** we begin to commit to the *ba/ka* process. The heart chakra is the energy centre of love and true self-knowledge, which is the province of the goddess **Hathor**.

The myth tells us that when Horus engaged in hand-to-hand combat with Set at the battle of Edfu, thereby losing one of his eyes, he came to the notice of the goddess from her palace at Dendera across the Nile. She promptly married him. From that time forward, he could only prevail.

On rising to the heart from the solar plexus chakra, and allowing our confidence and will-to-be to flow into its true home of love and under-standing, we bring Horus our radiant inner warrior to the notice of his beloved and beautiful wife.

The heart chakra is the sacred alchemical vessel where earth and spirit meet and marry. Appropriately, it is here that the **first sacred marriage**, or first level initiation, is celebrated.

As we link with the warmth and wealth of the goddess of love, we combine lower nature and animal instincts with spiritual essence. Hathor is not only the woman aspect of passionate and vengeful Sekhmet, she is also the human manifestation of transcendent Nut. Mother of Isis and Osiris, Nut is the celestial Cow who pours out the Milky Way from her breasts and swallows the Sun each night to give him new birth at dawn. Hathor then, contains within her, both Sekhmet's blood-drinking rage and passion for retribution, and Nut's transcendent submission and adoration. Hathor is woman *as* goddess, a principle to which every individual can aspire, in terms of love-in-relationship. Not only the living embodiment of stellar radiance, she is also heir to the volcanic forces of nature, which are unleashed and refined through her heart into desire for the beloved other.

Hathor is both fertility principle and exponent of the cosmic laws. The Egyptians recognised that growth and fertility reflected the influence of the stars. The sustenance of Egypt depended upon the yearly inundation of the Nile, which occurred when certain stellar patterns were visible in the sky.

The stellar patterns of Nut were ordered and grounded through the devotees of Hathor into the temple arts of music and sacred dance, and the passions of Sekhmet were transformed through her into the harmony of successful sexual relationship. Hathor Consciousness 'grounds' and realises both the primal passions of Sekhmet and the transpersonal celestial light of Nut into a fully rounded, sexually confident, loving, workable reality.

Two of her titles are 'Cow of Gold' and, in her more fertile guise, 'Lady of the Sycamore Fig'. As consort of falcon-headed Horus, she becomes 'Hawk of Gold'.

The word 'Hat-hour', or '*Hat-Her*' translates into 'the house of Horus', the hieroglyph depicting a hawk within a square.

There are recently channeled teachings from an extra-dimensional entity known as *The Hathors* which hold that the cults of Hathor were inspired by the light and wisdom of beings of light from another galaxy.*
*Kenyon and Essene. *The Hathor Material*

In the Temple of Hathor at Memphis, where statues of the Seven Hathors are nearly all that remain of this great centre of civilisation, it is easy to believe this. Seven beautiful faces of the goddess stand in a circle, each subtly different from the other, yet all with a slightly leonine cast and an ethereal almost extra-terrestrial quality to their features.

Hathor is represented in the Tarot as 'The Empress'. Crowned with the stars of Nut, 'The Empress' represents the inner principle that rules our lives with love. Of the entire pantheon, Hathor maintains the flame of sexual relationship.

If you are a man of note, found for yourself a household and love your wife at home as it beseems. Fill her belly, clothe her back; unguent is the remedy for her limbs. Gladden her heart so long as she lives. She is a goodly field for her lord. However, hold her back from getting the mastery. Remember that her eye is a storm wind, and her vulva and her mouth are her power.

From the instructions of Ptah-hotep

The ancient Egyptians, like their moderns descendents, did not advocate celibacy. Sexual satisfaction within marriage was deemed a prerequisite for balanced and healthy living. And so Hathor was greatly revered as goddess of health and happiness. Hathor herself cured the god Ra of a sulking fit during the battle of Horus and Set by dancing naked before him, peeping between her legs at him, until he burst into joyous laughter.

Hathor is Lady of the Dance. Her symbols are the sistrum, which is a musical rattle in the shape of an ankh, and the magic mirror – not merely an object of reflected beauty, but of the mirror of loving relationship, by which is obtained self-knowledge.

Murry Hope in her book, *Egyptian Magic,* writes that the cult of Hathor was filled almost entirely by women; men holding administrative posts only. The role of many priestesses, known collectively as *The Hathors*, was to embody the spirit and nature of the goddess. They danced through the streets at sacred festivals and ceremonies. Chosen for their beauty and grace, they were trained in the arts of music to manifest the heavenly order through their playing of instruments, their singing and sacred dances, which they performed naked, wearing only silver finger-cymbals and musical necklaces known as *menats*. In this way, Hathor, regarded and worshipped as the quintessence of feminine beauty, could actually appear for the people, and be integrated into their hearts.

Everything that links with Hathor is warmed, civilised and refined into an art form of itself so that it can be expressed through love and generosity. Hathor brings enjoyment, humour and appreciation of the abundance of nature. Like 'The Empress' in the Tarot she expresses the joy of giving, and a true understanding of how to give and receive from the boundless store of universal energy the richest bounties life has to offer – the gifts of love.

In addition, as we rise to the home and heart of Hathor from the perspective and vision of our divine child and sacred warrior, we may consider when, in the story of Horus, he first comes to the notice of the goddess.

In the penultimate fierce and terrible battle with *Set*, Horus loses one of his eyes. The lost eye, symbolising his personal vision, is given up to the heavens to light up the world and protect mankind. From henceforth, Horus possesses only a collective vision, it being the second eye that provides a personal viewpoint on the world. This can be interpreted to mean that when the solely personal view transcends to the collective view, the self becomes ready to admit the beautiful goddess of love into its heart. It is then that Hathor can be realised, and the first, the integral sacred marriage within the self may be celebrated. The solar plexus can commit to the heart. The marriage of solar plexus with heart was understood by the Egyptians as the **ba/ka** process, or the integration of personality with soul.

Our connection to the goddess force Hathor, causing the awakening of the heart chakra and the sacred *ba/ka* process, brings us closer to universal soul consciousness. To prepare for this, we need to address those areas in our lives which rule our intimate relationships with others, our sense of aesthetics and beauty (including our own), and the procreation and delivery of our heart's desires, or our *fertility*. 'Fertility' in this sense needs not be actual flesh-and-blood progeny, but the manifested fruit of our deepest creative urges, which we can now release into the world

The questions to ask in preparation for this are:

Am I in Love?

Everybody should be in love, and everybody can be in love. If you are already in an intimate relationship, then it is in your own power to engender the constant state of being-in-love within it. This is in your power to do. If you *decide* to open your heart, you can magically charge the shared energetic flow with your partner. If you are not in a relationship, you can begin by being in love with Life, by deciding to connect with its beauty and its wonder, especially the beauty of women. Then, if you really want one, a loving sexual relationship is far more likely to follow.

How truly appreciative am I of feminine beauty?

This is an important question. Too many of us in Western society have allowed our vision of feminine beauty to become distorted by the preferences of arbiters of fashion. Usually homosexual males, their preferences have naturally led them to exalt the boyish or waif-like, rather than the fully formed woman. This has brought about pathological outbreaks of eating disorders and punishing physical regimes. To connect with Hathor we need to enjoy and celebrate the feminine from a sense of love and abundance. This does not mean giving in to greed or self-indulgence, which are only the shadow results of starvation and self-disgust, but a loving connection to the beauty of the goddess in all her various appurtenances. In Hathor consciousness, we are able to recognise these imposed distortions, and can begin to enjoy the feminine form with appreciation for its softness, fullness and grace. If we love the female body for its intrinsic beauty, we lose the more masculine aspect of competitiveness in beauty, stimulated by Western commercialism, which perpetuates envy and prevents contentment.

Living in Egypt, a country which has a strong feminine collective and rejoices in its beautiful women, I have come to appreciate this factor greatly. Every Egyptian woman celebrates her femininity. One only has to look at the grace with which, even the oldest and most monumental village women, naturally comport themselves whilst walking in the street, or selling vegetables in the *souk*. When visiting them in the privacy of their homes, as soon as the men go out, there is a rush to find someone's cassette player, then the tables are pushed aside and the dancing begins. It is both wildly sensual and perfectly controlled; an art form which has been perfected from early childhood by women for women, only for each other and the private delight of their husbands. I believe it to be a direct legacy from the temple training, drawn from the Collective Unconscious of the goddess Hathor.

How ready am I to release my creativity into the world?

When we become less critical of others, we naturally become more relaxed about releasing our own creativity, and expressing our own natural desires. Creativity can only really spring from the true connection of what we *want* to express.

When we can salute and honour this in others, we find that we can more freely offer it ourselves. This is the two-way flow of heart energy – from Outside to Inside – that allows love and creativity to occur in the world. Creativity can be raw and natural; it does not have to be fashionable to be effective. It derives from love and we all possess it. When we connect to the heart centre, we begin to experience the 'fertilisation' process, which occurs when the *ka* body first connects with the creative *ba* (which has designed our physical and mental levels) . Thus, we become more conscious of the creative drive, which issues for us personally from the Universal Ba.

We may now consider the seven chakric gifts of Hathor and begin to claim them for ourselves. These 'heart' qualities need to be 'known by heart'. The attainment of them gives us knowledge and understanding of our 'heart-soul'. It is a worthwhile exercise in the process of refinement and transformation to compare each of Hathor's chakric gifts with its corresponding chakric gift of her more primal aspect, Sekhmet.

THE GIFTS OF HATHOR THROUGH THE CHAKRAS

ROOT:	*Abundance*
SACRUM:	*Pleasure*
SOLAR PLEXUS:	*Music*
HEART:	*Beauty*
THROAT:	*Harmony in Relationship*
BROW:	*Radiant Understanding*

CROWN: ***Grace***

ABUNDANCE: THE ROOT OF HATHOR

When we experience the rooted ness of the heart chakra, we tune in to a sense of the limitless **abundance** of nature. There is plenty for everyone on our planet. It is only fear, disguised as human greed that makes us believe otherwise. Greed is a shaky basis for the heart. To form a strong and rooted heart consciousness, we need to know that we have sufficiency. When we know that our needs are always met, this becomes true. Unfortunately, it does not happen the other way around. It is a sad fact of human nature that the more we are given, the more we feel we need. Without deciding from the basis of the heart to appreciate life, and give thanks for its bounties, we can allow a sense of deprivation and paucity to pervade our lives. When we celebrate abundance, we create it.

In Egypt, the words '*el hamdu l'illah*' (thank you God) are constantly heard. Gratitude is considered the primary step to enlightenment by the Sufis. They teach that one should be grateful for what one is given, and even more grateful for what one is not given. Knowledge of what to aim for and work towards is a blessed gift.

The gift of abundance, as is true of all the heart qualities, can only be realised when we decide to claim it. Then we can be generous with others and ourselves. We root ourselves to the limitless source of life to allow its blessings to flow through. The heart chakra is the first energy centre where there is a sense of oneself in relation to others. When we attain the root of Hathor and the heart, we claim the security of sufficiency and the perfect balance between giving and receiving which perpetuates abundance.

To refer back to the raw, untransformed aspect of Hathor, we can compare the gift of abundance with the root chakra quality of Sekhmet, which is **passion.**

This will help us understand how to claim abundance. Just as Sekhmet, in her primal sacral mode, draws earth energy up to motivate her being, Hathor, drawing from the same source, transforms it through the heart into the knowledge of plenty. Love can never run out. The more one loves, the more love there is. Love cannot be contained and it cannot be conserved. Love seeks to share, to be given freely. There can never be too much of it. Working from the root of the heart, we decide to open ourselves to the depths of universal energy so that we can share it with the world. We decide to receive as many of life's blessings as we could possibly desire, and bestow them wherever we go.

This gives a very safe sound structure for our heart and all its workings. We gain the knowledge of abundance.

PLEASURE: THE SACRUM OF HATHOR

When we have found the knowledge of abundance, we can open to the sacrum of Hathor, and allow her primal will to flow into our heart. This opens us to the gift of **pleasure**. As we gain knowledge and experience of our true pleasures, we take pleasure in life. We find pleasure easily. We express pleasure innocently. There are no guilty blocks to our pleasures. Love flows into the sacral centre, and we take delight, we are charmed, we can be sexually enjoyable and enjoying, but in all areas of life we can give pleasure by being pleased with it. We laugh readily, we are appreciative, and we are prepared to be surprised and entertained. We are good company to others and we enjoy being ourselves.

To express our pleasure is a precious gift of love. We take pleasure in giving pleasure, and we give pleasure by taking it. It is a two-way flow. Pleasure needs to be expressed and released through the heart. Secret guilty pleasures often lead to pathology and self-dislike. Open, honest pleasures bring self-esteem and physical health. Shared pleasures bring the gift of friendship. Intimate pleasure creates the fundament of happy marriage.

The raw aspects of pleasure, found in the sacrum of Sekhmet, are joy and righteous wrath. When these gifts are fully realised, we can transform and refine them so that they are released from the sacrum of Hathor as the sacred art of pleasure.

MUSIC: THE SOLAR PLEXUS OF HATHOR

Pythagoras taught that the universe was a symphony. He taught that every fragment of divinity resonated at its own note within it. It was the task of the aspirant to discover the truth of his own note so that he could consciously harmonise with cosmic vibrations to augment the music of the spheres. It is a beautiful idea. At the solar plexus of Hathor, the goddess of music and dance, we attune to our own resonance. We discover the truth of our 'note'. Just as a musician follows the laws of music to create beauty for others, we follow the laws of the cosmos to create beautiful thoughts and ideas of self.

We can now express ourselves at the personality level with knowledge of our real tastes and preferences. The colours and styles we adopt, the words we choose, the pitch of our voice, our aesthetics; all of these express our **music**. Our ideas become truly our own, they flow from our knowledge of self. Opening to the solar plexus of the heart allows the heart to 'sing', because when we find our music we 'ring true'. We begin to know and love our individuality, and express it with love. We create music by knowing who we are and expressing ourselves with consciousness. We learn our rhythms. Our life becomes a dance, the truth of ourselves, our song.

Sekhmet expresses **dignity** from the solar plexus. This can be thought of as the raw aspect of our **music** in the sense that the primal integrity of the lioness is her utmost truth of herself. Music, which is the physical manifestation of the cosmic laws, can only stem from truth. We can only resonate our music from what we intrinsically are. We cannot create music by copying others, or trying to be what we think others want us to be. We have to find our dignity first.

BEAUTY: THE HEART OF HATHOR

We rise now to the heart of hearts. The gift from Hathor's heart chakra is the knowledge of **beauty.** Beauty is 'heart-stopping', sometimes 'heart-breaking'. It is always heart lifting. When we know beauty, we see it everywhere because we begin to understand the **beauty of difference**. The heart of hearts understands both that which it is, and that which it is not. To celebrate beauty in others and the world outside is to share in it, to recognise it as living in one's own heart.

When we see something that is not at all beautiful – perhaps some cruelty which we do not understand, as it is far from our own heart – we can celebrate the fact that it is not in our heart. We see the beauty in the difference. We are shown our own beauty. We can perceive the ugliness as a dark reflection of our beauty. It no longer bewilders. It clarifies beauty for us.

We are all different. There is such beauty in the differences between us. There is pain in that too, but a heart pain, a poignant beautiful pain.

As a species, we are so beautiful to look at. We are perfectly proportioned and shaped in limb.

We have a wonderful symmetry of design. Our flesh and skin have plasticity and bloom, warm and soft to the touch. Our eyes, especially, are exquisite. We are each of us different, but not so different to be confusing. We each have a special personal stamp, physical imperfections which make us perfect. There is great beauty in our imperfections because they reflect our individuality.

Islamic artists and potters always finished their work with a thumbprint to give an individual imperfection to a masterpiece. The hand of God gives us the same.

If we were not imperfect, we would not strive for perfection. If there were no imperfections, we would not recognise beauty. In the heart of Hathor, we find beauty in difference and imperfection and we love it.

The raw aspect of beauty, found in the heart of Sekhmet is **power**. Beauty is extremely powerful. To emanate and celebrate beauty we must recognise it as stemming from our intrinsic power.

HARMONY IN RELATIONSHIP: THE THROAT OF HATHOR

When true knowledge of beauty rises from the heart to be released from the throat of Hathor, it issues forth as the art of **harmony in relationship.** Expression of the knowledge of beauty in the differences between oneself and others actually creates this gift. Understanding the beauty of differences gives us the ability to form harmonious relationships with everybody and everything. We can become a force for peace. Peace is not merely absence of strife; it is a power in itself. Knowledge of the gift of harmony in relationship promotes this power in our personal relationships and in our political ones.

When we operate from the throat of the heart, we communicate with love from a place of self-knowledge in recognition of the other. We negotiate from the knowledge of beauty. We do not expect everybody else to hold the same views as we do. We respect the differences, we enjoy them, and they serve to deepen our own truths.

When we negotiate from knowledge of beauty, we exercise choice and discernment in our dialogues. We find compassion, and can create accord.

The raw material of **harmony in relationship**, which we encounter in the throat of Sekhmet, is the gift of **enchantment**. We can understand this as the power to command attention. To be a force for peace we need firstly to be taken seriously.

RADIANT UNDERSTANDING: THE BROW OF HATHOR

When we rise from the throat chakra of Hathor to her brow, we bring our knowledge of the art of harmony in relationship to the level of spiritual wisdom. We realise how much we have learned in the promotion of peace. We have learned to listen, to respect different viewpoints in order to arrive at harmony. We can now receive the gift of **radiant understanding**.

This is the understanding that blesses and brightens that which it under-stands. Whatever or whoever is understood from the brow of the heart becomes more bright, more radiant, more powerful and positive. It has been subjected to loving scrutiny; it is regarded from the perspective of beauty and harmony. It therefore becomes more of itself. When we are perceived and understood from the heart and soul we do feel empowered and exalted, or *irradiated*. From the brow of Hathor, we can offer that gift to the world. We can understand with radiance. In the same way that a poet or songwriter irradiates the subject of his work, we bring light to anyone or anything that we have understood.

The raw material for Hathor's **radiant understanding,** arising from the brow of Sekhmet, is **exaltation**. This gift allows us to raise our perceptions in order to determine the higher meanings of events and situations. From the brow of Hathor we can realise them.

GRACE: THE CROWN OF HATHOR

We may now integrate all the preceding chakric gifts of Hathor into her crown. The goddess of love journeys through abundance, pleasure, music, beauty, harmony in relationship and radiant understanding to arrive at **grace**. To be in a state of grace is to be sure that one is in the right time at the right place, in accord with all the positive forces of the universe. Whatever happens, one can be thankful and appreciative for the gift of the experience. In grace, we do not seek to impose our will upon people or events. We move through life lightly, effortlessly, in the knowledge that we are blessed. We accept change with interest; we receive our lessons with thanks. We are gracious to others because we perceive them with compassionate consideration. From the crown of the heart, we can remain in grace, knowing we are blessed by the light of God.

Grace releases us from fear and the tyranny of self-will. The crown quality of Sekhmet, the *prima materia* to work with towards the attainment of grace, is **ecstasy.** Ecstasy is a climactic sacral release of *Kundalini* power where the boundaries of the sacrum have allowed a directed force of power to be liberated through the chakras to the crown. Grace is a culmination in the crown of all the heart gifts, which frees us from the prison of alienation and self-doubt.

Gaining personal knowledge of the gifts of Hathor 'grounds' us in understanding of our **ba** and the true nature of our heart-soul. We may now proceed with the personal affirmations of the goddess Hathor. These should be easily learned by heart, as they are already there.

PERSONAL AFFIRMATIONS ON THE GODDESS HATHOR
I can dance lightly on the Path to meet Myself
I draw from the Limitless Source of Life to give to Others
My beauty may change but will never diminish
I am always guided by Love

Once these affirmations have been learned and repeated with meaning we are ready to prepare for the ritual awakening of the goddess Hathor, the heart chakra and the *ba ka* process.

RITUAL CORRESPONDENCES FOR AWAKENING HATHOR

COLOUR:	*Emerald green; Rose pink*
PERFUME:	*Rose*
INCENSE:	*Rose-petals, Benzoin*
CHAKRA:	*Heart*
BODY:	*Ba/Ka Process*
ANIMAL:	*Cow*
TIME OF DAY:	*Evening*
SACRED SYMBOLS:	*Magic Mirror, Sistrum*
TAROT CARD:	*'The Empress'*

RITUAL PREPARATION, ALTAR, ANOINTING AND ROBING
Whilst preparing for this ritual, spend time and effort preparing as for a bridal ceremony or a meeting with a lover. Make yourself as beautiful as you can. Wash your hair and bathe your body in rose-scented water. Massage your skin with oils, groom your hands and feet, and dress yourself in a clean garment that pleases you. If it is **green** or **rose pink**, all the better. Adorn yourself with jewelry, and anoint your heart chakra with the sign of the Pentagram in essential oil of *rose.* Place two pink or green candles on your altar and a representation of the goddess of Love. Placing a photograph of yourself and your love partner upon it will bring greater harmony to, and magically charge your love relationship with, the gifts of Hathor. For this

ritual, it is a graceful gesture to place flowers in honour of the goddess, and some of your favourite fruit, or cakes and, if you can happily drink it, some wine or beer. Burn **rose-petals** and **benzoin** incense on a charcoal tablet, and play a recording of some gentle, harmonious music that soothes and uplifts you. Make sure that you will feel warm and comfortable, even luxurious, during the meditative work. Some extra cushions or a feather duvet on the floor will help. Evening time is good for this work, when the Evening Star, *Venus*, is rising in the sky.

Prepare your ritual space in the usual way, calling the Quarters, and creating your Circle of Power. Then light your altar candles saying:

'I dedicate this altar to Hathor, Goddess of Love, that I might receive her into my Heart'

VISUALISATION OF CHAKRIC COLOUR

Surrounding yourself with a clear green light, seat yourself comfortably in the centre of your working space. Spend a few moments 'grounding'. Close your eyes and direct a ring of emerald-coloured light in a circle all around the ritual area. Focus on your heart. Imagine a beautiful, silver framed, rose-coloured looking-glass standing before you. Passing across the mirror you see different faces appear, the faces of people you have known and loved, or have been important to your growth.

They smile at you before they fade and are replaced. Sometimes they may give you a message. Spend about five minutes on this, without thinking about it or consciously trying to summon anyone in particular. Just allow your heart to tell you who are sending you positive energy and blessings.

You may now begin your work on assimilating the qualities of the goddess Hathor as they proceed through your chakric system from root to crown, allowing each quality to activate your emotional imagination. This time, before you give thanks for each heart gift, actually **envision yourself** embodying each quality so that you create it, and **experience it emotionally**. Place yourself, each time, in a real and manageable situation where you are actually expressing the energy and essence of the gift itself. Experience it fully with your heart. All of these gifts are readily available to you; you can manifest them at any time, in any situation.

'I give thanks for my abundance.'
Create a scenario where you are manifesting the gift of abundance. Make it realistic and manageable.

'I give thanks for my pleasure.'
Take yourself to a place where you are in utter enjoyment. Look at everything around you, and register what pleases you.

'I give thanks for my music.'
See yourself in a situation where you are expressing your true self with power and focus.

'I give thanks for my beauty.'
Give yourself a beautiful heart-lifting experience.

'I give thanks for my harmony in relationship.'
Create a situation where you are expressing the gift of harmony and peace effectively.

'I give thanks for my radiant understanding.'
Allow a vision to form where you bless and empower with your understanding

'I give thanks for my grace.'
Experience yourself blessed and understood

Spend some time integrating this experience. **Was there a theme to your visions? Who else was with you? Did you recognise anybody? How do you think you can manifest these visions into your life?**

You can now consider yourself on the ray of the goddess Hathor and ready to perform the invocation. Stand before the altar, visualising the beautiful soothing presence of the goddess of love and beauty filling your space, and streaming through your heart.

INVOCATION TO HATHOR

Hail Hathor, Lady of Light and Pleasure,
Lady of the West, She of the West, Royal Lady of the Sacred Land,
Who art crowned with the Sun and The Moon,
The Horns of Sacred Plenty.
In Thy Right Hand the Ankh, symbol of the Eternal outpouring of
     Life,
In Thy Left, the Sistrum of the Cosmic Dance.
On Thy Breast, the Menad beaded with Stars.
Eye of Ra, Mistress of the Night Sky, Queen of Beauty and the
     Force of Love,
 Lady of the Sycamore Milk,
Pour Thy Love onto the Earth for men and women to live and love
And die in your worship.
Thou art glorious in Thy Power and Thy Grace.
Lady of the Majestic Movement and the Chanting Hymn.
Thy Voice is heard in the desert wind
And the great Sun himself rises and sets for Thee.

Whenever Sun and Moon meet together in endless sky,
Wherever music and laughter are born in the hearts of men,
Where Love is whispered and teased from the hot simoom,
And Forces grow wilder from the gathering sand,
And Love and Strength and Majesty smile as One
Thy Face is seen.

By the countless stars of the desert night
By the fierce hot kiss of the morning Sun
By the infinite Dance of the Tides of Life
By the trembling Beauty of the Sycamore Fig
By the power of the Lion, and the ageless wisdom
Of the Serpent of Love.

By the Meeting at the Gates of Death,
And the Knowing of the bounties of Fire and Passion,
By the Feast of Life and the Giving of Plenty
By the Joy of Beauty and by the Gifts of Lust for Life Itself
We call upon Thee to be with us now.
In Body and in Spirit
HAIL HATHOR!

Hail and Welcome.

Make yourself comfortable lying down, ensuring that you are warm, and attempt the guided meditation.

GUIDED MEDITATION ON THE SPHERE OF HATHOR

You are inside a Pyramid Temple made of translucent Turquoise.

You are lying alone on a cool flat surface.

You are perfectly calm and relaxed.

The stone Sarcophagus is open.

You become aware that you are lying in a shaft of starry light.

You begin to feel yourself being pulled gently upwards, flying into the light.

Your body is weightless. Your hair streaming behind, each pore, each cell of your body is breathing in the stars.

Up, up you fly, the night stars twinkling and glowing in the purple sky. Their perfume pervades with a heavenly essence, they vibrate with a delicious sound of clear sweet music, filling you with clarity and light.

Up, up you fly, the cool fragrant starry light imbuing your entire being with an ecstatic sense of freedom and bliss.

Every tiny molecule and atom of your body is being charged with pure energy and peace.

You are beautiful beyond imagining.

Below you, the Earth and the Planets spin like jewels.

The pure starry iridescent shaft lifts you higher and higher up to the vaulted arch of the Heavens.

Now you begin to feel a pull.

You gently wheel and circle in the sky, but some sort of gravitational tug is making itself felt at your heart level. It is similar to Earth's tug, but subtly different. Slightly lighter, with faster vibration, but more poignant, somehow sweeter, and older, as though it does not pull at your Roots, but at the very core of your Heart.

Now you long to descend.

You close your eyes, and wrap your arms and legs close to your body.

Down you go.

Smoothly, easily, rolling and turning, and quite softly and gently you land in a sweet, beautiful haze of emerald-coloured light.

You open your eyes.

You are in a summer meadow. Rich grass is velvety under your feet. Water bubbles silvery from a nearby spring into a sparkling brook. The sun shines, warm and mild. Bees and butterflies float past in the soft air. Birds are singing throatily and joyously from trees rich with creamy blossom.

And on the grass stand huge platters of delicious food: summer fruits, breads, honey, flagons of wine and sweet cool drinks of fruit.

All this abundance is here for you.

You settle yourself comfortably on the rich and luxurious cushions, and you recline there in the warm sunshine. Beautiful flowers are nodding all around, filling the air with their perfume. Adorable little creatures scamper past for your delight. You may stop them to pet and caress if you so wish, or simply smile upon them admiringly in their play.

Help yourself to some food and wine, savouring the beauty of the rich and vibrant colours on your plate, and in your goblet, smelling the magical scents of the aromatic gifts of Nature, sensing their higher purpose at the same time as enjoying to the full the varied and sensual pleasures they offer.

Allow the honeyed flavour of the wines to enhance your mood and deepen your senses.

Now everything seems a little brighter, a little deeper. A little richer, a little more meaningful and enjoyable.

Stretching your limbs, and settling your body comfortably into the luscious softness of the cushioned meadow, amid the fragrant freshness of the sweet Summer sunshine, and enjoying the gentle breeze kissing your face and hair, you may drift into a light sweet slumber.

In the distance, you hear the light high notes of children calling in play. These are your children; the fruit of your creativity whom you have released into the world to enchant and delight, growing at their own pace and rate.

Here in the garden of your Life, you feel the deep slow stirring of your own potential and power. Your own deep creative fertile force, at one with the Source of Life and Love.

Feel it stir. And love the stirring.

It comes from the matrix of the Cosmos; from the womb of the Great Goddess, whose child you are, and whose great creative pulse quickens in the centre of your Being.

Now you open your eyes to the glories of Nature, you stretch your sleepy limbs, you stand upon the emerald turf, and you reach your two arms up on your tiptoes to the blue sky.

Blessing the green meadow with your eyes, you extend yourself upwards, and you feel yourself rising, lighter and fresher up and up. Up you rise above the green grass studded with flowers, up above the meadow and the brook, up above the shining planet into your shaft of starry light, up into the indigo star-studded night.

Up, up you go, wheeling and turning, free falling and breathing in the fragrant stars.

And now Earth's pull.

The safe warm sweet heavy familiar tug of Planet Earth.

Down you come.

The gravitational Magic of Home.

Back you come.

Return to the Pyramid.

To the stone sarcophagus.

Back through the Turquoise Temple to the Temple of the Body.

Let the Temple and the Pyramid fade.

All is well.

Return to full waking consciousness refreshed and alert and ready to proceed with your life.

Having completed this, spend time in the usual way integrating the experience you have just undergone.

How did you feel during the meditation? Were you able to experience it emotionally? Were you able to rise and descend at will? Did you connect with the power of the goddess in your body?

Were there any children there?

If you are using the Tarot, you can ask any questions which arise from your heart. Some guidelines are suggested.

Questions you can ask the Tarot:

What is the nature of my present relationship to the goddess Hathor?

How may I most readily integrate the energy of the goddess Hathor into my life?

How can I improve my current love life?

How can I more readily express my (any of the) chakric qualities of the goddess Hathor?

If you prefer, you could try writing your question down in block capitals, taking care to be very specific. Then just let the answer flow through your pen on to the paper in your normal script. The discipline here is to *focus on one word at a time as you write it down.* This is a very powerful exercise to stimulate the true creativity, which proceeds through the *ba/ka* process from the Universal *Ba.*

You can eat and drink the altar food and wine. When you feel contented, you may thank the goddess Hathor for her presence, blow out your candles and close down in the usual way.

HAIL AND FAREWELL

CHAPTER FIVE

THE SACRED MARRIAGE OF HORUS AND HATHOR

FIRST LEVEL INITIATION BA/KA PROCESS: INTEGRATION OF PERSONALITY WITH HEART- SOUL

We are now ready to celebrate the **first sacred marriage**. We have traveled along the path of love from our primal roots and shadow to knowledge of our divine heart-soul. We can now commemorate and honour our union of the sacred principles Hathor and Horus. As a wedding of equal loving partners, it is both a serious undertaking and an occasion for congratulation and rejoicing.

The ancient Egyptians held yearly fifteen-day celebrations of the sacred marriage of Hathor and Horus at Dendera on the Nile, where they first met. Priestly representatives of the two gods would meet and marry, and the entire population of Egypt would enjoy two weeks of 'unbridled revelry'* (C.Jacq)

We can dispense with representatives. We are celebrating our arrival at, and connection to, the heart. Just as in any marriage, we can make a solemn commitment to honour and obey its dictums from henceforth and forever as the receptacle of our truthful self-knowledge. Unlike marriage with another person, it cannot deceive us.

Information is transitory, but to know anything 'by heart' renders it eternal. This is why the heart of the Initiate is weighed against the Feather of *Maat* in the Halls of Judgment. When our heart, with all its truthful self-knowledge, weighs as light as a feather, then we as 'the initiate' are already in Paradise.

In Western society, it is not an easy matter to proceed always from one's heart. Sometimes when I return to London, on the aeroplane I can actually feel my heart closing in preparation for the hard-line focus I'm expecting to adopt, away from the loving acceptance which I enjoy in my village at the Pyramids. I have to remember to keep it flowing and open, even in the relatively short time I am away. It is not easy, but is possible, and I am constantly learning that a hard-line focus need not at all prohibit a full and open heart. This is the reason we need make a commitment when we marry. Solar plexus and heart can come together in love and consciousness as Horus and Hathor. Even between those two closest divine principles within the self who are already connected, even ordained to be together, commitment still needs to made, so that, just as in any marriage, we can maintain their constant union. The *ba/ka* process brings the heart-soul and the personality into loving alignment and trust. When our heart and solar plexus centres, or personality and soul become separated from each other, we experience bereft senses of alienation. Commitment to the process of integration precludes this, because it is an avowed, growing, living process of love. It leads us to become love.

However, before we acknowledge commitment, we must prepare to work on the shared gifts of Horus and Hathor as they proceed through our chakric system, to give us deeper understanding of this inner marriage and the blessings we may achieve from it.

The balance of the archetypal principles of Horus and Hathor is very easy to understand in human terms. Closest to each other in essence, there is a heroic quality about the relationship between radiant warrior and beautiful maiden, with which we are all familiar from legend and romance. The knight must storm the castle to rescue the immured damsel; the avenging divine child who resides in the solar plexus finds his peace in the sealed alchemical vessel of the heart.

To prepare for the celebration of this sacred marriage we need to return to the qualities of the prospective god-forces, as we realised them individually in our previous work. Hopefully they have all become more conscious with regular use. Now we may blend or 'marry' two divine qualities at each level, so that they combine in love providing us with the fruits of their union, spiritual qualities which we can think of as 'Wedding Gifts'.

SEVEN WEDDING GIFTS
COMBINED QUALITIES OF THE SACRED MARRIAGE OF HATHOR AND HORUS THROUGH THE CHAKRAS

This part of the work integrates the separate qualities of the god and goddess so that we may begin to realise the dynamics of their marriage. Beginning with the root chakra gifts, working upwards, and meditating upon each separate and then each integrated quality, we will arrive at the freedom and grace of commitment.

The magical perfume blend of the sacred marriage of Hathor and Horus consists of one drop of **rose** essence to one drop of **neroli**. Before meditating on your Wedding Gifts, anointing all seven chakras with this blend, with the sign of the pentagram, will help in actualising them.

HORUS	WEDDING GIFT	HATHOR
ROOT: Obedience	*Prosperity*	Abundance
SACRUM: Determination	*Creativity*	Pleasure
SOLAR PLEXUS: Intelligence	*Art*	Music
HEART: Courage	*Self-Realisation*	Beauty
THROAT: Perfect Honesty	*Truth*	Harmony in Relationship
BROW: Vision	*Prophecy*	Radiant Understanding
CROWN: Glory	*Magnificence*	Grace

PROSPERITY: THE WEDDING GIFT OF HORUS AND HATHOR FROM THE ROOT CHAKRA

The first wedding gift we receive from the shared root chakra of Horus and Hathor springs from the marriage of **obedience** and **abundance**. This combination, bringing together recognition of the richness of life and adherence to the laws of nature, bestows upon us the blessing of **prosperity**. Whatever our undertaking might be, when the principles of Horus and Hathor combine in love on the organic root level, we can only prevail and prosper. However, we do need to commit to prosperity. It is a responsibility that we do not always want. Sometimes it feels much easier to be reliant on the help and prosperity of other agencies and organisations, which or whom we can always blame for our problems. At the organic root level, our concerns are with survival and nourishment. When we commit to prosperity, we allow ourselves to arrive at a position and stances where we can freely offer these things to others and the world. When we find that our obedience to the natural laws is organically in love with our belief in the abundance of nature, we have the fundamental constituents for prosperity.

Our commitment to prosperity helps to promote world order. In economic terms, marriage creates stability, stability promotes prosperity, and prosperity brings peace. Relating this ethic to the self, we begin our sacred marriage, or first level initiation, by making a commitment to prosperity, thus allowing our creative energies to flow freely without the preoccupations of poverty and neglect, and the irresponsibility of blame. We can then achieve independence and security, in the knowledge that we can only prosper in all that we undertake.

CREATIVITY: THE WEDDING GIFT OF HORUS AND HATHOR FROM THE SACRAL CHAKRA

On the sacral level where the primal will of Horus and Hathor combine in love, **determination** marries **pleasure**. The fruit of this union is **creativity** these being its necessary component parts.

Allowing ones true creativity to flow brings one to a truly blessed state. It is a mystical combination of resolve and enjoyment, which is timeless. It is intensely pleasurable or it is not true creativity, but it is also hard work, requiring concentration of will, and the ensuing self-discipline to continue and finish until the creativity becomes a full creation. In the Egyptian myth of Atum, the loving creator, we are informed that even he, on emerging from the Primal Oceans, went through a phase of resolution and resolve. Although he longed to create, he needed to determine the right way to do so. This explains the creative process in all of us. When we commit, on the sacral level to the marriage of Hathor and Horus, uniting our pleasure principle with our determination to succeed and prevail, we can be sure that whatever we undertake to create will bring blessings to the world and ourselves. Drawn from the divine part of our lower selves, yet also springing from the creative force of the cosmos which flows through them, our creations will be truly 'ours', with our own stamp of originality upon them, but they will be released and welcomed into the world to give others the pleasure they gave us to create.

ART: THE WEDDING GIFT OF HORUS AND HATHOR FROM THE SOLAR PLEXUS CHAKRA

From the personality ka level of self-awareness and directed will, or solar plexus centre, the separate gifts of Horus and Hathor are **intelligence a**nd **music.** When these gifts share in love, they combine to provide us with the Wedding Gift of **Art**. This brings us to the mindful state in which one's whole life becomes a conscious work of art dedicated to the divine. Then one can truly be an exponent of the 'artless art of Being', the holy state of loving service written about by Elisabeth Haich in her wonderful semi-autobiographical work, *Initiation.*

Claiming the individual gift of music from the solar plexus of Hathor means that we become conscious enough of our truth to be able to apply it to the *rhythm* or pattern of the universal 'symphony' with which we resonate. We then begin to recognise where we can personally serve the harmony of the cosmos. When this 'truthful resonance' marries our awakened intelligence from the solar plexus of Horus, we bring resonance and harmony to our alertness and the recognition of our life tasks. When we commit to art, we can create our own symphony as we go. Our whole life becomes a work of art.

SELF-REALISATION: THE WEDDING GIFT OF HORUS AND HATHOR FROM THE HEART CHAKRA

When our sense of **beauty** marries our **courage,** Horus and Hathor become one heart and one love. This union in the heart provides us with a spiritual sanctuary to which we can always return, in the on-going struggle to maintain **self-realisation**. The intelligence of the spiritual warrior rises to his heart and finds his courage; the music of Hathor flows into her heart, and there provides us with a constant sense of beauty. When these two qualities meet and mingle, they realise that they are, and always have been, part of each other. For courage *is* beauty, and nothing is truly beautiful without its courage. Courage, like beauty, displays itself as itself without seeking reward. Courage, like beauty, can always be found; courage, as is constant awareness of beauty, is the key to spiritual development. When courage marries beauty, the result is splendour. Courage and beauty brought together consciously as one, brings the certainty that we are always splendidly self-realising, and that wherever we may be in this process, it is always perfect. The process of self-realisation is the most beautiful thing about us and the most courageous. When we actively marry these two qualities from and in our hearts, we will experience not only own sense of **self-realisation**, but the perfection of everyone and everything else's

TRUTH: THE WEDDING GIFT OF HORUS AND HATHOR FROM THE THROAT CHAKRA

When we rise to the *ba* level of the sacred marriage of Horus and Hathor our **perfect honesty** marries with our **harmony in relationship**. This very potent combination produces the Wedding Gift of the counsellor healer, and consciousness changer, which is a powerfully charged **truth.**

As we activate the throat chakra, in our work on the sacred marriage of Horus and Hathor, we are preparing to express and communicate the blessings of this marriage into the world. Hathor has found her beauty, and Horus his courage, which in the preceding heart level came together as a constant, present realisation of self. At the *ba* level, we can combine their qualities for the benefit of humanity.

Harmony in relationship recognises the beauty in all the 'differences', and can express this in every way. Constant harmony is formed in relationship to everything else. Courage has arisen to the throat of Horus in order to open his throat chakra with the blistering power of perfect honesty. When these two qualities combine within us, we are really in a position to help. We can trust ourselves to be honest, fair and tactful, and powerful in self-expression, in full realisation of our own thrust to self-realisation and that of everyone else. We are able to recognise the beauty and magnificence of their process, and find the perfect expression to guide them towards consciousness of it. Now, everything we say or do is expressed towards this purpose. **Truth** releases the love for humanity, expressed by both principles in their separate ways, into a combined working channel for this love to do its very best in the world. When we live in **truth,** we are given higher truths to share. Truth and only truth opens the channels, or throat chakra, from the higher dimensions of Universal *Ba.* When we have natural access to these we can be of real help in the world. By loving the separate principles within and integrating them, we can help others to do the same.

PROPHECY: THE WEDDING GIFT OF HORUS AND HATHOR FROM THE BROW CHAKRA

Rising to the shared third Eye of Horus and Hathor, we combine in love our **vision** with our **radiant understanding**. This bestows upon us the spiritual gift of **prophecy**. This gift carries considerable responsibility, as the gift of prophecy should never be taken lightly, or, except in very special circumstances, spoken aloud. It is, of necessity, a secret gift. When Horus marries Hathor on the *khu/ba* level, our spiritual magical levels are awakened by love, and our understanding transcends the limitations of time and space.

Prophecy allows us to recognise how the divine plan is unfolding, from levels which have not descended to manifestation. These subtler levels have not yet formed into the personal self-will or *ka* levels of individuals. To express knowledge of them can cause confusion and fear in less awakened souls. It may even interfere with the unfoldment of the divine plan. Most spiritual disciplines are clear that whenever this occurs, it carries severe karmic repercussions for the perpetrator.

A good illustration of the misuse of prophecy is found in Shakespeare's *Macbeth*. In this highly occult work, the leading protagonist, Macbeth, is a nephew of the King. While out riding, he meets three witches who prophesy that he will succeed to the throne of Scotland. His highly ambitious wife then persuades him to murder his uncle, and seize the crown. The reasoning behind this stems from the idea that, as it is his destiny to become King anyway, the murder is merely an expedient act. However, the terrible act of regicide creates dreadful repercussions. Lady Macbeth goes mad, and Macbeth, tormented by guilt to megalomaniac state, murders all his detractors, is overthrown and killed. The play leaves us wondering whether, if Macbeth had not taken matters into his own hands, he would have succeeded in due course to rightful possession of the throne.

Prophecy allows us to glimpse into the future, but it is a gift of the higher consciousness which needs to be guarded carefully, and used only by the self in order to promote energy and consciousness along the 'right lines'. It is a special privilege, which we must withhold from those who have not earned it for themselves. If the gift of prophecy is released without care it will immediately be lost, and furthermore, the negative karmic repercussions it creates are borne by the person who releases it.

However, when we rise to the shared qualities of Horus and Hathor, which we can combine at the brow level of awakening, combining our far-seeing vision of Horus with the radiant understanding of Hathor, we should be able to recognise and respect the meaning behind the knowledge we are given. Radiant understanding irradiates everything and everyone it understands with perfect love, and vision confers the ability to see beyond the personal, to the transpersonal levels of universal consciousness. Prophecy is a gift, which we may only employ to help *prepare* others and ourselves for future stages of growth.

MAGNIFICENCE: THE WEDDING GIFT OF HORUS AND HATHOR FROM THE CROWN CHAKRA

At the crown of the sacred marriage of Horus and Hathor, these shining principles share their love as the combination of **glory** with **grace.** When we accept our glory with grace, we display **magnificence.** The ego, as Horus, has realised itself through love and commitment. Hathor, as the heart-soul, has recognised the struggle of the ego/personality to overcome the forces of chaos, and she smiles upon him. Our penultimate battle has been fought at Edfu; Horus has offered up his eye to protect the world, just as we have attained and understood the brow chakra gift of prophesy. Hathor has found her true soul mate at last. On every level but the final *khu* level, heart-soul and personality are married. On attainment of the *khu* level of Horus, the final battle brings glory. Horus prevails – evil is avenged, peace restored. Hathor's *khu* gift is grace. At their combined *khu* level, Horus and Hathor share in glory and grace. Now that he is husband to the goddess of love, he can accept his glory with grace. Her grace becomes glorious. Their love is magnificent. From his magnificence, Horus spares the life of his enemy. The ending is magnificent.

Magnificence stems from our own validation of our struggles, and it allows us to be merciful. Magnificence is simply magnificent. We are all capable of magnificence if we commit to it. Life gives us many opportunities to realise our magnificence if we acknowledge it.

The following 'mystical revelation' is offered as a symbolic paradigm of the shared qualities of the god-forces Horus and Hathor. It is not a pathworking, and does not need to be undergone in ritual conditions. Rather, regard it in the light of a mythic story, which can be read or listened to, to help put flesh and bones on the Wedding Gifts mentioned above.

MYSTICAL REVELATION OF THE SACRED MARRIAGE OF HORUS AND HATHOR

She is dancing in a long, wide temple of *shimmering turquoise. The floor, stretching out into space, seems to be a plateau of azure, above the clouds.*

There are alcoves and pylons, and pillars of gold, and inner sanctums in which stand ceiling-high golden statues. She feels utterly light and joyous, but completely centred and self-controlled. Her dance is measured, but her movements free and graceful. She is clad in beautiful garments of soft, clear colours; floating and diaphanous. Around her wrists and ankles are golden bells that chime with a sweet pure note as she moves across the shining floor.

She knows that he is nearby, and watching her. She knows exactly where he is standing in the hidden alcove. She dances up to him, and then, as he reaches out to touch her, away and lightly running, weaving between the pillars, laughing, hiding, teasing him with her long blue veil. He is radiant and golden; strong and impatient for her. He stalks her, his warrior instinct aroused and active. He might just catch the scarf; but she is lithe and effortless in her graceful evasions. He sits down upon the floor, the blue surrounding him like a shining sky. His silent discomposure pulls at her heart. Tentatively, she moves out of the shadows to stand beside him, poised for flight. Leaping to his feet with a whoop of pleasure, he seizes her, lifting her up into his arms, spinning her around. It is wonderful being caught by him. They laugh; and now they run together, hand in hand, whirling and laughing, her feet barely glancing over the shining turquoise, until she releases him with a kiss. They stop, suddenly quiet. They smile into each other's eyes.

Wordlessly, they take hands, and begin to move towards the inner portals of the temple. They experience each other's bodies aurically; the acknowledgement of need, each for the other, weightless and close fitting, like a cloak of rainbow light which merges and disperses through the spectrum.

There is a round, fathomless pool of dark blue water, which they gaze into together, sharing its secret insights and prophesies. Together they are forming the subtle shapes of their union. The pain of their separations gives definition to the shapes. It bonds them in love. They recognise the darker, deeper shades of their loss, as the outer limits of their achievements, and their plans. Without each other, they could not see the harmony of the shifting shapes and patterns in the depthless water. They entwine their arms around each other in recognition of their love and loss, and embraced, they move away from the pool. They pass a great golden bed, with wings, they smile with remembrance at what they no longer need and with clear and radiant appreciation for the joys they have shared.

They walk together across the plateau of blue cloud. There is another temple below. She will return to her home, and he to his. They will meet again; for they have met and married in love and grace.

RITUAL PROCEDURE FOR THE CELEBRATION OF THE FIRST SACRED MARRIAGE

Having studied and meditated upon all the above qualities and images, you may now prepare for the ritual celebration of the sacred marriage of Horus and Hathor.

Requirements for the Ritual Celebration of the Sacred Marriage of Horus and Hathor

This wedding represents an important initiation for you. You need to plan it with love. Plan for it in seven stages, thinking of each stage as a preparation to receive one of the seven wedding gifts. You could buy your ritual commodities on your 'obedience and abundance' day, or decide what you want to wear at your wedding on your 'music and intelligence' day. The important thing is to honour each stage by putting into actual practice the gifts of the two gods, and bringing them together in your heart.

For the ceremony, you will need:

One white candle, four tea-lights

Seven different crystals or gemstones

Incense and flowers of your choice

A new garment

Essential oil of **neroli** or **orange** and **rose**

A clean cloth for the altar

Ritual Preparation for the Sacred Marriage of Horus and Hathor
Seven Crystals

Choose beforehand seven gemstones, rocks or crystals. These should be of the seven colours of the chakras to represent each of the Wedding Gifts of Horus and Hathor. You can take them from your own collection, or you can buy them especially. In choosing, allow your intuition to be the arbiter of which quality applies best to each crystal or stone. The following guidelines are offered as suggestions.

Root chakra:	**Ruby, Garnet, Black Onyx**
Sacrum:	**Orange Jasper, Fire Opal, Carnelian**
Solar Plexus:	**Yellow Jasper, Topaz**
Heart:	**Emerald, Peridot, Malachite, Rose Quartz**
Throat:	**Turquoise, Lapis Lazuli, Blue Sodalite, Sapphire**
Brow:	**Amethyst, Purple Alexandrite**
Crown:	**Clear Quartz, Diamond.**

Cleanse your seven gemstones in salt and water and pass them through incense smoke. On a special piece of cloth, place them in a vertical line with each appropriately coloured stone at its chakric level. Call each one by name, as its Wedding Gift of Horus and Hathor. Thus, your crystals are called respectively: **Prosperity, Creativity, Art, Self-realisation, Perfect Honesty, Prophecy** and **Magnificence**.

These crystals now represent your inner Horus and Hathor Wedding Gifts. Wrap them up carefully and put them aside for the ceremony.

Ceremonial Site

This ceremony works very well out of doors. Choose a familiar place where you feel free and happy. If, however, the weather is cold or inclement, using your usual working area will do as well.

Witnesses

If you have been working alone you may want to share this moment with loved ones.

They need not actually be with you in the flesh. Send loving thoughts from your heart to your loving witnesses, as you prepare for the ceremony. During the procedure this will give you a proper bridal sense of your loved ones joy for you. You should take into account that brides also 'go away' from their 'families' to form their own matriarchies. Sorrow and joy mingle at weddings, but joy usually prevails.

Anointing, Purification and Robing

Buy a new garment that honours the occasion. Bathe and anoint your heart and solar plexus with a blend of **rose** and **neroli** or **jasmine** oil in the sign of the pentagram. Smudge your hair with your favourite incense. Spend time on your grooming. Take pleasure in your preparations.

Altar Preparation

If you are working outdoors, set a small space aside which faces you as you turn to the East to act as your altar. Place a cloth on the ground in this space, and arrange some flowers, salt, spring water and one white candle (a church candle is ideal) on top. Anoint your candle with your perfume blend, working from its base to its tip. Unwrap your crystals and place them in a vertical line on the altar in the chakric order you have given them.

Delineation of Sacred Space

Prepare your sacred space by calling in the Quarters and creating your Circle of Power. If you are working outdoors you will probably need four small glass candle-covers to prevent them blowing out. If they do blow out, however, allow them to do so. The symbolic lighting of them is the important factor in a ritual. Nature is the best judge in this case.

Visualisation of Chakric Colour

Go into the centre of the circle, sit down and surround yourself in a double ring of golden and rose pink light. Visualise the shining presence of the god and goddess blessing your endeavours with love and grace.

Welcome them into your space.

Meditate for a few moments on accessing your inner place of love.

Experience the golden glow of your inner radiance emanating into your heart and illuminating it. Feel this radiance as a freeing of energy, which flows through your heart and your chest, and up across your shoulders, releasing all unnecessary burdens, yet giving strength and square ness for the ones you freely choose. Let this energy now flow down your two arms. Release it through the open palms of your hands and let it sparkle out through your fingertips like gold dust, as the give-and-take of universal love.

Now rise and face the altar. Light your candle and say:

'I light this candle in commemoration of the divine light of love which will always and henceforth flow into and from my heart.'

Invocations to Horus and Hathor

You may recite the invocations to Horus and Hathor, see pages 142, 167

Commitments

When you feel ready, approach the altar and focus on your seven crystals.

Prosperity:

Starting with your black or red Prosperity crystal, hold it against your root chakra and deliberately visualise yourself in a situation where you are manifesting peaceful prosperity. Notice the *feeling* this gives you, and try to maintain it.

Acknowledge *aloud* that this prosperity serves you and others to create peace and harmony in the world, saying:

'In the names of Horus and Hathor, I commit to peace and prosperity in the sacred cause of my integration.'

Focus on charging your Prosperity crystal with the feeling that arose in you during your visualisation.

If you have managed this correctly this crystal is now programmed with your Prosperity, and may be used for any future work on this issue, provided it does not become exposed to different vibrations.

Placing it back in position, you may repeat this process with your remaining crystals. working sequentially, thoroughly, and without interruption. The better you can focus on each quality, the more powerfully programmed with it each crystal will be. Always make your commitments aloud, offering them in the sacred cause of your integration.

Creativity:
Holding the second, orange crystal against your sacral chakra, visualise yourself in a situation where you are happily engaged in a task of *fruitful* creativity. Integrate the feeling this gives you, and allow the feeling to flow into the crystal saying:

'In the names of Horus and Hathor, I commit to fruitful Creativity in the sacred cause of my integration.'

Art:
Holding the third crystal at your solar plexus, visualise yourself in the midst of a scenario where your natural and loving self-expression is uplifting and changing consciousness in others. Allow the feeling this gives to charge your yellow crystal, and acknowledge this aloud:

'In the names of Horus and Hathor, I commit to my Art in the sacred cause of my integration.'

Self-Realisation:

Holding your pink or green crystal against your heart, take yourself to a place where you can feel in perfect harmony with yourself, others, and your surroundings. Allow yourself to experience the beauty of all your experience, past, present and future:

'In the names of Horus and Hathor, I commit to my Self-Realisation in the sacred cause of my integration.'

Truth:

Take your blue crystal and hold it next to your throat chakra. Remember that this is a marriage of perfect honesty with harmony in relationship. Allow yourself to be placed in a situation where you have been granted permission to help, offer advice or guidance to another. Feeling both interest in and compassion for this person's situation, imagine speaking directly to them from the truth of your knowledge and experience. This person could always be you. As before, allow the feeling to flow up from your heart and into your throat, really concentrating on magically charging your blue crystal with the power of your feeling and voice. Then say:

'In the names of Horus and Hathor, I commit to my Truth in the sacred cause of my integration.'

Prophecy:

Take your violet crystal and hold it to your brow. Visualise yourself sharing the gift of secret Prophecy with the god, the goddess and your own Higher Self. You can both acknowledge this gift, and keep it safe. The image of Horus and Hathor gazing into their deep pool, supplied in the 'mystical revelation' on page 185 is a helpful one. Acknowledge the responsibility of this gift as you say:

'In the names of Horus and Hathor, I commit to holding the secret

gift of Prophecy in the sacred cause of my integration.'

Magnificence:
Spend a little time here to connect to a level of understanding where you experience yourself as being a part of a larger, greater consciousness, which nonetheless includes you integrally. When you feel you have achieved this, take your clear crystal and, holding it against the crown of your head, say:

'In the names of Horus and Hathor, I graciously receive the gift of Magnificence in the sacred cause of my integration.'

When you have completed your work on the seven Wedding Gifts of Horus and Hathor, you may wrap your crystals up in their cloth, bid the god and goddess **Hail and Farewell**, blow out your candles and close down.

To follow, allow yourself a joyous celebration, such as bottle of wine, a shared meal with friends, or a treat such as a concert, or best of all, a dance.

Blessed Be.

CHAPTER SIX

PTAH: DIVINE ARCHITECT

THE FIFTH LEVEL
THE THROAT CHAKRA. THE BA BODY

The next part of our journey along the path of love brings us to consciousness of the *ba* body or higher soul level, and the **throat** chakra. Here, we learn to express the magic of our true voice through the power of utterance. The Egyptians understood this power completely, which they termed *heka*. Many mystics and channels have posited that the Pyramids were built by the power of Sonics, and it is certainly true that they do 'sing'. Especially at Saqarra, the great necropolis for the ancient city of Memphis, there are some pyramids which on some days I have heard vibrating with high clear notes of their own.

As we arrive at the throat chakra and integration of our *ba* body, we activate and awaken the power and magic of the great creator god of the Memphite cosmology, **Ptah**.

Ptah is the divine Architect of the cosmos. It is through his great design that the higher patterns of life emerge and evolve. If the Nile is considered as the spiritual backbone of Egypt, or debatably the planet, Memphis is its throat chakra. It was here that the Egyptians held that Ptah created all things by *naming* them. Just as the Bible states that '*In the beginning was the Word, and the Word was with God, and the Word was God*', the Memphite tradition held that all thing were formed from vibration, or Sonics, which held the loving intention of the creative force of the god-head. The Giza Pyramids are a testament to this belief. Scholars and scientists are still baffled as to how a society without the wheel or iron tools could have arranged these huge blocks of granite into such perfectly proportioned and timeless structures.

Gazing upon them, as I do every day, and living in their presence brings deeper certainty as to the spiritual reasons behind the secrets of their construction. Whatever their uses were, I am sure that the Egyptians were able to manifest them because they knew how to align their highest purpose with their deepest desires. They are monuments to eternity, which demonstrate quite clearly, that with the right consciousness, it is possible to gain control over the density of the material world.

The first Pyramid, Zozer's Step Pyramid, clearly visible across the desert plain, stands at Saqarra, just a few kilometers away from Giza. This great site is the necropolis for the ancient and holy city of Memphis, which sadly no longer remains. The loving and powerful presence of Ptah, however, is still immanent there.

As a god-force, Ptah is wholly creative and positive. The Memphite Cosmo genesis places him as the main creator who, as the *Shabaka Texts* inform us:

gave birth to the gods; made the cities, established the principle divisions; put the gods in their places of worship; fixed their offerings; established their shrines; made their bodies according to the wishes of their hearts.

Then 'breathed' life into them by giving them their *Ren,* or 'true name'. This true name had great significance for the Egyptians who perceived it as having independent power. When the magician truly 'named' something, he imbued it with magic and substance. This magical power was known as **heka**. This is a very interesting idea as we connect with the god-force of Ptah within ourselves. The communicative energies of the throat chakra, arising from the heart, where all things are truly 'known', are the first exposition of real magic, or the effecting of powerful and positive changes in the world by the outer expression of real internal knowledge and love.

Ptah is usually depicted wearing a simple white robe and the close-fitting cap of the artisan, and holding the *uas*, or two-pronged staff of magric. He is not only a great magician, but also a simple and humble artificer; not only the great Architect, but also the wise, gentle, all seeing father. He has infinite patience and care for the smallest of creatures. He loves without censure; he listens and encourages. He was the only god in ancient Egypt who could be approached directly without the intermediary of the priesthood. In fact, most public squares and precincts had little kiosks devoted to the light of Ptah, where his priests and devotees kept a flame perpetually burning in a blue bowl. His energy, however, was so powerful that the priests of Ptah could only channel him in material form through sacred bulls, called the Bulls of Apis. Priests used to search the length and breadth of the Two Lands until they found a black bull-calf with appropriate markings, which included a scarab upon the tongue and a white square upon the brow. They would then bring him with great ceremony to Memphis, to ensconce him in the temple as the living voice of Ptah. The *Serapeum* or labyrinth of the sarcophagi of the sacred bulls at Saqarra has still, after thousands of years, the warmest and most powerful atmosphere I have ever experienced in a place of death or worship.

All the great initiates of the Memphite dynasties were entombed at Saqarra, notably *Ptah-Hotep* the priest-architect who designed the Step Pyramid. His tomb is a masterpiece of artisanship to the inspiration and love of Ptah.

The second sacred marriage along the path of love links Ptah to his wife Sekhmet, the fierce and primal lioness. This union which is totally creative and inspirational, symbolises the inner marriage of the conscious powers of throat (*sa*) and sacrum (*sekhem*) which the Egyptians believed formed the *Sahu,* or Integrated Initiate *   *SEE ROBERT MASTERS '*SEKHMET*'

The word 'ptah' means 'sculptor' or 'engraver'. I find it interesting to note that in the English language it is an anagram of 'path'. The Necropolis Texts refer to Ptah as the 'One Who Makes Lessons'. In his capacity as lord of the sacred Bull, and remembering that the sign of Taurus rules the throat chakra (Memphis being throat chakra of Egypt), Ptah has great resonance with the Tarot card of 'The Hierophant'. This card represents both arche-typal Teacher, and the astrological sign of Taurus.

Ptah Consciousness is both an earthly and a heavenly force. An energy that shines its light onto the spark of spirit residing in matter, to free it and release it into union with itself. Particular to Ptah, though, are the qualities of concentration to finite form, and consideration, the loving attention to detail that turns craft into Art and breathes magic into communication. On the highest level of human achievement, it has created the Pyramids. On the more personal, when linked in love to the mighty passion and fire of Sekhmet, anything one truly desires to create can be manifested to the glory of God.

Ptah Consciousness relies upon the realisation and use of virtue. Virtues are spiritual tools, which we need to hone by constant use, and apply to the creative process of our evolution towards divinity. They provide us with the spiritual equipment necessary for the on-going task of growth; and we can always find them if we know their names.

Our *ba* body is the higher soul consciousness, which designs our lives. Our virtues are the tools which we use to manifest that design.

Now that we have celebrated the first sacred marriage, and have integrated our personality and heart-soul, we are ready to receive the more powerful influxes of light, which descend from universal *ba*. We are ready to work with our magic. Both the fifth and the sixth chakric centres are concerned with the power of magic. Here we prepare for the magical work of awakening the inner god-force Ptah. This is potent work, which we can regard as the first real use of our latent magical powers. The Western Mystery Tradition defines magic as the ability to effect 'change', or transformation, by the power and use of the true will. Our magician-ship can be regarded as the conscious process of self-transformation, and the ability to attain our full potential by accessing and integrating our own higher Will. Using the Pyramids as an example and inspiration, we can meditate upon the qualities of the Creator god Ptah, to become conscious of the higher design of our life. We can then employ those qualities and virtues to manifest that design into the world.

As we embark upon this process of magically re-creating our lives, we prepare to integrate our lower nature with the higher design of our life, which we can ritually celebrate as the sacred marriage of Sekhmet and Ptah, or **second level initiation.** Firstly, we need to realise the qualities of the god-force Ptah as they flow through our chakras. Consciousness is rising to integrate our *ba* body, the loving aspect of our soul-nature, which has designed our bodies and personalities, and it is necessary that we should be prepared, to work in accord with it. The magical levels that we awaken to henceforth, design lives and effect change. They have greater ramification in the world, and so we need to approach them with even more responsibility and mindfulness than before.

Questions we need to address in ourselves, to prepare for connection to the *ba* body and awakening of Ptah in the throat chakra, relate to our plans and projects as well as our use and realisation of virtue.

'Do I always mean what I say?'

If you are a 'games player' in your relationships, or enjoy weaving fantasies about who you are, and what you mean to do, it is time to stop. You will not develop magically if you make unrealistic promises, or issue empty threats. As we progress along the path of love to the *ba* level, we must take responsibility for the words that issue from our throat. A magical life requires that we always try to be conscious of our words and the thoughts that shape them. Naturally, we are only human, and there are times when we speak hastily and imprudently. No deep harm will occur if our words are true. If however, we are deliberately misguiding others or ourselves, we will not be able to connect with our higher levels, and, if we are releasing power from the lower levels without connection to the higher, we can cause real damage. At this stage, we need to be clear about what we want, and peaceful in our expression of attaining it. This cannot be if we are saying things we do not mean to create effect.

Do I engage in malicious gossip?

When we feel frustrated or restricted in our relationships, we can resort to malicious gossip. Even if we do it lightly, it is very harmful indeed. Kindly thoughts towards those who wish us harm, transform malicious intention. Engaging in gossip perpetuates it. When our magical power is developed, speaking ill of our friends and associates has dire ramifications. From this point forward, it is good practice only to speak positively about anyone in his or her absence. This will create positivity, and support magic.

Can I listen to others without immediately thinking about myself?
This is a good test of magical ability. Listening is learning. The closer we listen to others, the more we learn about life. Listening requires that we give full attention so that we can digest what we hear. When we have digested the knowledge properly, we are in a position to help. If we immediately refer to our own problems without listening, we help no one, least of all our self.

Having addressed these searching questions, we can proceed along the path of love, by realising the gifts of Ptah through the chakras.

THE GIFTS OF THE GOD PTAH THROUGH THE CHAKRAS

ROOT:	*Patience*
SACRUM:	*Order*
SOLAR PLEXUS:	*Design*
HEART:	*Knowledge*
THROAT:	*Heka (Magical Utterance)*
BROW:	*Wisdom*
CROWN:	*Cosmic Consciousness*

PATIENCE: THE ROOT OF PTAH

Patience is not resigned waiting or deliberate tolerance to inadequacy. It is a *full engagement with the present task of being*. This means being fully conscious of the moment and the different levels within it. God, as represented by Ptah, has care and attention for the tiniest detail of life as well as for the most magnificent of his creations. Engagement with the immediate task-in-hand is the most positive and powerful step towards the manifestation of miracles. Here at the root of the throat we are concerned with the basis for our magic and our released creativity. Patience gives us the most reliable basis to operate from, because when we find it, we pay full attention to what we are doing and where we are. We take full interest in the moment.

Magic is a science; all the sciences require patience. When we are being truly patient, vibrating to the power of the moment, we do not ask 'when?' Scientific breakthroughs and magical phenomena happen when everything comes together to allow them to do so. If we long for them, we must place that longing into our work on making them happen. We must be present. If we chafe at the restrictions of time, or the limitations of our understanding, we will never overcome them. We do not try to be patient; this is a contradiction. We find complete interest in what is actually happening, and our anxious restrictions melt away.

ORDER: THE SACRUM OF PTAH

Placing our energies, thoughts and ideas in **order** provides a reliable structure for them to manifest in the most positive way that our higher and lower natures dictate. We can escape neither Nature, nor our unconscious destiny, but if we recognise and **order** the one, we may become conscious and fulfilled in the other. We are told that the god Ptah 'orders the principle divisions'. Awareness of our principle divisions exist in the sacral chakra. When sacral consciousness rises to the *ba* level, we find order in our existence. We 'know where everything is'. We know how we can access the energies we need, to create what we want to do with our lives, and what we need to 'transform'. We work in harmony with the laws of the cosmos because we can recognise our self as a living manifestation of it. To find order we must be aware of the laws. We understand the cosmic laws as operating though us. We see divine order and our self as a part of it.

DESIGN: THE SOLAR PLEXUS OF PTAH

Having gained the consciousness of cosmic law and order from the sacral level of the throat, we rise to the *ka* level of Ptah, where we can freely express our sense of individuality and originality in magical terms. We become aware of our own **design**. The creative *ba,* having designed our life, operates through it in consciousness.

Here is a chance to be both truly creative and spiritually awake to the potential of self. A very powerful and positive exercise here to awaken your magic of **design** is to think about designing your perfect day in two year's time. When you have finished the exercises on realising the qualities of Ptah, you will be ready to initiate the manifestation of your own design. Start with considering exactly how, where and with whom you would choose to wake up on the morning of this perfect day, and end with going to sleep at night. Account for every moment of your day, being both as daring and as realistic as you can be, to provide yourself with an ideal day. Spend as long as you need to make it good, and really yours, without stinting yourself, or exercising undue control over others. When you feel it is sound, manageable and well fitting, write it down. Place it on your altar with a blessing; we shall return to it later.

KNOWLEDGE: THE HEART OF PTAH

To know anything, for **knowledge** is much more than information, we need to have it 'by heart' so that we never forget it. The Egyptians placed the heart as the organ of all knowledge, in the understanding that true knowledge was imprinted on to the soul, and thus everlasting. As already mentioned, it was the heart of the Pharaoh which was weighed against the Feather of Truth in the Halls of Judgment.

Self-knowledge lives in the heart of Ptah. From the heart of the throat, we can create real magic because it comes from our deep and eternal knowledge of self. Our magic will live because it is real, it stems from our heart's truth. We will now only manifest or transform that which we know is true for us, and conducive to our purpose. It is released from our heart through our throat. We know what we are in our heart, and our heart knows of what we are capable.

In the myth of Atum Ra, when he became aware of his heart, he knew that his true name was Ptah. He uttered the word, and he became him. This radiant solar creative force pronounced his name so that he could express the loving attention to detail which lived in his heart – the knowledge of creation.

HEKA: THE THROAT OF PTAH

The throat chakra of Ptah is the absolute throat, the throat of throats. From this level, the *ba* body magically utters its design to manifest itself. Magical utterance or **heka** is the directed power of the spoken (or written) word, which issues from true heart knowledge through the throat. Heka requires all the gifts of the magician: knowledge, power and love. It also requires directional focus. When true heart knowledge is properly directed from the magician who has realised the appropriate virtues and qualities, into thought form, it manifests.

The god Ptah says in the ancient texts that his '*tongue is the agent of his heart*'. His creations, arising from his deepest knowledge, were, when released by his utterances, given independent power. So can yours. Have the courage given by true self-knowledge to utter *your* truths that they will manifest for you in ways more beautiful and powerful than you can presently imagine. They will then return to you in love and consciousness.

In order to exercise the **heka,** you must first be sure in your heart of what you want. Then, in your sacred space, speak the words, declaiming them clearly, whilst visualising yourself actualising your desires and creating the real and positive emotions which spring from their actualisation. For example, if you really desire to be in a committed, happy relationship, you may say:

'In two years time I wake up in the morning next to my beloved wife (husband).'

You will feel the love and commitment in your heart as you speak these words, and you will experience the sleeping warmth of your beloved partner. If you are not already in a marriage, you will not create the face and form of the other person; you will merely create the feeling of them. It is the feeling that carries the heka into manifestation. Like the Lord Ptah, your heart directs your tongue.

If you feel that two years is too long a time span, then make it shorter. I suggest two years as a manageable creative magical period. I have found that if you give yourself two years to manifest your hearts desires, and you work clearly and powerfully with your heka, then they can manifest far quicker; sometimes even in weeks.

WISDOM: THE BROW OF PTAH

The gift of love-in consciousness, **wisdom** is the capacity to see truth beyond the apparent, to recognise the beauty of different truths and the similarities of their essence. When we rise to the *khu/ba* level of the throat chakra, we are able to see truth in everything and act accordingly. We do not judge others harshly because we can see where they are 'coming from'. We see how we can help them, and how we cannot.

A very good illustration of wisdom comes from the 'Instructions of King Cormac'. Cormac was perhaps the greatest kingfrom Irish antiquity. His words have been handed down from the druidic bards to the chroniclers of the 9th century. I include them as particularly favourite inspirational words.

King Cormac is asked about his habits when he was a lad.

I was a listener in woods

I was a gazer at stars

I was blind where secrets were concerned

I was talkative among many

I was mild in the mead hall

I was stern in battle

I was gentle towards allies

I was a physician of the sick

I was weak towards the feeble

I was strong towards the powerful

I was not close lest I should be burdensome

I was not arrogant although I was wise

I was not given to promising though I was strong

I was not venturesome although I was swift

I did not deride the old although I was young

I was not boastful although I was a good fighter

I would not speak about anyone in his absence

I would not reproach but I would give praise

I would not ask but I would give.

For it is through these habits that the young become old and kingly warriors.

COSMIC CONSCIOUSNESS: THE CROWN OF PTAH

Arrival at the crown level of Ptah and the *khu* level of the throat brings awareness of the greatness of existence, and the perfection of its workings. We can now claim the gift of **cosmic consciousness.** At this stage we realise that we have become co-workers in the divine plan of the universe; we understand and adhere to its laws, and can allow its greatness to work through us.

Having contemplated the chakric gifts of Ptah, we are ready to make his personal affirmations. As before, enounce them clearly, with meaning, until they sound very firm and strong.

PERSONAL AFFIRMATIONS ON THE GOD-FORCE PTAH

I am always approachable by those that I can truly help

Each day I consider how I may improve my life

I do not blame; but I do give praise

My heart directs my tongue

RITUAL PROCEDURE

You may now prepare for the ritual awakening of the god-force Ptah. It is best to conduct this work in the morning. Before you begin, spend some time singing, or reciting poetry. If you feel you have difficulty with clarity of speech, diction, a stumbling vocabulary, or even making yourself heard, wearing a turquoise or lapis-lazuli pendant at throat level can help to correct this.

Ritual Correspondences for Awakening Ptah

COLOUR:	**Blue**
PERFUME:	**Lavender**
INCENSE:	**Juniper berries, Thyme leaves**
CHAKRA:	**Throat**
BODY:	**Ba Body**
ANIMAL:	**Bull**
TIME OF DAY:	**Morning**
SACRED SYMBOL:	**Uas**
TAROT CARDS:	**'The Hermit', 'The Hierophant'**

Altar Preparation, Purification, Anointing and Robing

After bathing, anoint your throat chakra in oil of **lavender** with the sign of the pentagram. Dress in a clean **white** or **blue** cotton garment. Place a blue candle and a representation of Ptah on your altar. If you do not possess a picture or statue of Ptah, you could place one of your own working tools, or any representation of a loving creative force. Burn some **thyme leaves** or **juniper berries** on a charcoal tablet. Read over your design to make sure that you are perfectly satisfied with it. When so, pass it through the incense smoke and place it on the altar.

Delineation of Sacred Space

Create your sacred space in the usual way. When you call the Quarters and create the Circle, make sure that you enounce each word with clarity and power.

Then approach the altar and light your blue candle, saying:

'I dedicate this altar to the divine Ptah, that I might release the magic of my true Voice into the World.'

Visualisation of Chakric Colour

Seat yourself comfortably in your space, and surround yourself in a cool blue light. Practice activating your chakras, meditating on the qualities of the god Ptah as they proceed from your root to your crown.

> 'I give thanks for my patience.
> I give thanks for my order.
> I give thanks for my design.
> I give thanks for my knowledge.
> I give thanks for my Heka.
> I give thanks for my wisdom.
> I give thanks for my cosmic consciousness.'

Imagine yourself as a living *uas,* or two-pronged staff of power, with a sparkling crystal tip. Experience the cool sparkling fire of the gem flowing down your spine to your two feet, penetrating and sinking into the earth below you. Feel the volcanic power of the earth below you refining as it rises to meet it. The power meets and mingles in your full and happy heart, which directs the power up and out into the world, through the clear, open channel of your throat.

Now practice the following chant for at least five minutes.

*ANKH – PTAH- SEKER- ASR.** 'words of power' Brian and Esther Crowley.

'Eternal Life in the Three-fold Principle of the Godhead, known as 'Ptah- Seker- Osiris'

As your lips form the words, remember the *uas,* and focus on the light power flowing up through your legs, and down from your crown, meeting in your heart, and directing itself upwards like a controlled fountain of light into a clear and resonant sound, which issues magically from your throat.

Fill your space with the strong and loving vibration of this sound. Experience the love of Ptah flowing out of your throat, and blessing the world. When you have chanted enough, stand and face your altar, and repeat the Invocation simply and from your heart. Think about every word as it passes from the page, to your eyes, to your heart, and out of your mouth into your space. Visualise the gentle, loving strength of the god descending into your space and blessing you.

INVOCATION TO PTAH

*Hail
Ptah,
Lord of
Right and
Teacher of Virtue;
Gentle giver of the
rightful name, Who
breathes your Love on the
work-tools of living to steady
Creation's holy flame, Let Thy
Light be our guidance, Thou Maker
of Lessons, when learning to master the
craft of Life's art. Eternity speaks in the
form of thy Sculpture, for all that we can be is
known in thy heart. By Perpetual Structure of the
Laws of Heaven, By the Smallest stone from the
upturned Plough. By the perfect shapes of unfolding
Nature. By words of the wind in the highest house. By the
Temple of Learning, and gifts of Magic. By the blessings Of
Lessons and the knowledge of Right. By the quiet joy of application, and the Light of Wisdom, we Thy Children call upon Thee to
be with us now In Body and in Spirit. HAIL PTAH! Hail and Welcome.*

Make yourself comfortable and attempt the guided meditation.

GUIDED MEDITATION ON THE SPHERE OF PTAH

I would like to acknowledge my friend, the poet Suzanne Miller, who first dreamed this Ptah work.

You are standing barefoot on soft golden sand. Before you the sun is rising, casting a roseate glow over the landscape. The desert is warm and friendly, bathed in pink and golden light, stretching out to a green fringe of trees at a distant oasis. Behind you, facing the sunrise is a beautiful Temple of white stone. You have just emerged from its high doorway to welcome the bright new day. In the clear morning air, the sky is near, almost as though you could reach up and touch it with your fingertips. You are wearing a long white gown, and the morning light is touching you, too, with its rose and gold. The tender rays of the dawning day stroke your head and stream into your heart, filling it with simple gladness. It feels like the dawning of the World. With solemn joy, you dance to greet the day. With each simple and stately movement, your body becomes a vessel of Love for the energy of Creation.

Your dance over, you sit down upon the sand. By your side, you see a small wand. It is made of wood and on its tip is a sparkling blue crystal. You take it up and attune your personal energy to its clear light vibrating power. You turn the wand round, examining it minutely. You see that it bears a hieroglyph, which only you can understand. This is your Name. Look at the hieroglyph and let your eyes drink its secret message for you. Now you take the wand and write your Name into the sand in your own language, in beautiful flowing script.

You speak your name aloud into the new morning. It resonates clearly in the fresh empty world. The morning receives it gladly.

You spend a moment or two assimilating the power of your Name. It gives a new sense of stability.

As you do this, you become aware of a magnificent warm strong presence at your side. You see that a great black, winged bull has joined you. He has moon-shaped horns and a white square upon his brow. His liquid eyes are shining with strength and intelligence. You gaze into them; they are pools of power and grace. You climb up on to his back. He lifts you up into the blue morning and you go sailing up above the clouds into the sunlight until you see far below you a gleaming city of alabaster and white marble. As you approach, you see that the city is still being built. Artisans and artists are there, applying their skills to matchless standards. Exquisite murals adorn walls of breathtaking beauty of proportion and design. It is a dazzling and noble sight.

The Great Bull lands gently and firmly. You wander around freely. All is a-bustle with energy and action. However, it is not noisy or dirty. All this work is being conducted with grace and calm. You feel privileged and exalted being in the midst of it. There are statues, and watercourses, fountains and temples, public buildings and private homes, all yet uninhabited. On each public square, however, there is a beautiful kiosk in which burns a lamp of blue crystal. The calm clarity of the flame fills you with inner peace.

At length you come to a tall white Pyramid building, which draws you with its warmth and beauty. The door stands ajar, and as you approach you see that it bears your True Name; the one you wrote upon the sand. You enter gladly. A staircase leads upwards, streaming light. The sound of golden notes of music pours down from the light. You run nimbly to the top; the light, the music draws you, your whole being responding to their clear purity.

At the top, a beautiful presence awaits. A tall smiling figure in a white robe with a close-fitting cap, stands holding a two-pronged staff with a blue crystal tip. He emanates kindliness and love. The light and the music seem to be radiating from him. Smiling his blessing deep into your eyes, he seems to be waiting for your question. You know that he loves you with a completeness of understanding, without judgment or censure. You know that you can ask him anything. As you smile up into his eyes, you become aware that there is something incomplete within your heart. There is a virtue or a quality you have lost, mislaid or forgotten how to use to perfection. There is something in the tool-bag of your being you have left aside for the moment, and the empty feeling of it makes the word burn in your heart.

However, the Great Architect just smiles, and points to the floor at your feet. With surprise and delight, you pick up a little golden hammer and chisel. Ptah indicates that you may use these sacred tools to carve your virtue into the temple wall. The stone wall is soft under your golden chisel; the hammer light and steady in your hand. With pride of precision, you carve the name of your special virtue into the temple stone. Now it is truly yours. The blessing of Ptah's light approves and sanctifies your effort. With a light heart, you receive his blessing, and turn to return down the long staircase out into the now empty street.

The winged Bull is waiting. You climb up, and he soars with you into the evening sky.

Feeling his power under you, and the enormous love in his great heart beating for you, you feel calm and trusting like a small child. At length he brings you back to your temple in the desert. He lands with a rush of mighty wings and you slide off, relaxed and sleepy. The day is over. All is well. You settle back on the sand to rest and dream. You are safe; grounded; home. In a little while, you may return to full waking consciousness, alert, refreshed and ready to continue with your life.

Integration and Grounding
Did you see a hieroglyph on the wand? Did you receive a new name? What virtue(s) did you require?

Take special note of the 'Name' you may have received during the meditation, and any 'Virtue' you felt you required. Write these down on a separate piece of paper, and any other words that might have occurred for you.

When this part of the procedure feels completed, take your design from the altar. Read it out aloud, clearly visualising every event as you say it, and experiencing its emotions and sensations truthfully. When this is done, say:

'I dedicate this Design to the highest I can attain, in full acceptance of my capacities and limitations.'

Ignite it at the altar candle and let it burn out in the thurible or incense-burner. You can do the same with any Virtue or Name you might have received, on its different piece of paper. You have now released the magically charged Design of your Life into the world, and the power of Ptah will bless and shape it for you, so that all that is best in it for you can in due course manifest

After a suitable time of contemplation, thank the god for his presence, bidding him:

'HAIL AND FAREWELL'

Blow out your candles. Throw your paper ash out of the window so that the winds take it, and close down

Blessed Be.

CHAPTER SEVEN

THE SACRED MARRIAGE OF SEKHMET AND PTAH SECOND LEVEL INITIATION

CONSCIOUS INTEGRATION OF THE AUFU AND BA BODIES

THE SERPENT AND THE STAFF
Power and Wealth

We can now prepare to celebrate the sacred marriage of Sekhmet and Ptah.

Traveling along the path of love from sacrum to throat, we have transformed raw Sekhmet serpent power into the consciousness of love in relationship as Hathor, in the heart. This is the very transformation Ra effected when he tricked Sekhmet into 'drunkenness', or ecstasy. We, however, managed this transformation by meeting the courage and intelligence of Horus in our solar plexus.

At this stage, our consciousness refined and rose from the primal boundary issues of Sekhmet, to recognition of our humanity. This was a painful and difficult transition. As Horus, we had to find the consciousness of humanity to locate the 'evil within' and the determination and skills to vanquish it. However, to give us recognition of our internal 'enemy' along the path, we have had the company of our own shadow (*khaibi*) in the form of Anubis, the dark half-brother of Horus, whom we first encountered at our root. Anubis gives us understanding of the shadow, Sekhmet and Horus, the power and courage to meet it.

Horus, like Sekhmet, is a mighty retributive solar force, albeit a much more conscious one. The part of the journey we travelled from Sekhmet to Horus, raised and refined our primal powers and boundary issues from the divine animal (*aufu*) level of consciousness to the divine human (*ka*). The gifts of Horus brought our human intelligence into awareness, so that we became conscious of our own weaknesses and strengths. We could celebrate our heroism and valour in adversity.

At this stage we 'came to the notice' of the sleeping Beauty in our own heart. She woke up to us as Hathor. Our heart welcomed its 'avenging' hero. Our *ka* had vindicated past evils. Our personality was true, and our heart could marry, or integrate with it. The transformation from Sekhmet to Hathor became conscious. Personality integrated with heart-soul. The *ba ka* process took place.

We celebrated this process as the sacred marriage of Horus and Hathor. We committed to acceptance and realisation of seven precious gifts. In acceptance of these gifts of prosperity, creativity, art, self-realisation, truth, prophecy and magnificence, we prepared to awaken to the powerful and loving presence of the creator god Ptah.

We raised and refined the raging serpent power of the Kundalini, which we first encountered in the sacrum, into the magical staff of power or *uas* of the great Architect, Ptah. The serpent and the staff entwined in love. The serpent staff is a powerful alchemical symbol of magical creativity.

Now that we have a deeper understanding of its purpose and value, it is time to meet that raw power again.

This is an appropriate place to return to our source. Our relationship to the source changes as we develop and transform, but the primal roots of our beginning will always be there. If we cut ourselves off from them we will wither, or harden and atrophy. Now that we have arrived at the magical level of Ptah, where we may begin to effect change in the world, it is of supreme importance that we re-connect in love to the power and ferocity of our primal Lioness, and the intoxicating intransigence and truth of our lower Will.

The sacred marriage of Sekhmet and Ptah is not so easy to understand in mythic terms as that of Horus and Hathor. The chakric points are further apart, and the subtle bodies much more different. Yet the wild, bloodthirsty, rampaging lioness who resides in our sacrum is partnered in love with the humble and gentle craftsman, who lives in our throat Together they form the cranial sacral link, which is integral to health and wholeness. They need one another. In Egyptian civilisation, the great Pharaoh Rameses linked along the Nile the great spiritual centres of Memphis (throat) to Thebes (sacrum) to celebrate this marriage from the very body of Egypt.

The ancient Egyptians termed the initiate who had formed the connection between the throat and sacral centres, the *Sahu,* or 'he who had integrated his subtle bodies'. This integration allowed him to manifest the royal prerogatives of the tamed Lion, the prerogatives of 'power' and 'wealth'. The alchemical symbol for transmuted consciousness is 'gold'.

The controlled solar energy of the tamed Lion brings gold, but wealth is a burdensome responsibility for the uninitiated. The higher self will not bring it into manifestation unless this inner marriage is consummated in love. It is a serious undertaking, and although it is a time for celebration, it is time for sober reflection. Power and wealth are great responsibilies, and we must prepare for them properly.

Egyptians still regard gold as the ultimate token of married love. Every *fellah* woman in the vegetable market is bedecked in golden earrings and bangles to denote her married status; betrothal gifts are invariably, when economically possible, of this sacred and precious metal. At my own wedding, my husband presented me with a bridal gift of a magnificent golden 'glove', a bracelet and five golden rings intricately wrought together for my left hand. Although we are not rich by Western standards, subsequent birthdays and anniversaries bring me more. I wear it all with pride, as a proper and radiant symbol of my husband's love and his continuing commitment to our married state.

Western Europeans are generally ashamed and uncomfortable with wealth; we hide it and hoard it in insurance bonds and Unit Trusts. We do not display it comfortably and simply as a reward for a loving life as the Egyptians do. When in London, I am constantly being warned by perfect strangers not to wear my gold in the street. The Egyptian market women, who live at a basic level of subsistence, sincerely admire it and robustly congratulate me. Wealth, of course, is a relative matter, but a *sense* of wealth, well-being, generosity of spirit, and pride of love will emerge from the realised golden solar force of Sekhmet, in communion with the wisdom of the great design of Ptah. Undergoing the second sacred marriage gives us the power to love the world. In order to promote love in the world, we do need to feel powerful and rich in ourselves.

Preparation for the Sacred Marriage of Sekhmet and Ptah

This sacred marriage integrates our *aufu,* or physical intelligence, with our *ba,* or eternal soul consciousness. When this integration is complete, we can enjoy our spirituality from a physical level, and vice-versa. We can be conscious of continuous self-healing. In preparation, we need to balance three areas of our life. These are **power, well-being** and **purity**. We need to consider how integrated they are. It is all too easy to apportion blame when we are sick or unhappy, thus missing the point of our choices. Feeling wronged is a dangerous luxury; as we commit to a magical life, we need to be responsible. Therefore, before we embark upon celebration of the sacred marriage of Sekhmet and Ptah it is important to question the truth of our needs and to consider how conscious we are about meeting them. Here are some examples.

Power:

    How honest is my will?

    Am I controlling others out of fear?

    Am I doing too much to prove myself? To make myself in expendable?

    Do I 'give in' too readily?

    Do I pretend for a 'quiet life'?

    Do I refuse things that I really want?

    Can I control my temper?

    Do I weep when I am angry?

Well-being:

Do I take delight in things every day?

Do I eat too much/too little?

Do I drink or smoke too much?

Do I enjoy getting bathed and dressed?

If in relationship, is lovemaking a favourite occupation?

How ready is my laughter? My tears? My smile?

Do I give myself enough sleep? Exercise? Stimulation? Restful occupation? Congenial company?

Am I as comfortable in my body as I might be?

Purity:

How does my behaviour match up to my highest ideal?

Have I honoured the needs and wishes of others?

Do I bear a grudge? If so, how does it affect me?

Have I been candid lately? If not, why not?

Am I content with my own company?

Do I consider my dreams?

Am I growing in consciousness?

Do I love enough to give freedom?

Do I notice nobility in others? Graciousness? True courage? Decency? If not, why not?

Am I incurring debt? Paying it back?

If so, how pleased am I to be doing it?

Am I preoccupied with constant thoughts of another?

Am I as peaceful with myself as I might be?

Asking these questions gives insight into how power, well-being and purity are balanced in the self.

THE SEVEN WEDDING GIFTS

The next part of our preparation requires meditation and contemplation upon the combined qualities, or Wedding Gifts, of the sacred marriage of

Sekhmet and Ptah as they proceed through the chakras.

Anointment of the appropriate chakra with a blend in equal parts of **musk** or **patchouli** with **lavender** oils, in the pentagram sign, will help to give focus to the process.

WEDDING GIFTS OF THE SACRED MARRIAGE OF SEKHMET AND PTAH THROUGH THE CHAKRAS

PTAH	WEDDING GIFT	SEKHMET
ROOT: Patience	**Serenity**	Passion
SACRUM: Order	**Justice**	Joy/Righteous Wrath
SOLAR PLEXUS: Design	**Integrity**	Dignity
HEART: Knowledge	**Everlasting Love (The Sphinx)**	Power
THROAT: Heka	**Manifestation**	Enchantment
BROW: Wisdom	**Communion**	Exaltation
CROWN: Cosmic Consciousness	**Eternity**	Ecstasy

SERENITY: THE WEDDING GIFT OF SEKHMET AND PTAH FROM THE ROOT CHAKRA

When we love our **patience** and our **passion** enough to marry them, we arrive at the blessed state of **serenity**. This Wedding Gift from the root chakra provides us with deep security because in it we find complete engagement with our life and our tasks. From serenity, we know that we are self-perfecting. Our consciousness is devoted to the ultimate achievement of perfection, and we can be fully alive to the process. Our serenity blesses everyone. It never incurs envy. In serenity we gain and promote a profoundly pulsating connection to the power of life, desiring nothing but what it offers us, yet remaining open to change and experience.

JUSTICE: THE WEDDING GIFT OF SEKHMET AND PTAH FROM THE SACRAL CHAKRA

Justice, or *Maat,* was integral to the life and purpose of the Pharaoh, who administered it to himself and his subjects in every thought, word and deed. The Egyptians held it in such reverence as a quality that they gave it a goddess of its own. The Rule of Maat ensured that peace, prosperity and unsurpassed creativity prevailed throughout the kingdom. Acknowledging our sacral issues from the marriage of Sekhmet and Ptah gives us an integral sense of **order**, which, when it links in love to our **joy** and **righteous wrath**, administrates them, so that they may be applied with directness and truth. The Tarot teaches that the principle of justice exists within the cosmos to balance polarities, so that, without swinging from one pole to the other, creative energy can occur. Awareness of polarity exists in the sacrum; when our two creative principles Sekhmet and Ptah combine in love from this level, they bring understanding of the rule of balance. We know unthinkingly what is right for us. We gain the authority to redress our transgressions and correct our excesses, and gain compassion for those of everyone else. When we discover our own justice principle, we do not need to judge others. When we live by the Rule of Maat, our heart can be as light as the feather of truth.

INTEGRITY: THE WEDDING GIFT OF SEKHET AND PTAH FROM THE SOLAR PLEXUS

From the solar plexus of this sacred marriage, Sekhmet's **dignity** meets and mingles with the true **design** of Ptah. This gives us the focus of real, unshakeable **integrity**. When we can claim this gift, we achieve the freedom of self-empowerment. We are aware of the 'design' of our personality, and what will uphold it. We also have the dignity which comes from recognition of our intrinsic nature. The fruit of the marriage of these qualities, **integrity** ensures that we will always be true to ourselves and our calling. With integrity, we live in honour; our *ka* body having formed its code of belief and behaviour, which we choose to live by, in thought word and deed. In integrity we are who we want to be, and we maintain whom we like being, by conscious thought and conduct.

EVERLASTING LOVE: THE WEDDING GIFT OF SEKHMET AND PTAH FROM THE HEART CHAKRA

As commitment rises to the heart chakra, the Wedding Gift of Sekhmet and Ptah springs from the sacred vessel where earth energy and spirit meet. Sekhmet's **power** meets with Ptah's eternal **knowledge**. We find the knowledge of **everlasting love**. This gift reminds me very much of the Sphinx. With the body of a lion and the head of a man, the Sphinx gazes out towards the rising sun with timeless love of humanity, and ineffable knowledge of the divine. The love that emanates from its presence is almost tangible. When the primal force of Sekhmet and the creative love of Ptah meet from their hearts, the result is a love of self for self that is both protective and unconditional. It allows us to love with absolute certainty. When we realise this gift, we know we can express ourselves fully in the service of light and evolution. We know that whatever and whomsoever we love, our love will always be with them; will always support them; and will always promote their growth and well-being. This is the love that transcends time and space. This is the love which seeks to love for the sake of loving. It can never run out, and it is never wasted. From the shared heart of Sekhmet and Ptah, we can find this love for others, the world and ourselves.

MANIFESTATION: THE WEDDING GIFT OF SEKHMET AND PTAH FROM THE THROAT CHAKRA

We can now raise our consciousness to join the voices of Sekhmet and Ptah. The mighty roar of the lioness and the creative Word of the 'Giver of the True Name' meet and marry from the throat chakra, to manifest our desires and purpose. The **enchantment** of Sekhmet links with the **heka** of Ptah, and we effect **manifestation**. Manifestation is the ability to bring into concrete reality that which both our higher and lower selves want and desire. Proceeding from **everlasting love**, these desires accord with the cosmic plan and can only unfold to the glory of God, and the benefit of humankind. The Pyramids are a perfect example of this idea. They simply could not be manifest. Perhaps the Egyptians were able to manifest them from the design of Ptah merely because it was in the order of the cosmic plan that they should. The fact that they are there certainly gives us insight into the wonders of Egyptian consciousness, and ensures that we continue trying to unravel its mysteries.

When we marry from the throat chakras of Sekhmet and Ptah, we too can manifest time defying achievements. Our manifestations, arising from everlasting love, will have their own power and purpose, which we have been able, through work and consciousness, to bring into the world.

COMMUNION: THE WEDDING GIFT OF SEKHMET AND PTAH FROM THE BROW CHAKRA.

When **wisdom** and **exaltation** come together consciously from the brow chakras of Sekhmet and Ptah, they create the alchemy of **communion** with the higher worlds; the immeasurable riches of connection to the divine. The queen of the beasts and the gentle artificer join their higher vision in love to share in the creative process of God. When we can connect these two aspects of self from our *khu/ba* bodies, we gain insights and inspirations which effect powerful changes in the collective. We see where and how we can promote the creative vision of the universe. We have access to our inner plane guides and masters, and they to us. We can commune with them; their insights are ours.

ETERNITY: THE WEDDING GIFT OF SEKHMET AND PTAH FROM THE CROWN CHAKRA

When we attain the crown of this sacred marriage, Ptah's cosmic **consciousness** mingles with Sekhmet's **ecstasy**, or abandonment to innermost and highest truth. Our *aufu* and *ba* levels have integrated. We are ready to experience mystical glimpses of **eternity**. We attune to the creative flow of universal energy from which we proceed, and to which we will return. One mystic said that 'eternity is a sense of the continuing present'. At the crown chakra of the sacred marriage of Sekhmet and Ptah, we know that we are eternal, that life is eternal, and that the actual present is eternal for us.

I experienced the following 'revelation' in meditation, after a visit to Abu Ruach, which is the northernmost Pyramid on the sacred alignment of Giza. The Pyramid itself is hidden behind a high peak on a vast, deserted, crumbling area, closed to the public, which can only be reached on horseback. It was a painful, arduous, even dangerous, journey; the steep slopes were stony and harsh on the horses, and it necessitated passing through tracts of land, which sang with negative power, made even more unpleasant by the lowering presence of huge electricity pylons whispering balefully in the silence. Several times, I despaired of finding it. It was a hot morning, and I feared for the horses in the afternoon sun. However, when we came to it, it lay open to the sky, and descending deep into the earth, ancient, untouched, and vibrating with stellar power. When, subsequently, I asked for a revelatory illustration of the meaning of the sacred marriage of Sekhmet and Ptah, it was to this place that I was taken. This 'revelation' then is offered as an imaginative aid to stimulate the necessary qualities for the integration of the god-forces involved, and to hopefully provide insight into the purpose of their union.

As you follow the revelation, allow the images to appear, as though it were a Pathworking, but *follow* it rather than engage with it, more as though it were a radio play, than a guided meditation.

MYSTICAL REVELATION ON THE SACRED MARRIAGE OF SEKHMET AND PTAH

Under the dark sky, lit only by strong starlight, she stands on the open hilltop. Beneath her feet, below the ground, there is a vast Pyramid Temple Complex of golden stone. She has ascended its secret shafts and passageways to come and commune with the stars. She awaits his coming. All her work in the Temple below is concentrated towards these meetings.

Her knowledge of the celestial patterns informs her of when to expect him.

She is wearing a dark heavy ceremonial cloak chased in patterns of gold. Its high collar masks her face; its weight gives her complete awareness of the deep heavy powers of Earth below her. However, there is no weight of responsibility in her heart. Just a wide-open feeling of connection and serene anticipation.

Then on the horizon, a golden disc of light appears in the sky. It is a golden vehicle with wings of light; the Winged Disc. She stands motionless, but the joy in her heart flies to meet it.

Now it is landing some distance away from her on the Pyramid hilltop. The light parts at its centre as though it opens, and from the surrounding darkness, he emerges to meet her.

He is a magnificent presence of light; his cloak is golden and flowing, billowing around him, incandescent. He shimmers with love and radiance. The light radiating from him makes his shape seem like a bird with golden wings, a Phoenix. He has come from the Other Place. The Place of Gold where the other Pyramids are. She is here to receive his blessing of light, with which she will later irradiate the Temple Treasury.

As he advances to greet her, the energy- field between them creates a communion of tremendous purity and power. They stand together on the high point over the Pyramid, beneath the stars. They are in perfect alignment with the clearest point of the Constellation of the Lion. He needs her life force; she must exchange it for his Light, which she needs to illumine the Gold.

Her life force streams up to her Crown, and she feels it irradiating him, strengthening his Light. He needs her Fire, her depth, the dark sustenance of her fuel. She loves to give it to him. It gives him the ability to share his radiance with other Star Temples all around the Planet. She gives him all her trust and truth. He cannot be who he truly is without her. Without question she performs her joyful duty, with silent and serene majesty she receives his Light.

The night passes in an eternal moment; the Earth turns from the perfect alignment. It is time for him to leave. Soon the Sun will rise. She has work to do. She climbs down the steps inside the secret shaft of the Pyramid, in a deeply held concentrated trance, holding all the radiance she has received from him. Gentle hands remove the dark and heavy cloak; now she must keep his energy within the cloak of her body. She is entering a deep square pool of blue water, filling the water with her radiance, yet maintaining it within herself. The water is being charged homoeopathically with her essence; with their shared essence.

Emerging from the pool, she is robed in a dark simple garment, smooth and soft on her skin.

She enters the Treasury. There are huge golden statues, sacred artefacts, regalia and chests of coin. She walks around the Treasury irradiating the gold, sanctifying it with the presence of her love. Now she is finished. She may rest. She is helped into her own golden bed, where she glides into deep and peaceful sleep.

RITUAL PROCEDURE FOR CELEBRATION OF THE SACRED MARRIAGE OF SEKHMET AND PTAH – AS A SECOND LEVEL INITIATION

Choose a time for this ceremony when you do not have a particularly heavy work load. The ideal time is over a weekend, or on a holiday. As you are welcoming power and wealth into your life, it is a positive gesture to provide yourself beforehand with a token piece of gold jewellery to commemorate the experience. A ring or a pendant depicting Sekhmet or Ptah would be perfect.

Ritual Requirements

For the ceremony, you will need:

One blue and one orange candle, four tea lights

Essential oil of musk or patchouli and lavender

Incense of thyme leaves or juniper berries, and frankincense

A small drum or tambourine

A new garment

An item of gold jewelry (as mentioned)

Representations of Sekhmet and Ptah

A clean altar cloth

Flowers for the altar

Ritual Preparation

Prepare and plan for your sacred wedding in seven stages, using each stage as an exercise in preparation for realising each sequential Wedding Gift of Sekhmet and Ptah. Take particularly careful note of your dreams and visions during this time.

Stage 1. Serenity:

Focus on a simple task, which you have been deferring, and give it your full attention. Put all your energy into completing it with enjoyment.

Stage 2. Justice:

Try to clear up any outstanding debts/quarrels, which preoccupy you.

Stage 3. Integrity:

Write down your personal 'code of honour'.

Stage 4. Everlasting Love:

Open your heart to all those you love and have loved, and bless them. Thank them for being who they are, for teaching you how to love.

Stage 5. Manifestation:

Practice voicing your true desires.

Stage 6. Communion:

Contemplate on your inner plane teachers and guides. Form your mind to meet theirs. Try some automatic writing or channeling.

Stage 7. Eternity:

Try to let go of your attachments, and just *be*.

Ceremonial Site

This ceremony requires some drumming and dancing. Your usual temple space will serve, but if you feel the need to conduct your ritual in a special place, make sure it will be private and spacious enough for you to move around.

Witnesses

If you have been working alone up to now, you may wish to have this ceremony witnessed. This is a more powerful ceremony than the last one, and it is best if one person only witnesses it. This must be a close and trusted friend, teacher or partner.

Purification, Anointing, Robing and Altar Preparation

Bathe or shower, clothe yourself in a new garment, and anoint your throat and sacral chakras with a blend of musk or **patchouli** and **lavender** in the sign of the pentagram

You may adorn yourself with anything that occurs to you, as long as it allows you to feel radiantly powerful.

Prepare your altar with a **clean cloth**, **flowers**, a **blue** and an **orange** candle, and representations of both Sekhmet and Ptah. Burn a blend of **thyme leaves** or **juniper berries** and **frankincense** to prepare and purify your space.

If you have provided yourself with a golden wedding gift, pass this through the smoke, and. place it on the altar for the moment.

Delineation of Sacred Space

Create your sacred space, this time delineating its boundaries in a circle of your own magical energy. As you create the boundary, see it as a glowing orange colour then repeat it, this time in a cerulean blue. Set your four tea-lights at the four directions and call the Quarters and create your circle of power in the usual way.

Re-familiarise yourself with thee Personal Affirmations (see p120), and the chakric qualities of the goddess Sekhmet. Acknowledge the goddess rising within you to attend her bridal, yourself preparing for your sacred wedding.

Go to your altar and light both the candles, saying:

'**I dedicate this altar to the Sacred Marriage of Sekhmet and Ptah within myself, that I might realise their divine qualities in Love.**'

Pronounce the invocation to Sekhmet (see p123), accompanied by a *tabla,* tambourine or sistrum; or clap your hands, tap your feet or dance instead of using a musical instrument.

This completed, sit or lie down. Relax your body. Go through again the personal affirmations on the god-force Ptah, and the qualities of the god through the chakras, this time pronouncing all the words clearly and with meaning. Visualise each word as you speak it written on the air in a translucent blue colour. Remember to concentrate on the qualities themselves, trying to experience them inside you.

When you are ready, you may chant:

'***Ankh Ptah Seker Asar***' for as long as it feels right to do so. While you chant, imagine yourself *as* the goddess Sekhmet. If it helps, you can use the images provided in the 'mystical revelation' in the previous pages.

Make the invocation to the god Ptah. Welcome this energy into your space.

Imagine a stream of light linking both your sacral and throat chakras. Feel this light interchanging from a deep orange into a clear blue and back again.

Now you are ready to receive the Wedding Gifts of the sacred marriage of Sekhmet and Ptah, from root to crown.

Now you may make your commitment. Stand before the altar. If you have provided yourself with a gold adornment, you may now put it on, saying:

'**In honour of this occasion and in the service of the Integration of my Higher Self with my Primal Will, I commit to attainment of my: Serenity.**'

Experience your root chakra glowing with the holy light of serenity.

'**Justice.**'

Feel all the joys and anger residing in your sacral centre ordering into the clarity of rightness.

'Integrity.'

Feel your natural dignity radiating from your solar plexus, combining with the design of your life and being. Begin to experience the beautiful, golden structure of who you are, and commit to constant, conscious expression of it.

'Everlasting Love.'

You are already in a state of timeless Love. Undertaking this ritual commitment has placed you there. Give thanks for the gift of it, and, in your heart, make a pledge to treasure it forever.

'Manifestation.'

The power and majesty of your innate divinity is rising to your Throat. Now you say:

'May my words bring forth the power and love of God.'

Then continue:

'Communion (with the Divine).'

Experience the exalted nature of this undertaking, and the wisdom it brings you. Allow yourself to experience a vision here, and register it carefully in your mind.

'Eternity.'

Feel the combined energies of Sekhmet and Ptah flowing into you at crown chakra in love and consciousness, linking you to your beginnings and your spiritual future.

'AND THUS DO I WELCOME POWER AND WEALTH INTO MY LIFE.'

Turn aside from the altar, and relax. Spend some time 'grounding' in any way that feels appropriate for you.

What visions and emotions occurred for you during your Commitment? Which of the Wedding gifts came easily, and which did not? What was the vision you received during your commitment to *Communion?*

Questions you can ask the Tarot

What is the nature of my relationship to my power? My wealth? How may I improve this?

How may I most readily attain the gift of any of the seven Wedding Gifts of the sacred marriage of Sekhmet and Ptah?

Blow out your candles, and bid the god and goddess

HAIL AND FAREWELL

Congratulations!

Blessed Be.

CHAPTER EIGHT

ISIS: QUEEN OF HEALING AND MAGIC
THE SIXTH LEVEL

THE BROW CHAKRA. THE KHU/BA
PROCESS

ISIS

Oh Isis, Queen of stars
Veiled in night and day,
Who has uttered the spell
With the magic of her perfect mouth
Who gives new life to the lifeless
Who gives us radiant Horus,
Grace us with intuitions light.
We come as supplicants to that secret place
Where your face shines through the luminous Veil
Where the moon rests by your feet
Where the waters of lives force flow.
Mother of Nature in its most secret, sacred aspect,
We honour you and come
As seekers to your all-seeing presence.

Suzanne Miller 1996

We now attain the sixth level of the system, which takes us up into the **brow** chakra, the *khu/ba* process and the realm of the goddess-force **Isis**. Isis is the daughter of Nut and Geb, the wife and sister of Osiris, and the mother of Horus. The first actual Queen of Egypt, she is concerned with rulership and wise administration. Her sacred symbol is the Throne, which she wears upon her crown.

Isis and her darker sister, Nephthys, both ruled as queens over the land of Egypt. Their concerns and pre-occupations are more to do with issues of work and consciousness, such as administration, succession and societal structure than the primal and creative expressions of divine feminine power as expressed by Sekhmet and Hathor.

However, both Isis and Nephthys are in their separate ways, powerful magicians. The ancient Egyptians made no distinction between spirituality and magic. All their Pharaohs, scribes, architects, doctors and healers were initiated into extremely high levels of magical lore and practice. Magic was understood be the essence of divine meaning that pervades all life, and the magician its earthly exponent.

Magicians, in today's terms, are those of us whom, with proper under-standing of and insight into the more subtle levels of existence, can make manifest on the material level that which serves humanity best. In the words of the Renaissance philosopher and alchemist, Pico della Mirandola, '*The true Magician works in God's cause*'.

On contemplating and attuning ourselves to the principle of Isis, we commit to the arts of magic, and begin to claim for ourselves their subse-quent gifts of wisdom, service and healing. Having awoken to the power and the glory of the inner gods, we can now integrate them with responsibility. As part of the ritual awakening of the brow chakra and the goddess Isis, a dedication ceremony is included, as a commitment to the arts of magic and their sacred use. Isis speaks for herself in the following statement from the ancient texts.

The Words of Queen Isis

I am the wife and the sister of Osiris.
I am mother of King Horus.
I am she that rises in the Dog Star.
I divided the earth from the heaven.
I showed the path of the stars.

I ordered the course of the sun and the moon.

I devised business in the sea.

I brought together woman and man.

I taught men to honour images of the gods.

I revealed mysteries unto men.

I consecrated the precincts of the gods.

I broke down the governments of tyrants.

I compelled women to be loved by men.

I made an end to murders.

I devised marriage contracts.

I ordered that the true should be thought good.

I decreed mercy to supplicants.

I protect righteous guards.

With me, the right prevails.

I am Queen of the rivers and winds and seas.

No one is held in honour without my knowing it.

I am the Queen of the thunderbolt.

I stir up the sea and I calm it.

I inspect the courses of the sun.

With me, everything is reasonable.

I set free those in bonds.

I am the Queen of seamanship.

I make the navigable unnavigable when it pleases me.

I created walls of cities.

I brought up islands out of the depths and into the light.

I overcome fate.

Fate hearkens to me.

Hail, O Egypt that nourished me.

'I am the wife and sister of Osiris. I am mother to King Horus.'

The most important factor about Isis, the first statement she lays claim to, is that she is 'The wife and sister of Osiris'. Her identification with her Love, exemplified by her husband/brother, supercedes any of the considerable administrative gifts and magical powers that she owns. Her entire life is dedicated to the purpose of serving Osiris consciousness, and healing the terrible rift in herself and Egypt, caused by his murder. Moreover, eventually, through her efforts she is rewarded by being united with him in the highest spiritual realms. This factor can be thought of as representing the process of integrating our *khu* and *ba* bodies, called here, *khu/ba*. The *khu* represents our highest spiritual body, but it can only be accessed by the true aspirant to the magical path, and only by way of the *ba* body. The loving, powerful *ba*, longing to return in wholeness to Universal *Ba*, finds peace and respite from the exigencies of denser levels of consciousness by integration or 'marriage' with the purity and light of the immortal spiritual soul, or *khu* body. The ancient texts are clear that the *khu* is 'associated' with the *ba,* and can only integrate with the lower bodies by its 'association' or 'marriage' with it. When this happens, the divine will of our *khu*, working through the *ba*, connects and integrates all our other bodies. Thus *khu-ba-ka-aufu* bodies become one, and we can interact 'with the gods', or gain rulership over all aspects of our life.

Here, Isis represents our own bright feminine inner ruling principle; the love of our own soul, which constantly works to serve our growth and renewal. Our eventual *khu/ ba* integration is symbolised by Isis' quest to re-member Osiris, to heal and integrate the 'Land of Egypt'. Isis brings Osiris to rulership of the living and the righteous dead, or the marriage of our brow and crown chakras, which, when we finally arrive at its celebration, brings us to self-sovereignty over both our earthly and our spiritual consciousness.

The tale of Isis is a deep and compelling illustration of the soul's constant quest in incarnate form to understand and realise itself through love. She represents humanity's need to understand the value of separation from the divine in order to return to it through choice and consciousness.

She is also that part of ourselves which suffers and grieves, and searches for wholeness in order to bring forth and nurture our creativity (Horus), only to release it into the world so that it may *avenge,* or expiate the suffering.

All true creativity has the salt of sorrow in its bones and marrow. As Isis claims to be the 'mother of *King* Horus', consciousness of our losses and fragmentations from spirit brings us to creative and moral sovereignty.

'I am she that rises in the Dog Star. I showed the path of the stars. I divided the earth from the heavens. I ordered the course of the sun and the moon.'

These statements reflect knowledge of cosmic and stellar patterns, which was integral to the considerable achievements of the Egyptians. The laws of magic are based on them. They are to be found in the studies of alchemy, astrology, Tarot and the Cabbala. One of Isis' titles is Isis Urania, or 'Isis Unveiled', in which she is celebrated as the presiding genius of astrology. These subjects, which have fascinated great thinkers throughout the centuries, are readily available to the modern aspirant.

'I am Queen of the rivers, the winds and the sea.'

Isis is Queen of the seas, or the unconscious. In western occultism she has great resonance with the Cabbalistic Sphere of the great Waters of Binah (the Hebrew word for *understanding*), which is the first aspect of the divine as Mother. 'Binah' is the dark and bitter Seas of *Marah* from which we have all sprung. In astrological terms, Binah relates to the planet Saturn, whose concerns are with order, structure and harsh lessons. Binah as such is the Sphere of Limitation and her vision the Vision of Sorrow. The idea behind this is that everything that is formed from the creative thrust of the Universe is brought forth in pain and travail. This is her correlation with the principle of Isis. Isis must not only exemplify all the qualities of divine queenship, but she must also know and experience the terrible pains and sorrows of humanity. The Ancients regarded the inundation of the Nile – which occurred when the Dog Star was prominent in the Heavens – as the tears of Isis, weeping for her lost love.

The Pyramid texts say that Isis 'orders business in the sea' and makes the 'navigable, unnavigable when it pleases her'. This is surely a veiled allusion to the *business* of healing and integration; of bringing (in a professional therapeutic sense) to the conscious mind, all the sub aqueous secrets of the dreaming dark. She also claims that, as part of her structured approach to rulership, she 'devised marriage contracts' and 'compelled women to be loved by men.' However, one of her loveliest attributes, where we encounter her on rising to the intuitional awakening of the brow chakra, is as the lady of revelation where she 'brings islands up from out of the depths and into the light'.

Like the 'High Priestess' of the Tarot (whose lovely Esoteric Title is 'The Priestess of the Silver Star', whom she most closely resembles), Isis too holds the Law in her lap. Shining under her veil, and, like the 'High Priestess', enthroned between the two pillars of Sorrow and Joy, she rules with wisdom and compassion and, of course, with magic or full cognisance and exposition of the cosmic laws. Unswerving in her passionate loyalty, as fixed in her principles as a guiding star, she nonetheless expresses her deepest and most agonising feelings freely and unselfconsciously. The island of feminine energy is brought up through suffering and travail into the light of birth.

'I overcome Fate. Fate hearkens to me.'

This is probably the most important claim of Isis. It teaches us that, if we manage to live by the laws set down for us in her statements, we overcome *karma*. If we can be utterly reasonable, forgive those that ask us for forgiveness (decree mercy to supplicants), protect the righteous, think good thoughts, honour our marriages, and so on, we can change our fate. Our present fate is the outcome of all our previous choices, but with Isis we can create a new and shining destiny. We too can 'rise in the Dog Star'.

Therefore, we may see that Isis Consciousness combines profound and painful emotion, powerful magical and administrative qualities, with the quest towards self-rulership and wholeness. To rule, one must first know how to serve. To serve others properly one must firstly know the deepest and most painful aspects of oneself. Humility, compassion and self-knowledge are prerequisites to the safe handling of power.

The quest of Isis, her immeasurable love and dedication to her eventual integration, denote the exact requirements in us to achieve this blessed state

FROM THE BOOK OF THE DEAD

We stand before the Masters who witnessed the Genesis,
Who were the authors of their own forms,
Who walked the dark circuitous passages of their own becoming.
We stand before the Masters who witnessed the transformation of the
body of a man into the body in spirit,
Who were witnesses to Resurrection when the corpse of Osiris entered
the mountain and the soul of Osiris walked out, shining.
When He came forth from Death, a shining thing, His face white with
heat.
We stand before the Masters who know the histories of the Dead,
Who decide which tales to hear again
Who judge the books of Lives as either full or empty
Who are themselves the authors of Truth.

And they are ISIS and OSIRIS, the Divine Intelligences.
And when the story is written and the end is good
And the Soul of Man is perfected
With a shout, they will lift him into Heaven.

And so, as we rise and awaken to the principle of Isis, at the brow chakra, connecting with our *khu/ba* process, we can consider ourselves ready to heal, guide and direct others. As Isis 'rises in the Dog Star', so can we be prepared to set an example, to be a 'star', or a living exemplar of the qualities of united power and compassion which will serve to inspire and provide spiritual comfort wherever we go in the world. The power of high magic and revelations of true meaning of the patterns of life will be ours, if we commit to use them always, from a place of humility and compassion, in the service of evolution, and in respectful cognisance of the laws of the cosmos. In this way, we can link back to our spiritual home. And if the journey is constantly undertaken, the 'end' will always be in view, and we too can be 'lifted into Heaven'.

The questions we need to address in preparation for the ritual awakening of the brow chakra, and the *khu/ba* process are:

'Am I prepared to dedicate my life to love itself?'
'Do I proceed from a firm understanding of order and rightness?
'Could I be unswerving in my commitment to the Light?'

When you feel prepared to proceed, you can contemplate the gifts of Isis as they enfold along your chakric system.

THE GIFTS OFTHE GODDESS ISIS THROUGH THE CHAKRAS

ROOT:	*Sorrow*
SACRUM:	*Search*
SOLAR PLEXUS:	*Consecration*
HEART:	*Healing*
THROAT:	*Revelation*
BROW:	*Intuition*
CROWN:	*Wholeness*

SORROW: THE ROOT OF ISIS

The deepest vision of Isis is the vision of **sorrow**. From the root chakra of Isis, where we experience ourselves as organisms on the surface of the Earth, we attune to the ephemeral nature of life. We can begin to understand from deep emotional levels our part and place within it. When we can safely experience the sorrows of the limitations of earthly existence, we stop prevaricating, and we commit to our growth and wholeness. From the root of the brow, our sorrow is the safest, most reliable place from which to start. When we recognise the beauty of sorrow, and can admit that our losses and privations bring us closer to our truest self, we are safe. With sorrow as our security, we are in no danger of abusing or mishandling our gifts. While we are alive on earth, we are always vulnerable to change, and we cannot control the destinies and choices of those we love. These are sad facts for us to bear. When we connect fully with the sorrow this give us, we gain insight, healing powers, and the real ability to direct and guide others. Sorrow never seeks to manipulate, it does not concern itself with trying to save itself from pain or disaster. It knows how to release. It has great beauty and depth, and from the root of the brow, it is our fundamental safety.

SEARCH/ADMINISTRATION: THE SACRUM OF ISIS

As the light of Isis rises from root to sacrum, the deep, undersea strength of our ancient sorrow activates our primal will, and is transmuted into the beginnings of the quest for wholeness. We are given the vision of our **search**. As Isis searches for the lost limbs of her beloved lord, so we too embark on our journey towards healing and integration. We also attain the vision of **administration**. We 'see' how our lives need to be ordered. Sacral energy rising to the brow chakra allows us to recognise what needs to be done so that we can rule our lives with consciousness whilst searching for meaning in everything we undertake. We do not get lost in trivia. Isis 'deems', 'decrees', 'orders' and 'compels'. She also 'protects', 'inspects' and 'teaches'. These words denote considerable administrative gifts, which we can attain when we open to the sacral level of our *khu/ba*. The commitment to a magical life requires that we realise them. As we search for wholeness, and the return to spirit, we must be clear and self-commanding. We need the focus and the self-worth to recognise and value the truth when we find it. The 'missing limbs' of our forgotten immortality have been scattered and hidden from us, by our own weaknesses and confusions. We now find the strength and clarity to recognise them again.

CONSECRATION: THE SOLAR PLEXUS OF ISIS

In the centre of our Isis self, the quest for wholeness becomes focused as a conscious life task. From the golden solar plexus centre of the brow, we dedicate ourselves to each moment of the process. When we are firmly conscious of the meaning behind our task, we see that everything along the path of love is holy, and we make it so. We attain the gift of **consecration**.

As Isis, who rules as Queen of both Heaven and Earth, gladly offers herself and all her gifts in the task of re-membering Osiris, so might we from this level of self, make the conscious commitment to put our own talents and attributes into the service of our self-realisation, and to the highest good. Now everything we do, every task or chore we undertake, becomes sacred. As part of her quest, Isis takes a menial post as a nursemaid to the Queen of Syria. When we reach the solar plexus of the *khu/ba* process, we bring sanctity to all that we undertake. When we can consecrate each moment, nothing ever feels lowly or tedious again.

HEALING: THE HEART OF ISIS

When conscious commitment to attain our wholeness rises to the heart of Isis, it flows through its sacred chambers as **healing**, for others, the Universe and us. We have traveled from 'sorrow' through 'search and administration' to 'consecration'. Now we can experience healing light, flowing into and from our heart. We may bless and heal wherever we go, and we may receive blessings and healing. It becomes completely natural. We do not necessarily have to advertise ourselves as healers, or magicians, but we can realise that, with simplicity and truth, our understanding and compassion can always prevail over our confusions and fears.

REVELATION: THE THROAT OF ISIS

As universal energy flows from the healing heart of Isis up into our throat chakra, it opens to reveal the highest truths in the simplest and readiest ways. As Isis 'unveils' herself through us, we receive the meanings behind events and circumstances, so that we may reveal them to others through natural self-expression. We receive the gift of **revelation**. Isis' claim to 'reveal mysteries to men' becomes realised through the throat of our awakened brow chakra. We are given words of wisdom to comfort and inspire others, and the 'keys' to the missing dimensions we have been seeking.

INTUITION: THE BROW OF ISIS

Here we attain the gift of gifts on the ray of Isis. At the brow of the goddess of spiritual wisdom, we open to our own inner teachings or '*in tuition*'. **Intuition** does not refer to psychic powers such as clairvoyance, clairaudience or telepathy, which are faculties of the lower astral plane. It is a highly developed inner *guidance*, which recognises the patterns of Universal energy as they flow from divine will into earthly cause and manifestation. The light of our intuition, shining from the brow of Isis will allow us to recognise meaning and patterns in life, and to know truth enough that, as the goddess claims to do, we can 'overcome Fate', or the exigencies of *karma*. When we can see behind the 'veil' we can 'bring islands up out of the depths and into the light', or provide spiritual structure and safety for others. We too can 'create walls of cities' because we can now recognise the necessity of our illusions of mortality. The 'city' becomes a symbol of civilisation, which protects and strengthens our consciousness. We are not seduced or distracted by the outer world; we have traveled through it arduously and long, in our search to find our own guiding principle. On this search, we have learned to love our lower levels enough to integrate them.

WHOLENESS: THE CROWN OF ISIS

The crown of Isis is **wholeness**. United with both her dark sister and her lost lord, she stands, in joyful welcome to all who might approach her, behind her husbands' seat upon the Throne of Heaven. The *khu/ba* process is completed. The bright feminine ruling principle has finished her task. She is integrated with the dark feminine and the bright masculine. Osiris is remembered. At this stage, we can connect with our magical *khu*. The spark of indwelling divinity is released into our consciousness. We achieve peace, because we can trust our judgment. We can begin to do very good in the world.

Having contemplated these gifts of Isis, and committed to realising them, you may now attempt the personal affirmations of the goddess. This time it is important to learn them by heart, so that they become a working mantra for you.

PERSONAL AFFIRMATIONS ON THE GODDESS ISIS

My deepest feelings are my truest guide

My Life is a sacred journey towards my wholeness

I tread the Three-fold Path of Love, Power and Knowledge

Every real loss brings me closer to myself

Ritual preparation for awakening the goddess-force Isis

This work is best undertaken on the rising of a new moon. Take time beforehand to contemplate the story of Isis and what it means especially for you. Pay particular attention to your dreams during this period. Do not shy away from or repress any painful emotion that emerges. If you experience unfocused feelings of sadness and loss, realise that these are appropriate and pertinent to your inner work, and that it is necessary to be in touch with them in order to integrate them, so that they need never overwhelm, nor incapacitate you. In fact, the reverse is true. Your sorrow is the safest and soundest basis of your work on the ray of Isis.

During your preparation period, try to emulate the queenly and noble aspects of Isis in your daily life. This is not a time for mischief or gossip, or sharp practice in business. If you have any unpleasant tasks to finish up, do so with consciousness and self-forgiveness. Remember that Isis eventually even forgives Set, knowing that there must be a place in the Universe for the forces of evil and corruption, if they are rendered powerless by the self. And there is nothing as effective as forgiveness to disempower negativity.

Meditate upon the personal affirmations and chakric gifts of the goddess-force Isis, daily during the preparation period. A few days should suffice. During this time, follow a light vegetarian or fish diet, and abstain from excess.

Ritual correspondences for awakening the goddess-force Isis

COLOUR:	Violet
PERFUME:	Violet, Sandalwood
INCENSE:	Sandalwood chips
ANIMAL:	Sparrow hawk
CHAKRA:	Brow
BODY:	Khu/Ba
TIME OF DAY:	Moonrise
SACRED SYMBOL:	A Throne
TAROT CARD:	'The High Priestess'

If you now feel ready to undergo your dedication, read over carefully the commitment provided as 'Dedication Speech' on page 258. The ritual awakening to the principle of Isis can be included as part of your dedication ceremony. If you do not feel ready to make the commitment, then you may proceed as usual, excluding the passage concerned with and devoted to dedication.

Altar Preparation, Purification, Anointing and Robing

Choose a time in the evening, if possible at the time of a new moon, to proceed with setting up your ritual space. Place a **silver** or **violet**-coloured cloth on your altar, together with a representation of the goddess Isis. This does not have to be an actual statuette. If you do not possess one, you could use something that expresses the nature of this goddess for you, such as a picture of the crescent moon on the sea, a nursing mother or a grieving widow, or even a sparrow-hawk Also add a silver or violet candle to the altar. Light **sandalwood incense**, purify your ritual area and leave the incense burning on the altar.

Bathe or shower, and dress in a white or violet garment. Provide yourself with a veil of filmy material in a violet or amethyst shade. Pass your veil over the incense smoke. If you have silver or amethyst jewelry you wish to wear during your ritual, make sure it is cleansed in salt and water and passed through the altar incense smoke before you wear it. Anoint your brow chakra with essential oil of **violet** or **sandalwood**. You might like to dab a drop or two of this on your veil.

Delineation of Sacred Space

Create your sacred space in the usual way, calling the Quarters and creating your Circle of Power. Place your veil over your face.

Visualisation of Chakric Colour

Take yourself into the centre of your space. Sitting down, allow yourself to be encompassed in a pool of violet and silver light. Visualise a shining silver Pentagram star above your head, with silver and violet light pouring down from its points, bathing you in tranquility.

When you feel ready, proceed to your altar and light the candle saying:

'I dedicate this altar to the Goddess Isis that I might understand the Mysteries of Life.'

Go back to the centre and offer thanks for the gifts of the goddess Isis as they proceed through your chakric system, allowing the feelings they produce in you to manifest as fully as they can.

'I give thanks for my sorrow.
I give thanks for my search and my administration.
I give thanks for my consecration.
I give thanks for my healing.
I give thanks for my revelation.
I give thanks for my intuition.
I give thanks for my wholeness.'

Then repeat the above personal affirmations on the goddess Isis that you should have by heart, in a soft but meaningful tone.

When this is completed, rise and face your altar to repeat the following invocation, again softly, but with as much emotion as you can muster.

INVOCATION TO THE GODDESS ISIS

Hail, Great Isis! Queen of Earth and Heaven
Mother of Life in Her most sacred ways,
Thy gift is the truth of our painful Becoming
Under the safety of Thy loving gaze.
Wife to Osiris, Mother of Horus
Lady of Journeys, Queen of the Sea,
Wherever we search, and how far we may travel
Our hope and our harbour reside but in Thee.

Thou art she that rises in the Dog Star.
No-one is held in honour without Thy Knowledge
Protector of righteous guards, and bestowed of order and brightness,
Thou deemed that women should be loved by men
And made an end to murders.
Thou bring Islands up out of the depths and into the Light
Lady of Moonlight and Revelation
Patroness of the Healing Arts
And mighty Queen of the rich Black Lands.
Veiled in Nature, many-coloured
Lady of Sorrow and haven of all our joys.

By the power of Silence and the mystery of Becoming
By the deepest secrets in the Oceans of Time
By the mystery of Marriage and the boundless Waters of the
Essence of Life
By the grace of Intuition and the many-coloured Veils of Nature
By the Wisdom of Existence and the ordered Laws of the Cosmic Tides

By the new-born cries of fatherless creatures
By the glory of Order and the wholeness of Right
By Love and Peace, and Search and Magic,
We Thy children, call upon Thee to be with us here and now
In Body and in Spirit.

HAIL ISIS!

Hail and Welcome.

This next part of the ritual is optional, and applies only if you feel ready to make your dedication commitment.

Dedication Speech
Remain standing before your altar and, concentrating on every word, say:

'I stand before this altar which has been dedicated to the Goddess Isis.

I have brought myself here of my own free will and in loving
    testimony to the Divine.

I therefore offer myself in loving service to the Cause of Wholeness,
    which is the Crown of the Goddess of this place.

I desire to become wise in the love of the Gods, who are the One
    God,

 To become strong in the aid of Man and Woman,

Learned in the Arts of Magic and Healing

And skilful in their ways,

To balance the Three-fold Rays of Power, Love and Knowledge

And to work ever in the service of Evolution.

Thus do I make my Commitment.

So Mote it be.'

Turn back to the centre of your space, once you have performed the dedication speech; spend a little while integrating this. When you are ready, make yourself comfortable, and proceed with the following guided meditation.

GUIDED MEDITATION ON THE SPHERE OF ISIS

You are in a boat on a huge lake of shining water. The surface of the water is fragrant with blue and white lotus blossoms. Your boat is being rowed over the shining surface by silent oarsmen. It is taking you far out to the centre of the lake where there is an island. Your progress is calm and unhurried, but there is a sense of purpose. Beside you in the boat you have a canine companion – a beautiful black dog. He is like a person, a man to you. You trust him completely. He protects you, and helps to sharpen your senses and your instincts.

It is quite late in the day. You will need to be at the island before the sunset. The boat glides over the water in the late afternoon sunlight, creating a light breeze that refreshes you.

As you near the island, you see a great number of other boats gathered before it in the water. Some of them are magnificent, burnished with gold and faience and with furling painted sails; some are simple fishing crafts. There is a beautiful calm silence. All the occupants of the boats are waiting for you in peaceful respect. They are aware of your arrival, but nobody watches you, you must pass amongst them as though you are invisible.

Your boat grounds. You disembark. The dog walks at your side. There is a violet-coloured pathway leading you to the side door of a temple, which is like a pavilion with a large open terrace facing out to the water. The door opens to receive you both, and you pass into a wonderful anteroom, which glows with rainbow colours. In silent meditation, you prepare yourself for the ceremony. One by one, you receive the glowing colours of the room into your auric body. You receive the blood red of your 'sorrow', the flame hue of your 'search', the gold of your 'consecration'. Then you receive the bright green of your 'healing', the clear blue of your 'revelation' and the violet of your 'intuition'. The colours merge into a shining rainbow spectrum veil, which is your 'wholeness.'

You feel the force of the new Moon which is about to rise from her cloak of sky. You feel her unveiling her slim crescent for the first time this season, bringing new fertility to the land and deeper wisdom to the people.

You feel the falling force of the setting Sun, about to shed his deep, dying glow over the water as he bestows his farewell blessing.

You attune to your Rising Star, climbing to the dazzling height of its power at this moment and about to burst into view.

The colours in the room veil you in shimmering light.

You are ready.

You stand up and move towards a small table on which is placed a silver vial. You pick up the vial, and holding it in your left hand, you and the dog pass through the anteroom onto the open terrace, where a silver throne has been placed for you, facing out at the water's edge. You are aware of everything. Not a ripple passes over the surface that you cannot feel. It is so still. Not a murmur from the flotilla. But you can feel the hearts and minds of the people focused upon your task. You face the sunset. The sky is like fire, the water, molten gold.

At the exact moment when the Sun disappears below the horizon, both the Moon and the Star will rise in the sky. At this point, you will reveal yourself to the people, you will cast the contents of your saver vial into the water, and the lake will flame with glory.

As the energy heightens, you feel the colours of your aura refining and dancing; your veil of light is clearing, opening the collective Veil. The starlight is pouring into you, the Moon is piercing your heart. You feel every emotion; you feel everything.

You sit upon your throne, the dog at your feet, your rainbow veil gradually releasing, as its colours quicken and vibrate to the pulse of the conjoining Moon and Star, in the dying glow of the Sun.

You place one hand upon the dog's neck.

The moment is here. The Sun is down. The Star and the Moon appear together in a violet sky. Your veil lifts, you are revealed. You throw the contents of the silver vial into the water. The lake becomes like a sheet of flame. The holy light is bathing the boats in gold. The lake is a shining beacon. Starlight pours down. Everything is ablaze with energy and pure power. All flesh, all form, all matter upon the lake and below it, receives the influx.

You leave your throne.

In the anteroom, there is a couch. You lie down; the dog puts his two front paws upon your feet. Leaving your body, you travel to the pinnacle of the pure beam of light where the Worlds meet and mingle. In quiet ecstasy, you join your beloved other. Looking down, you see the island, the temple and the boats on the lake. You see everything and everyone on the lake of flame; you see your own body safely held by the loving care of the dog. All is charged with light. You can see the light clearing the lost and lonely passageways in the hearts of the people, opening them to the power of Truth and Love; burning away the dross of fear. You hear their cries. You are painfully aware of every sorrow, every joy, and you can see the patterns of their individual vibrations as they flow into the wider streams and tides of Universal energy. They are revealed to you, just as you were revealed to them in that one moment before the liquid from your magic vial turned the lake to flame.

The Moon is luminous, fresh and young, her pale horns shining with a delicate gleam. Her message calms you, you are aware of your own renewal. The sparkling starlight fills you with hope. You send a blessing to the assembled company in the boats below you, and a message to sail their crafts with trust and mindfulness into the oceans of life

Now you are ready to descend. You can feel the warm strength of your canine protector gently guiding you home; home to your sleeping body in the temple on the lake.

You flow into the warmth of your body.

You become aware of the security of its limits. The transcendent beauty of the stellar pattern is echoed in its form. You smile; and the dog removes his paws from your feet. The room is dark now; the rainbow colours have merged into a velvety blanket of peace.

In your own good time, you may let the room in the temple fade, and return to your full waking consciousness, refreshed and ready to resume your life.

Remove your veil. Have a good bodily stretch and a drink of water. Then 'ground' your recently accomplished meditational experiences in your preferred fashion.

Which of your 'veiling' colours were more readily acceptable to you? Did you set the lake alight? Were you able to see energy patterns arising from the boats? How did it feel being 'revealed'? Did you recognise your beloved other?

Questions you can ask the Tarot:

What is the nature of my present relationship with the goddess Isis?

How can I best develop my intuition?

In which area of my life can I best serve my higher calling at present?

How can I realise more readily my (any of the) chakric qualities of the goddess Isis?

When you feel you have finished, bid the Goddess **HAIL AND FAREWELL,** blow out your candles and close down.

Blessed Be.

CHAPTER NINE

NEPHTHYS: THE DARK SISTER

Before proceeding on to the seventh level, and the Mysteries of Osiris, I feel it important to include, as an optional appendix, a background chapter on the principle of Nephthys.

This is not work which necessarily needs to be part of the system, but I consider it a beautiful energy to attune to on certain occasions, and very helpful in providing a deeper understanding of principle of Isis. One can, after all, learn so much more about how to manage one's brightness, when one can look confidently at the shadow. I have not given Nephthys a chakric placement, although it was tempting to place her at the lower brow level. She works very well on the root level, as a substitute for her son, Anubis, **once the system has been completed**, and further work is felt to be important on organic, or Shadow issues.

Certainly a goddess-force in her own right, and not merely the shadow aspect of Isis, Nephthys can be employed as a helpful medium, whenever it is felt that a quiet space for reflection is particularly needful, when external pressures cause the inner self to become immured in mundaneness, or when ones creative imagination requires an extra stimulus. Nephthys is a law unto herself, she cannot be forced or commanded, only understood and persuaded into conscious awareness. I have not subsequently provided invocations or exercises to awaken her as part of this system, but I *have* included her, and thus opened the way for you to find her for yourself.

Lady of Sorcery and Deception
Nephthys, the dark sister of Isis, is the daughter of Nut and Geb, wife of Set, the lover of Osiris, and the mother of Anubis.

Like her bright sister Isis, she is a goddess of the moon, which, because of its nature of waxing and waning, is understood to be dual. Within the dyad of Isis and Nephthys, Isis is the waxing, beneficent force of the moon, whilst Nephthys exemplifies its more menacing, waning quality. As the moon can be said to rule the tides of life, like Isis, Nephthys is also Lady of the Waters and the Seas.

As we have seen, Isis 'orders business in the sea', and is concerned with the 'navigational' matters of commerce and administration *on* the sea. Nephthys however, connects us to the dark nutritive powers of its depths, from which all life has emerged.

In psychological terms, she is the passive aspect of the feminine psyche, yielding and negative, the Jungian *shadow anima*, largely unrecognised and unconscious.

Queen of shadows and sorcery, she is usually defined in her relation to others, rather than in her own right. In Egypt, she held no cult of her own.

Nevertheless, she is a tremendously powerful and loving force, and when brought to conscious awareness, she helps us to effect subtle and powerful changes in the outer world.

Nephthys is rich and fertile, but married to the sterile and homosexual dark Lord Set. She thus disguises herself as her sister to lie with Osiris, becoming pregnant with the Shadow god, Anubis. It is not at all clear whether this was an act of collusion with Isis, who was perhaps too occupied with her husband and her administrative duties to conceive a child. Anubis, conceived of the bright Lord by deception, is in himself, both light and dark. As we have seen, he grows to play a primary role in the mysteries, acting as mediator between the realms of light and shadow. He is also the one to find the last missing member of his father in the search for his re-memberment.

The secret behind this myth points to the employment of Nephthys' arts in a betrayal, which holds wider knowledge and prescience than the immediate and obvious. The Egyptians understood that our unconscious often guides us to do things which society and conscience deplore, but which nonetheless in hindsight, turn out to provide deeper insight and self-knowledge than rigid adherence to a strict moral code.

In working with the principle of Nephthys, we need to remember that, although she is married to the dark lord, she abandons him when he perpetrates the dismemberment of Osiris, to rush to the aid and support of her sister and the forces of light. She shares in the laments of Isis, and commits to help recover the fragments of Osiris. Together, the sisters set up temples in the places where they find the fragments, where Isis teaches of his love and laws. The dark sister is needed to maintain concealment of the gradual process of re-memberment. Until the body of Osiris is complete, they must hide the collected pieces in a 'secret place'.

Nephthys plays an extremely significant dual role. She is comfortable and committed to the dark forces of the material world, symbolised, by Set, *but only up to a point*. She is adulterous, but understandably and pragmatically so, as she is unfaithful with Osiris, the Lord of Heaven. Her illicit love is for fairness, peace and order. She betrays both her brother and her husband, and possibly her sister, but the fruit of her betrayal, Anubis, becomes the Psychopomp and god of Embalming, able to travel freely between the worlds and witness with balanced understanding the weighing of the heart in the Halls of Judgment.

The Gods, as the *Book of the Dead* informs us, are the 'authors of their Own Forms, who walk the dark circuitous passages of their Own Becoming'. Like the Archetypal forces of truth that reside within us, they do nothing by mistake. The crimes and transgressions of Set and Nephthys teach us the value of separation from the world of spirit that we may return consciously and willingly to it.

This is echoed in the Judeo-Christian myth of the fall from Grace, and the expulsion from the Garden of Eden. It is Eve, the feminine unconscious, who tempts Adam, the conscious masculine, to taste of the fruit of Knowledge of Good and Evil. To the intuitive and passive is ascribed the inner wisdom to taste of life's experiences, both light and dark, in order to know, to understand and to *choose* to return eventually to the light of God, the true home of the indwelling spirit.

Nephthys, both passive and intuitive, is however no Eve, but a powerful and magical presence in her own right, fruitful and alluring. Queen of the Dark Waters – the rich amniotic fluids of earth, from which we draw our secret psychic powers – she rules the irrepressible forces of unconscious sexuality, revealed through fantasy, which show us truths about our deepest desires and motivations. Although deceptive and dangerous, when coupled consciously, *through choice*, with the order and real sorrow of her bright sister, she leads us unerringly (albeit tortuously and circuitously) to the Source.

Nephthys is secretive and elusive. Her ways and means are occult, or *hidden*. The Pyramid texts refer to her infrequently, and there is little written material about her. Of course, this is the whole point of her. Nephthys needs to be found, and, most importantly, found *within*.

The Tarot Card 'The Moon', with its strange and sinister symbolism, almost smells of the rich, fertile silt at the bottom of the great pond of life. It is to this place that she draws us; to the wealth of the Undersea, the unbridled flow and force of fantasy – hidden, magical, dangerous, deceptive, alluring and brim-full of feeling. Nephthys, like her sister Isis, is ruled entirely by emotion. Unlike Isis, she holds the lower force field of power. She is not an easy principle to work with. Meditating on Nephthys takes us to those levels of feminine power that the conscious mind is usually hesitant and squeamish about descending. However, descend or not, those levels *are there*. Fantasy, fuelled by feeling is an abundant force field of psychic power. Stirring up the silt, releases power into conscious imagination. When Nephthys is understood, the inner psychic world is a clearer and a far more exciting proposition.

The following hymn, correspondences, affirmations chakric qualities and Pathworking are offered as a loose structure for the work of contacting the energy of Nephthys. As the Dark Lady of the pantheon, she rules those areas of hidden power that emerge from the subconscious through clairvoyance, dreams or trance. As such, she is more of a 'wild card' in this system, and so I have not provided ritual procedure for her awakening; preferring to leave this to the personal preference and imagination of the aspirant. The realm of Nephthys is a shadowy, secretive landscape, as the goddess herself is elusive and mysterious. She does not fit neatly on to the path of love, but knowing and loving her, as I do, I could not leave her out.

RITUAL CORRESPONDENCES FOR THE PRINCIPLE OF NEPHTHYS

COLOUR	Aquamarine
PERFUME	Lemon, Sandalwood
INCENSE	Camphor
CHAKRA	Root; Lower Brow
BODY	Ka Body
SACRED SYMBOL	Bowl, chalice
TIME OF DAY	The darkest hours before dawn
TAROT CARD '	The Moon'

HYMN TO NEPHTHYS

Bosom Companion born of Tomorrow
Silvery Sister of Darkness and Light
Magical Mistress of Secrets and Sorrow
Maiden of Mystery, Queen of the Night.

Priestess of Drowsiness, Dusk and Duality,
She of the Shadows
Queen of the Ka,
Hold me ethereally, dream me inside of you
Draw with enchantment
Wherever you are.

THE GIFTS OF NEPHTHYS THROUGH THE CHAKRAS

Whilst contemplating the gifts of Nephthys, keep in mind the corresponding chakric gifts of Isis, to act as a bright mirror. The comparisons are extremely useful.

ROOT:	Concern
SACRUM:	Imagination
SOLAR PLEXUS:	Sorcery
HEART:	Guilt
THROAT:	Concealment
BROW:	Illusion
CROWN:	Self-Importance.

PERSONAL AFFIRMATIONS ON THE GODDESS NEPHTHYS

I can reach down into my Shadow to discover my Light
I never conceal anything from myself
Everything I dream is true
I can always be found by that which is truly mine

GUIDED MEDITATION ON THE SPHERE OF NEPHTHYS

It is dark night. You are standing, quite alone, facing the empty shore of a seemingly boundless ebb tide. The green sea is far, far away beyond the horizon; it seems on the Other Side of your world.

This is a landscape of flat, ribbed sand, dimpled with rocks festooned with slippery weed; starred with glittering salt-ringed shells, merging smoothly into endless sky.

The Moon is thin, a mysterious waning wafer of cold silver light.

However, the air is warm and close, like a veil. There is a rich dank smell of seaweed, brackish and briny.

It is completely silent. The silence is a deep dark power within you. You are aware of the minutest detail of the life about you. In the drying rock-pools you can hear the marine creatures' concern for their survival. Your bare feet can feel the Dead Sea salt in each grain of sand. The pull of the distant tide resonates in every cell of your quiet blood. And you are content. In this wide and quiet place, you feel lost and found in an eternal moment of becoming. There is great richness for you in this lone and bare landscape; there is timeless promise of the inevitable turn and rush of the incoming tide.

Nothing can disturb your solitude. You are completely at one with the open and defenceless shore.

You turn your face to the slender crescent of the Moon. She tells you nothing. This almost pleases you. There is nothing you wish to know. Yet her fading rays caress you with the blessing of recognition. Her secrets are shared.

You walk slowly out from the shore towards the long flat line of the distant sky. Your breath is light and even, your step easy and sure. You seem to make little shadow on the sand against the distant horizon. If you were not so completely conscious and aware of everything around you, and above you, and below you, you could almost believe you were not here.

Now you find a flat smooth rock, which accommodates the contours of your body perfectly. Settling yourself to watch and wait, you fill your being with the deep rich silence of the night. It is your night. The dark pinpoint gleam of the stars in the rockpools, the dry salt, the soft air, the secretly smiling Moon; all this is for you. All this is you. At this moment, you require and desire nothing more.

However, you require nothing less.

As long as you sit.

And for a long time you sit and face the thin straight line of sky.

Communing with the hidden Moon, and the fading, drying organisms of the Sea.

Immeasurably calm. Serenely powerful.

One deep part of you awaits the return of the raging rich life of the Sea.

The brilliant fish, the smiling dolphins, the cries of the gulls, the ships and winds, the rushing torrent of tide.

It is all there, somewhere else, far and near, within you and dreaming.

The Moon and the Sea belong to you, but in this calm and silent term of waiting, they can rest and wait within, and everything can be just as it is.

And it is perfect.

You take a frond of seaweed, which is curling at your feet. Clinging to it is a white starfish shell. You place it as a diadem around your brow.

And your inner vision opens to the deep mysteries of the Sea; of the Life within it, distant and present, and indestructible. You remember your life in the Womb of the sky. The stars and shells of your past and your future. And the organic growth of your quiet becoming.

And the Deserts which once were the Sea.

The rich salt glistens in the pale starlight. The declining Moon beckons and forbids. Just as you do.

When the moment of distant turning comes, you will rise from your throne of rock, and turn to shore. You will take with you the surge of life with the morning sunlight on the bobbing waves.

But that will come. This moment holds that promise within it.

You are all that is, and were, and ever will be.

Your dream of yourself is your deepest truth.

In a little while, you may let the landscape and the starlight fade, and return to your full waking consciousness, refreshed, composed, and ready to resume your life.

Blessed Be.

Questions you can ask the Tarot

How can I become more conscious of my Nephthys principle?

What is the nature of my relationship with my sister(s)?

How can I best control my imagination? Guilt? Sorcery? Illusions? Self-importance?

What do I need to conceal from others?

CHAPTER 10

OSIRIS: LORD OF THE LIVING AND THE RIGHTEOUS DEAD

THE SEVENTH LEVEL
THE CROWN CHAKRA. KHU BODY

We now reach the uppermost and final level of work. At **crown** level, we are concerned with the integration of all that has gone before. In addition, as we rise to the crown of **Osiris**, and we assume our *khu* or higher magical body, we are able to re-member all the disparate 'limbs' of the divine principles within us, and combine them in the cause of self-sovereignty. We approach the crown of Osiris from the throne of Isis, and so we are primed and ready, not only to meet and integrate the bright Lord within ourselves, but to 'marry' the power of our higher intuition as Isis, to our transpersonal levels of spiritual love and understanding as Osiris. As we rise to this point of sovereignty, we are prepared to celebrate the last sacred marriage, that of our brow and crown chakras, as the third level initiation, the sacred marriage of Isis and Osiris. A union that holds within it all the mysteries and revelations, all the sorrows and joys, all the fertile passions and the barren loneliness of every true and meaningful love story in the world.

Osiris is the son of Nut and Geb, the husband-brother of Isis, the lover-brother of Nephthys, brother of Set, and father of Horus and Anubis. He is both a life-giving force and god of the Afterworld and the Dead. The cult of Osiris was probably the most long lasting and popular in the whole history of Ancient Egypt. The first divine King, every Pharaoh had to strive to become his living embodiment to qualify for the sacred responsibility of rulership. The myth and sacred history of Osiris holds at its heart the deepest mysteries of spiritual attainment, and the clearest insight into psychological process. The principle of Osiris as sacred king holds intrinsically within it the core belief in the Saviour God that has filtered down into Western Consciousness from Egypt as the main tenet of mystical Christianity. In this sense, Osiris is understood as the bright lord, the radiant son who incarnates in flesh to teach the principles of love and order on earth, is sacrificed to redeem humanity, then resurrected and assumed into heaven, from where he henceforth casts his loving light onto the children of earth. After death and purgation, if the scales are correctly balanced, the immortal spiritual soul of an individual may dwell with him in Paradise. When his father Geb sacrifices his passionate embrace with Nut, the stellar wisdom of the cosmos, in order that manifestation can occur in human consciousness, he 'releases his seed into the sky' so that his bright son Osiris may inculcate the principles of divine order into earthly consciousness. Material existence, being subject to the laws of dispersion and renewal, it is the dark son, Set who is the perpetrator of these, whilst the bright son Osiris, must undergo the process himself, to 'redeem' consciousness.

This redemption creates the 'bridge' between the higher and lower levels of existence, or *'the subtle and the gross'*. This idea of the bright sacrificed god appears in nearly all of the Western Mysteries. In the Nordic tradition, the god Odin hung upside down on *Ygdsrassil,* the Tree of the World, in order to bring humankind the sacred gift of the runes. In the Celtic tradition, the Corn King was sacrificed yearly to the Goddess at *Llugnassa,* or Lammas. The Bible states that God the Father so loved the world that he offered up his [only begotten] Son to save it. This offering-up, or sacrifice of the first-born or favoured son, has great resonance in all three of the Western theological doctrines. In Judaic, and the later Islamic tradition, Abraham, the father offers up his favoured bright son Isaac to the Lord, who tells him that his willingness is enough and that the sacrifice of a goat will suffice. To this day, in Egypt this mystery is re- enacted yearly as the Feast of the *Eid Kabir.* On this day, each household ritually slaughters a goat, which surely symbolises the presence of the Setian Satan. In my village, the fresh blood of a goat is daubed on the wall of any new home, shop or even car, to ensure its safety and prosperity. The butchered meat is then distributed amongst the needy. The Christians celebrate this principle in the omnipresence of Christ who is sacrificed daily in Holy Mass when the 'grain' of the Holy Eucharist is ingested, just as Osiris 'lives on in the barley'.

Osiris represents all that is 'beloved' in the masculine principle. He is beloved by his people, by his father, by his wife, and so beloved by his posthumous son Horus that his whole youth is concentrated on the purposes of his avengement and vindication. To *be* so beloved, it is necessary to love unconditionally. Unconditional loving is a constant act of sacrifice, where the ego is offered up to the higher force of wisdom. Being beloved, although it is the deepest desire and need of the human condition, is not anything one can demand by force or obtain by strategy. In order to achieve 'beloved ness' one must begin by setting the example of love, and simply doing it with trust and open-heartedness as an act of faith. In due course, faith will assuredly be rewarded, and one will become beloved. This is the lesson behind the Biblical injunction to 'love one's enemies'. The power of love is the greatest force in the cosmos. It is the 'green fuse' of the Earth god Geb, and the creative Word of Ptah, as well as, in its subverted form, the furious envy of Set. Osiris, like Odin and Jesus, teaches us by example. Nothing can be truly learned unless it is by and from love. Fear instills patterns of behaviour, but love brings the real desire to learn which springs from the need to share in consciousness with the beloved teacher. This is the lesson of the dynamic between Set and Osiris. Being greatly beloved can bring about the subsequent problems of envy and resentment. Trustfulness sometimes leads to betrayal, but mistrustfulness assuredly brings about the greater self-betrayal of alienation and the tyranny of pre-occupation and doubt. Osiris, the Lord of Light, is a shining exemplar in the adoption of attitudes and behaviour, which are healthy for the soul, and conducive to the continuance of its well-being. This is the path of sacred kingship.

As we have seen from the story of Isis, Osiris has three definite and different aspects of sacred kingship which in Egypt were thought of as:

Osiris Ruling
Osiris Slain
Osiris Risen.

The principle of **Osiris Ruling** places him as lord of agriculture, or king of the '*Black Land*', where he expresses himself as the wise and sensitive priest-king, concerned with sensible administration and the dissemination of a belief system based on sexual equality, peace and order. This in itself is enough to make him beloved by his wife and his subjects. In this respect, we can understand Osiris Consciousness as the mindfulness of right action; the awareness of what will serve the collective, of which as individuals we are each a connected part. Also in this capacity, to understand and be in harmony with the energy of growth.

As **Osiris Slain** he emerges as the trustful brother who is dismembered by the forces of jealousy and corruption. At this outrage it is said in the sacred texts 'the gods wept', so that we return to the idea of Osiris as the sacrifice of the favoured Son, and beloved of the gods. Here we can consider our own dismemberment, which will make the divine spark of Godhead within us 'weep'. This more interior aspect of Osiris Consciousness serves to remind us of the 'missing bits' that every fragment of humanity has. We are none of us perfect; if we were we would not need to be here. Osiris was as near perfect as can be imagined, and he was removed from this sphere of existence to show us how we may attain perfection, and be with him in Paradise. The dismembered parts of the psyche hold the key to our eternity.

In his capacity of **Osiris Risen** we see in the extraordinary commitment of Isis, his feminine counterpart (and thus the love that he has left behind to re-member him and leave issue), the deathlessness of love. In his resurrection, we ourselves become part of that beloved ness. As Osiris advises Horus from Heaven in his fight against the wrong-doing and ill-intent of Set, so the beloved ness of our higher selves can guide the forces within us in our journey through the trials and perils of material existence.

We must remember though that although Osiris is, like his father Geb, both trusting and sacrificial, he is in no way effete or ineffectual. The power of Osiris is like the mighty inundation of the Nile. The sacred symbol for Osiris is the *Djed,* or column. This is a strange and compelling phallic object, with four different levels of existence arising from its shaft. It can be said to represent the life force of consciousness that Osiris *is* – the great Spirit of Earth arising into the powerful and ordered structure of the trinity of life, death and re-birth. The powerful life-force of his father Geb (*Osiris Ruling),* the chaotic stellar energies of his brother Set (*Osiris Slain),* and the inner brightness and beloved ness of Osiris himself (*Osiris Risen)* harness and harmonise into the thrusting and erect *djed* column which has its own perfect symmetry of design.

Osiris Consciousness is then perhaps the most wonderful and mysterious individual god-force we encounter in our quest to self-sovereignty. For Osiris ultimately is about self-rulership and integration of the subtle and the gross inner levels. Osiris is Lord of the Good Dead. The whole mystery of mummification, arising from the death of Osiris, was to maintain consciousness of the material world or mortal flesh, as *aufu* from the *Dwaat (ka).* This being achieved, the divine spark of self, or *khu*, which was symbolised by Osiris, could still maintain rulership on all levels. When the gods wept for the death of Osiris, they wept 'tears of honey, resins and incense', all perquisites for the mummification process.

The dismemberment of Osiris actualises the whole Alchemical credo of '*Solve et Coagula*', or 'dissolve in order to unite' or ' analyse in order to synthesise'. The myth of Osiris teaches us that to arrive at the real integration of body, mind, soul and spirit, which was the goal and aspiration of the Egyptian initiate, we must undergo *all* of life, including its shadows and terrors. We cannot hide from them, for like the jeweled casket, they are made specifically to our measurements. It takes great courage to trust, but the example of Osiris teaches us that it is a necessity on the path of love to be so aware of the in-dwelling spirit, that we can rule ourselves wisely and well 'from Paradise'.

Hail, you are Osiris the great on the riverbanks, at whose wish Hapy emerges from his cavern.

Hail, you are Osiris, the falcon on earth, the falcon of electrum within the sky.

Hail, you are the maker of grain, he who gives life to the gods with the water of his limbs, and bread to every land with the water that takes form under him.

(Ancient Egyptian text)

PREPARATION FOR THE RITUAL AWAKENING OF OSIRIS

On preparing for your ritual awakening to the god-force Osiris, it is important and helpful to go over all your notes of the preceding work along the path of love. We have now reached the apotheosis of the journey, and it is an appropriate point to make a deep reflective study of the personal experiences that you have undergone thus far. Before attuning to the principle of Osiris, in his three separate aspects, it is necessary to understand the lost and dismembered parts of yourself before you may re-member them, and assume the Crown of sacred kingship. As you do this, you may notice certain patterns emerging, which will help you to create a reliable framework for the future rulership of your life.

You are now at the perfect place to make an evaluation of your growth and progress by looking carefully at all the symbols, images and emotions that arose from your subconscious during the awakenings of the six god-forces you have encountered so far. See where there have been correlations between them, and disparities. Take a kindly and non-judgmental view of your progress, noting which principles came easily for you, and which were more resistant. Be aware that consciousness of the difficulties you sustain is a major factor in overcoming them. Look back at your life and consciousness *before* you embarked upon the journey, and mark its progress up to where you are now. Spend some time reflecting upon the external events in your life during the process, and how your inner work may have affected, or even caused them. Consider if this is different in any way from how you would have dealt with things before.

An invaluable discipline for self-rulership to instigate during this procedure, if you do not already perform it, is to spend the time between waking and sleeping at night going over the events of your day, and assessing *without censure*, how, during your waking hours, you have ruled your life.

However, to assist you in your evaluation of the journey thus far, the following questions are offered as a guideline.

ANUBIS: My Shadow Guide

Have I been aware of my accompanying Shadow on my journey thus far?

How well has my accompanying Shadow helped me to understand my fears and resistances?

Am I closer to my spiritual goal? Have the goal posts moved at all? If so, does my inner goal seem more realisable?

Have any of my values changed or shifted since I began this work?

SEKHMET: My Pride and Passion

Am I able to access readily both my anger and my joy?

Am I relaxed and comfortable with my sexuality?

Is my self-expression always natural?

How confrontational can I be when necessary? Has this developed at all?

HORUS: My Sense of Self

Do I have a clear sense of my true gifts?

Have I courage and confidence to offer my true gifts to the world?

What is the underlying essence of my relationship with my parents? Has this improved?

Do I consider myself honourable?

How ready am I to face a challenge?

HATHOR: My Love and Beauty

Are my relationships generally as harmonious as I want them to be?

Do I enjoy intimacy?

Is my outward appearance as pleasing to me as it is to others, and vice-versa?

Do I have sufficiency?

How ready am I to laugh, dance or sing, or to offer comfort, nourishment or inspiration?

PTAH: My Plans and Projects

Do I know what I want to do with my life? Am I getting on with it to the extent of my capacity?

Am I as able to concentrate as I need to be?

Are other people listening to me seriously? Do I listen to others?

Am I virtuous?

Is my life improving?

ISIS: My Wisdom and Spirituality

Do I consider myself equally powerful and compassionate?

Can I master my emotions?

Can I be content with my own company? Keep my own counsel?

Could I always recognise and trust my intuition?

Is my every day working life meaningful?

When you have satisfactorily completed your self-assessment, an accompanying lightness of heart will inform you that you are ready to awaken your inner principle of Osiris, rising to the crown chakra and connecting with your *khu* body.

In preparation, you may contemplate the seven chakric gifts of the god Osiris. These gifts have great resonance with Christian virtues. The mysteries of Osiris can live on in the teachings of Christianity. As we prepare to integrate our 'soul' nature as Isis or 'brow' levels, with our 'spirit' or 'crown consciousness', we will see that the seven chakric gifts of Osiris are integrations of all the previous chakric gifts of the lower levels. Every divine quality we have been realising on our journey along the path of love has been a preparation for the assimilation of the seven 'Christian' virtues we can commit to realising as we gain consciousness of our divine purpose at the crown. When we assume the crown of Osiris, we gain sovereignty over our life and death. The following gifts are our tools, our creed, and the expression of our love.

THE GIFTS OF THE GOD OSIRIS THROUGH THE CHAKRAS

ROOT:	*Trust*
SACRUM:	*Service*
SOLAR PLEXUS:	*Sacrifice*
HEART:	*Acceptance*
THROAT:	*Teaching*
BROW:	*Resurrection*
CROWN:	*Sovereignty*

TRUST: THE ROOT OF OSIRIS

At the fundamental level of the crown chakra, and the magical *khu* body, we need to realise the gift of **trust**. Osiris trusts himself and his processes, even to his dis-memberment. At the crown level of consciousness, we can begin to place our trust in Holy Spirit to guide and protect us. We have found the impersonal powers of love and goodness, which proceed from our highest levels of consciousness to work through us, and we trust them. On a more personal level, we can realise the trust in others, which leads them to find it in themselves. We can begin to rule through trust. All the root chakra gifts, from Anubis to Isis, have led us to this most beautiful quality, which is basic to our spiritual integration.

Anubis:	*Instinct*
Sekhmet:	*Passion*

Horus:	*Obedience*
Hathor:	*Abundance*
Ptah:	*Patience*
Isis:	*Sorrow*
Osiris	*Trust*

Just as integration with the magical *khu* body depends upon realisation and integration of the preceding less subtle bodies, Osiris consciousness is the integration of all the god-forces we have awakened beforehand. The crown chakra awakens when energy flows freely from the other six chakras. In the same way, the vital gift of trust is the amalgamation and integration of all the previous root chakra gifts from the 'lower' gods. On the root level, we began with 'instinct'. Our first root level lesson was to learn to listen to and trust our instinctual responses. At every stage, we have been learning the lesson of trust, until here at the root level of Osiris, we realise self-trust, and trust in God.

SERVICE: THE SACRUM OF OSIRIS

At the sacral level of the *khu,* we connect with our spiritual and magical desires. The primal will and desire of the spirit is to serve. **Service** is the gift from the sacred phallus of Osiris. From here, we offer ourselves in the service of light. Our primal will, asserting itself from the crown chakra, sublimates Kundalini energy into the *khu*. Our desires to procreate integrate with spirit. We live to serve.

Anubis: *Preservation*
Sekhmet: *Joy/Righteous Wrath*
Horus: *Determination*
Hathor: *Pleasure*
Ptah: *Order*
Isis: *Search/Administration*
Osiris: *Service*

From the first sacral gift of Anubis where we learned to 'preserve' our energies, we have been arriving gradually at the realisation of service. As Osiris is the integration of all that has gone before, the gift of conscious service is the integration of all the preceding divine desires. Service is a powerful force and a supreme desire. The desire to serve supercedes any other.

SACRIFICE: THE SOLAR PLEXUS OF OSIRIS

Sacrifice is a very powerful force. To 'give something up', literally means to 'give something *up*', or make a material offering for a higher, spiritual reward. As mentioned earlier, the sacrificial aspect of the god appears in most mysteries. Without sacrifice, there can be no redemption. At the solar plexus level, concerns are with the lower, ephemeral nature of existence, the personality aspect of self, which changes from life to life. When this energy reaches the spiritual levels of Osiris and the *khu*, personality itself is released. From the solar plexus of the crown chakra and the *ka* aspect of the *khu* body, we receive the gift of willing **sacrifice**. The ego is now strong and realised enough to let go of itself. It is the crowning reason for all the previous solar plexus gifts.

Anubis:	*Training*
Sekhmet:	*Dignity*
Horus:	*Intelligence*
Hathor:	*Music*
Ptah:	*Design*
Isis:	*Consecration*
Osiris:	*Sacrifice*

Osiris offers himself up to the highest good to bring redemption to the world. He releases himself as Osiris into Osiris consciousness. Willing sacrifice is meaningful to the will of God only when the ego has become strong and real enough for it to know what it is doing, and why it is doing it. It has resonance only when there is no personal agenda around the sacrifice. It is an act of love and faith. If we consider all the previous solar plexus gifts, we realise that our willing sacrifice of the 'self' has arrived from recognition and integration of all of them. From 'training' to 'consecration', we have been strengthening our sense of self, so that when we reach the mysteries of Osiris we can love the self enough to let go of it. We can then allow it to guide us from the highest levels. 'Trust' and 'service' have paved the way for us to release our sense of being who we are, into whom we could be. The sacrifice is blessed. The self is free.

ACCEPTANCE: THE HEART OF OSIRIS

When love rises to the heart of Osiris, it opens to receive the divine gift of **acceptance**. We are now ready to accept divine grace, and to be accepted into its light. The two-way flow of energy through the heart allows us access to spiritual love, to give and to receive it freely. From the heart of the crown we love without restriction or stipulation, because we are able to accept every stage of the journey as real and valid. We understand each aspect of self, loving our 'dismemberment' because it has brought us to the place of acceptance. It has taken seven heart gifts to bring us here, and we acknowledge and accept them all.

Anubis:	*Loyalty*
Sekhmet:	*Power*
Horus:	*Courage*
Hathor:	*Beauty*
Ptah:	*Knowledge*
Isis:	*Healing*
Osiris:	*Acceptance*

The most lovely and loving gift we can accept from our highest heart self is the gift of acceptance itself. We are then welcomed into the Kingdom of heaven, within our own being.

TEACHING: THE THROAT OF OSIRIS

The beloved ness of Osiris brings us to the gift of **teaching** from the throat or *ba* level of the *khu* body. When we can realise the divine gift of **acceptance** from the heart, it rises to our throat, to promote itself as divine doctrine of love and law. Our teaching comes naturally from the example and premise of love. We teach by being who we are. We show the way of love, because we become love. Our teaching is the integration of all the previous throat chakra gifts along the path of love.

Anubis:	*Learning*
Sekhmet:	*Enchantment*
Horus:	*Perfect Honesty*
Hathor:	*Harmony in Relationship*
Ptah:	*Heka (Magical Utterance)*
Isis:	*Revelation*
Osiris:	*Teaching*

At the throat of the crown, we integrate all those previous gifts into our being and can express them in our teaching, as our teaching.

RESURRECTION: THE BROW OF OSIRIS

At the brow of the crown, the *khu/ba* of the *khu,* we gain a sense of re-memberment and **resurrection**. The self, offered up to the highest, at the solar plexus of the crown, reasserts itself as fully awakened and re-connected with the divine. We understand and recognise our own processes of dismemberment, and fragmentation. The higher kingdoms are available and accessible to us. We have 'risen' above the 'tomb of matter', but we love and value it as our own temple of learning and light. Everything makes sense. We 'see' with the eyes of spirit.

Resurrection is the result of the integration of all the previous 'brow' level gifts of the gods.

Anubis:	*Impartiality*
Sekhmet:	*Exaltation*
Horus:	*Vision*
Hathor:	*Radiant Understanding*
Ptah:	*Wisdom*
Isis:	*Intuition*
Osiris:	*Resurrection*

In the Christian Gnostic tradition, which drew upon the mysteries of Osiris for its initiations, 'resurrection' was an analogy for triumph over the tyranny of lower nature, when the aspirant finally prevailed over his fear and greed, to reach the 'kingdom' of his spirit. He could then 'remember' his true self and be at one with the light of God.

SOVEREIGNTY: THE CROWN OF OSIRIS

The crown of crowns, the ultimate quality and gift of Osiris is the gift of **sovereignty**. At the *khu* level of the *khu* body, we rise to self-Rulership. We assume ultimate responsibility for our lives, and we commit to living them from a place of spiritual consciousness. We live in light, truth and awareness. We recognise all levels of our being, and we oversee them with clarity and compassion. We attain peace and prosperity; we commit to achievement. The 'land of Egypt' is analogous to our own life. Sovereignty is the result of all the preceding gifts of Osiris, as well as all the preceding crown level gifts of the gods. It is both an on-going task and a fulfilment of self. It is a sacred commitment, and a powerful resolution. It brings us to divinity, and divinity to us. It both ties and frees us. It glorifies and humbles us. We 'walk with the gods' in the company of our lowest aspects of self. Nothing is too lowly for our notice, or too exalted for our recognition. We live in consciousness, and we learn as we go. We integrate on all levels.

| Anubis: | *Freedom* |
| Sekhmet: | *Ecstasy* |

Horus:	*Glory*
Hathor:	*Grace*
Ptah:	*Cosmic Consciousness*
Isis:	*Wholeness*
Osiris	*Sovereignty*

As the final and ultimate quality and gift of the god, we can see sovereignty to be an integration of all seven-crown chakra gifts of the gods, and all the chakric gifts of Osiris.

SOVEREIGNTY:
(Trust, service, sacrifice, acceptance, teaching, resurrection.)
You may now perform the exercise of reciting the personal affirmations of the god Osiris, firmly and authoritatively, until you know them by heart – which of course you do already.

PERSONAL AFFIRMATIONS ON THE GOD OSIRIS
My Higher Self always directs me
My indwelling divinity brings peace and prosperity to my Life
I always trust in Love
I can only return to myself.

Ritual Procedure for Awakening the God-Force Osiris
We may now prepare for the ritual awakening of the god Osiris, the crown chakra, and connection to the *khu* body. The following correspondences are offered to help.

Ritual Correspondences for the God Osiris

COLOUR:	White
PERFUME:	Lotus flower, Spikenard
INCENSE:	Myrhh
CHAKRA:	Crown

BODY:	Khu Body
TIME OF DAY:	Night
SACRED SYMBOLS:	the *Djed* Pillar, the Crook and Flail
ANIMAL:	Heron
TAROT CARDS:	'The Emperor', 'The Hanged Man', 'Judgment'

Altar Preparation, Anointment, Purification and Robing

Choose a time for this work during the hours of darkness.

Set up your altar, placing upon it a **white candle** and a symbolic representation of the god Osiris. It is a good idea to add anything that you wish to charge with the power of your sovereignty, such as your desk diary or personal organiser, or even your current bank statement, if you feel you need a boost to your financial capacities.

Burn some **myrhh incense** and pass through the smoke any item you wish to charge and purify. Purify your room with the incense and leave it burning in its thurible or censer on the altar.

Bathe or shower, and anoint **all your chakras** with oil of **lotus**, **spikenard** or **myrhh** with the shape of the pentagram. Dress in a clean white garment, preferably new.

Delineation of Sacred Space

Prepare the sacred space by calling in the Quarters and creating your Circle of Power.

Go to the centre of your space and sit down.

Visualisation of Chakric Colour

Concentrate on the whole process you have undergone from the beginning of your work along the path of love, from the root level of Anubis to the brow of Isis, allowing the different chakric colours to immerse and enfold you as you rise to your crown.

As you do this, acknowledge the gifts of each god-force within you as your focus passes upwards.

Feel your crown chakra opening and multi-coloured diamond light pouring through your complete chakric system, clearing and intensifying each separate colour as it descends. Experience yourself sitting in a translucent pool of shimmering iridescent light.

When you have satisfactorily completed this, go to your altar and light the white candle.

Say:

'I dedicate this altar to the Lord Osiris that I may rule myself and my life from Paradise.'

Go and sit comfortably in the centre of your sacred space and perform the exercise of realising the qualities of the god Osiris through the chakras from root to crown. You may do this in silence if you wish, although murmuring the word to yourself does help to actualise it as a quality. This time the exercise will work as a two-way process. Each word will appear for you from your crown, and descend to its rightful place, formed from its diamond fountainhead into the sparkling coloured light appropriate to its chakra.

Thus, the first quality '**trust**'will appear for you as a sparkling ruby red light, flowing down from the top of your head, down your spine, and into your root. When it reaches your root chakra, you will experience '**trust**' as a warm, rosy glow, which then radiates upwards into your sacrum.

When this happens, you will be ready to receive the word '**service**' as a brilliant flaming, orange-coloured light. This will activate and inspire you so that the passionate desire to serve grows and brightens, and flows upwards into your solar plexus.

Here it receives the golden light of willing '**sacrifice**' and you will naturally offer a precious feeling up to your heart.

As you do this the green energy of you '**acceptance**' will flow into and from you. This is the most beautiful sensation, and one you will want to share with the world.

Therefore, the sparkling blue of your '**teaching**' will flow down from your crown chakra, subtly altering your heart's rising green into a clear vibrant blue, and releasing it through your throat.

As the blue '**teaching**' vibration is released, you will experience it deepening into the peaceful violet of '**resurrection**' in your brow. In addition, here you will *remember* your divine Self.

Having remembered your Self, you will now connect consciously to your Crown of Osiris, and may claim at last the diamond of light, the white Double Crown of united Egypt, the gift of your '**sovereignty**'.

Now you are ready to stand before your altar and perform the invocation, which is really more of a prayer than an actual invocation. This can be done simply and *sotto voce,* but most importantly, with love. Osiris is such a beautiful and holy energy to attune to that he is reached or approached rather than summoned. Osiris must leave behind on earth those closest to him, and even they are only able to 'commune' with him. Isis, with all her power, magical knowledge and all-encompassing love, can only bring him back for one sacred moment, with just enough time for his seed to flow into her womb. To affect this, she must hover over him in her guise of the sparrow hawk, for it only his from his sacred phallus, symbolizing the divine Creative principle, that she may receive his life force to nurture and rear.

As you prepare to adopt the crown of your journey, you can feel yourself accompanied by all the disparate parts of your divine Self, personified by the shining *neters* of Ancient Egypt that you have awakened and integrated during your past work.

They are strong and alive within you and for you, and you may call upon them any time you need them, for you know now where they dwell, and need only make the connection. In their luminous company, you can now approach the throne of your sovereignty.

Anubis! Sekhmet! Horus! Hathor! Ptah! Isis!

INVOCATION TO THE GOD OSIRIS

Hail, Beloved Osiris,
Lord of the Living and the Righteous Dead,
Who offers up Thy Body to redeem the World
Bringing
To Heaven's gate the green fuse of Geb
As it flows through the Land, in the whisper of the Barley
Through Thy infinite Love of Rightness
And Thy understanding of the needs to be Wrong,
Thou have shown us the Way to Paradise
To Trust and Perfection.
Thus, we may know Thee as Lord of Light, Eternal King of the
  Celestial Realm.
Crowned doubly; Sacred King of Life and Death
Both Realms united under Thy Love and Law
By the Sacred Trust of Kingship.
We come to Thee
That we may emulate Thee
To learn to rule our lives, and know our deaths
In passionate love with Wholeness
And thus to reign
From Paradise
With the Glory of True Judgment.

Osiris Ruling

(Place your two arms crossed over your breast in the manner of the Pharoah with his Crook and Flail)

Osiris Slain

(Open your arms to shoulder level)

Osiris Risen

(Raise your arms)

HAIL OSIRIS!
Hail and Welcome.

Lie down with forearms crossed over your breast. Breathe deeply and evenly, and when you are ready, undergo the following guided meditation.

GUIDED MEDITATION ON THE SPHERE OF OSIRIS

You are lying on hard-baked mud. There is a faint smell of river water. You are some distance away from the slow, low, brackish water. The dark sky is wide above you. Clouds occlude the stars. The landscape is empty. There are only dry reeds and papyrus. Your body, clad in only a breechcloth, feels faint and spare. But you are not cold. The night is warm. As you lie here, hardly breathing, you can sense the slow ebbing of your life-force in accord with the falling river. You are quite calm and in accord with Nature. You vital energies are fading and slipping into the deep dark centre of the riverbed. It is like being gently tugged into an unconstrained and natural sleep; the slow inexorable sleep of the Great Tide of Night. Your fluids harmonise with the dying Nile. Your body is becoming gradually more light and dry, like a fallen twig, or a hollow reed.

As you lie here, on your bed of baked river-mud, thoughts of your life drift across your waking consciousness. Almost idly, you can think of the parts of yourself you have forgotten or ignored. Parts of yourself you have disliked and cut off; parts of your being you have been too lazy or afraid of to acknowledge or recognise.

And you can lie here, easily sinking into the dreaming half-world of the dry half-dark.

Here is a last chance to let yourself think of your failures. You can let yourself think, without fear or self-censure, of where you were unable to engage in or recognise your richness, your magnificence. You can gently admit here, with the ghost of a smile, where you have allowed the Others' jealousy, envy and malice to prevent your talent, your greatness, and your sovereignty. You can think quite simply and without emotion, of where you could have been majestic, imposing or successful, if you had chosen differently. (five minutes)

As you do this, there is a distant almost imperceptible movement in the clouds above you.

This brings a strange feeling of discomfort to your body.

There is a rising of energy in the earth below. It makes you restless. You do not like it. You frown.

But the energy rises.

The wind lifts.

The sky brightens.

*And without your wanting it at all, the earth energy surges up and **the river starts to rise**.*

In your heart, in your veins, in your bones, the sap is rising.

You no longer feel resentful. You experience a dawning wonder.

It is painful but it is glorious.

You stand. You face the inundation.

It is fast. Furious. Inexorable.

The mud is black and rich. The water is bubbling, rippling, flowing.

Your energy is alive – full and fast. Your vitality more than matches the fierce fresh flood of the flowing tide.

The sun is rising before your eyes; the water sparkling, a million rainbow drops. A kingfisher swoops upon the surface. You see the richness, the fertile beauty of your life. You feel the youthful potential ever-growing in the Kingdom of your being.

You hear the sound of human voices.

Coming along the bank to greet you is a little procession of people you know and trust.

They are bringing you a tall crown and some shining robes.

You have arrived at your own re-birth. You have effected your own resurrection.

Welcome to the Rulership of your life.

In your own good time, return to your full waking consciousness, refreshed, renewed and ready to resume your life.

Integration and Grounding

Did you manage to let yourself undergo the process of dying?

What images of your dismemberment did you receive?

What was your inundation like?

Who was there to greet you?

Questions you can ask the Tarot

What is the nature of my present relationship with the god-force Osiris?

How may I most readily integrate this energy into my life?

How may I recognise my Rulership? My Dismemberment? My Resurrection? What particular aspect of myself can I use to integrate these three?

How may I best attain my (any of the) chakric qualities of the god-force Osiris?

Having completely understood and integrated this experience, close down in the usual way, blowing out your candles, bidding the god and all attendant guardians,

HAIL AND FAREWELL.

Blessed Be.

CHAPTER ELEVEN

THE SACRED MARRIAGE OF ISIS AND OSIRIS

THIRD LEVEL INITIATION

Perfect Judgment
'The Return to the Beginning'
From the Book of Coming Forth By Day

I stand before the masters who witnessed the genesis, who were the authors of their own forms, who walked the dark circuitous passages of their own becoming. I stand before the masters who witnessed the transformation of the body of a man into the body in spirit, who were witnesses to resurrection when the corpse of Osiris entered the mountain, and the soul of Osiris walked out shining. When he came forth from death, a shining thing, his face white with heat. I stand before the masters who know the histories of the dead, who decide which tales to hear again, who judge the books of lives as either full or empty, who are themselves authors of truth. And they are Isis and Osiris, the divine intelligences and when the story is written and the end is good, and the soul of man is perfected, with a shout they lift him into heaven.

Now we can prepare in gladness for the celebration of the mystical marriage of Isis and Osiris. This loving connection between the brow and crown chakras allows the earlier two sacred marriages to retain constant harmony within and with each other, from both earthly and cosmic levels.

It will proceed from a conscious integration of higher purpose with lower need, and from a place of joyous union. It is based on trust and sorrow, and yet it can be understood at its crown to be capable of omnipotence and omnipresence. It is a solemn commitment to give ones all in the service of light and right. It brings rewards of the Throne and Crown of power and perfect judgment.

Isis and Osiris must undergo separation, ordeal and crippling loss to rule forever together from the Halls of Paradise. However, no matter how far and how much they *are* separated, they are never separate from each other. This fact holds the deepest and most profound truth about the mystery of love and marriage. Just like any lovers, Isis and Osiris need to celebrate their separations, to learn just how constant and together they choose to be. In their mystery of '*solve et coagula*', they echo the tragic truth of their parent's marriage. Nut and Geb, as 'Heaven' and 'Earth' are separated by their father Shu, 'the breath of Life'. While we live and breathe, we have a sense of our divine spirit being separate from our waking consciousness. The story of Isis and Osiris tells us how we may reunite these lovers, and integrate our divinity into our life.

The passion of Isis and Osiris is immortal, even death-defying, and wholly productive in a sense of Rulership, if not in terms of conventional family life. Their relationship is a shining example of wholeness in marriage, where the individual principles together make up more than the sum of their parts. However, theirs is a particularly remarkable love story in the sense that it is the only love story in mythic terms where it is the feminine that is put to the arduous task of rescuing the masculine, releasing him into his truest self. We can interpret this as the considerable power of our inner 'feminine', or intuitional self, which separates from the 'masculine' (or often fragmented 'left-brain', logical self) in order to integrate consciously with it in entirety, thus releasing its power into the world, for the higher good, or achievement of 'perfect judgement'.

Isis and Osiris have three distinct levels or phases to their union, which correspond to the dynamics of any committed relationship, especially marriage. These phases echo the three aspects of Osiris, as 'Osiris Ruling', 'Osiris Slain' and 'Osiris Risen'.

It begins as a blessed and productive working relationship where they rule together over the Black Lands of Khem, teaching the laws of rightness and order, and inculcating art and agriculture into the collective. This symbolises the golden period of 'in love ness' which initiates and stabilises every love relationship, where the blessedness experienced by the lovers is celebrated and shared with the world. As golden and blessed as this period is for them, it attracts dispersion through the impersonal power of malice, acted out by Set.

The second phase begins with the tragedy of Osiris' murder and subsequent dismemberment by these forces of envy and malice, when their relationship moves into a yearning separateness. Now, Isis, as both the inner intuitional self and practical 'earthly' consciousness, sets to repair the damage. At the same time she is demonstrating great conscious awareness of the limitless force and power of love. Her motivation for this stems entirely from her own love. She does not consider her status or role as queen. She sets an example of deeply personal commitment to the process of healing and integration, expressing herself freely, powerfully and passionately. Thus, she adds far more to the collective good, than if she had acted out her queenly duties, whilst privately grieving. It is during this period that she is able to conceive, nurture and release the divine child into the world, who grows to redress the wrongs she has personally suffered.

This symbolises the stage of relationship where there is recognition of differences and discrepancies, pain at the loss of its golden beginnings, and awareness of the power of jealousy and envy within the self. It is, nonetheless, clearly the most creative and fertile stage in earthly terms. Up until this point, Isis and Osiris have not produced offspring. Only an earlier 'golden days' connection to the Shadow aspect of the feminine, symbolised by Nephthys who conceives by subconscious deception, has there been any thought of future generations. While Isis and Osiris were ruling, they were so immured in their personal relationship, they had no thought of procreation.

The third phase or level of the sacred marriage of Isis and Osiris celebrates their choice-centred union. Isis, united with her dark sister, remembers Osiris. The intuitional self becomes whole, and shares in conscious love with the logical, conscious self.

Now, the sacred marriage of Isis and Osiris is conducted from the highest level, the level of 'omnipotence' where all who approach the Throne of that marriage can be welcomed, blessed and rewarded.

And so, to approach that Throne in our ritual celebration of the final sacred marriage along the path of love, we need to be aware that all three of these levels or phases are in some way being played out and enacted in our daily lives. Just as the battles between Horus and Set are being fought daily and constantly in our lives, so are the mysteries of Isis and Osiris brought to bear in all our committed relationships with each other and with ourselves, and with the most mystical and important relationship of all – the relationship within each of us, which the Egyptians, through their mythology and symbols, bequeathed to us; the marriage that exists between our Heaven and our Earth.

As we approach the celebration of the sacred marriage of Isis and Osiris, and we consciously re-unite our *khu/ba* with our *khu* consciousness, we may re-connect with the chakric gifts of Isis and Osiris, and marry them together. The seven wedding gifts, which spring from this marriage, are gifts of the highest consciousness. Some are gifts to which perhaps we may only aspire. However, we must not be daunted. Even if we can only aspire to them, we shall still derive benefits from doing so. Realisation comes after effort, and eventual realisation is only possible if we try.

We need to meditate upon them carefully before we meet them as part of the later ritual procedure. They are powerful and transcendent qualities, and it is important to prepare for their access so that we might use them with wisdom and discretion.

To help realise each quality of the sacred marriage of Isis and Osiris, anoint the appropriate chakra with a blend of the essential oils of **violet** or **sandalwood** with **lotus** or **myrrh**, in equal proportions in the shape of the pentagram.

WEDDING GIFTS OF THE SACRED MARRIAGE OF ISIS AND OSIRIS THROUGH THE CHAKRAS

ISIS	WEDDING GIFT	OSIRIS
Root: Sorrow	*Belonging*	Trust
Sacrum: Search	*Fertility*	Service
Solar Plexus: Consecration	*Hope*	Sacrifice
Heart: Healing	*Faith*	Acceptance
Throat: Revelation	*Redemption*	Teaching
Brow: Intuition	*Omniscience*	Resurrection
Crown: Wholeness	*Omnipotence, Omnipresence*	Sovereignty

BELONGING: THE WEDDING GIFT OF ISIS AND OSIRIS FROM THE ROOT CHAKRA

On the root level of the sacred marriage of Isis and Osiris, our **sorrow** marries our **trust**. This creates a poignant dynamic which brings us to the deep, emotionally rooted feeling of **belonging**. To unite trust with sorrow ensures that we can never be lost. When we can both trust sorrow, and know that that trust itself will probably bring us sorrow, then we know that we belong, to both heaven and earth. We know that we are both children of nature and living sparks of the stars. We can never be alone, we will always be supported, and our growth is assured. We belong to God and God to us. There will always be a place for us, which we can feel is our home. There is a limitation in belonging, but there is great safety too. There is both sorrow and trust in being at home. We leave home many times on our various journeys, but we can always return. Our true home is our self. We trust in life with all its sorrows, because life belongs to us, just as we belong to life.

FERTILITY: THE WEDDING GIFT OF ISIS AND OSIRIS FROM THE SACRUM

On the sacral level of primal will, Isis' **search** and **administration** combine in love with the **service** of Osiris. In joining these gifts, we apply our will and passion to finding the truth, from a full desire to serve ourselves, the collective and God. We vivify everything we attempt with the innermost seed of divine light that allows it to grow and blossom into the true glory of itself. We create **fertility**. This wedding gift makes life rich, full and flowing, full of surprises and delight. When we open ourselves to the passion of life, and can move with the combined forces of **search, administration** and **service,** we enter into a world where everything that we plant with mindfulness bears fruit that will support and nourish whoever tastes it. Our plans and ideas flourish because we are always looking for the best place to sow them, where they will do the most good. We cultivate and harvest our gifts and natural resources because we offer them in the service of humanity and to the highest good. We can even distribute them fairly, because we have realised our administrative gifts. This wedding gift of Isis and Osiris from the sacrum brings riches from the 'black land' of our consciousness. Where we love, serve, seek and administrate, we flourish.

HOPE: THE WEDDING GIFT OF ISIS AND OSIRIS FROM THE SOLAR PLEXUS

As love raises to the united solar plexus energies of Isis and Osiris, our **consecration** reaches out to sanctify and strengthen our willing **sacrifice.** This is a very holy combination which bestows the virtue of **hope** upon our lives. Hope is an inspirational quality of the mind. It springs from a constant decision to adopt deliberate positivity, a conscious courage to believe the 'best'. In infinitely more cases than not, it allows the best to happen. Even in those cases where it does not seem to do so, it probably has. This combination has the flavour of the true *sanyassin* who goes naked out into the world with a begging bowl, unencumbered by all that might distract him from his spiritual truth. Both Isis and Osiris give unstintingly of themselves, in love and consciousness to their shared task of Rulership. From the solar plexus, where we radiate our light into the world, the star of the hope they give us acts as a beacon of illumination. When we think positively, we create light, freedom from doubt and we open doors to higher possibilities. The marriage of consecration and willing sacrifice releases us into the actuality of our positive potential. When we hope, we fix upon our highest guidance, and we follow its light. We grow towards the 'blueprint' of self, which our innermost self knows to be true. Hope allows us to become who we truly are. From the solar plexus level of Isis and Osiris where they join in consciousness of themselves as themselves, we can celebrate our potential divinity, and our truest aspiration. We consecrate our lives to the highest and holiest, and we release or 'willingly sacrifice' our ego selves to that end. We gain the blessing of hope.

FAITH: THE WEDDING GIFT OF ISIS AND OSIRIS FROM THE HEART CHAKRA

From the heart chakras of Isis and Osiris, they love each other from **healing** and **acceptance.** This special alchemy brings knowledge and practice of unconditional love, or **faith.** The component gifts of Isis and Osiris mingle in the hearts sacred vessel to produce the nectar of the gods, the flowing force of love that keeps the stars in their spheres, and blesses each moment in time with its greatness and power. Faith is free, constant and regenerative. It is immeasurable and infinite. To find it, we need both to heal and to accept ourselves, others and the lost divine. When we find it, we are healed and accepted. We are 'found'. We know who we are, we know love, and we know that we will always know it. In faith, we are love.

REDEMPTION: THE WEDDING GIFT OF ISIS AND OSIRIS FROM THE THROAT CHAKRA

At the throat level of communication and magical expression, Isis and Osiris marry **revelation** with **teaching.** This combination of qualities results in the mystery of **redemption.** To redeem, as re-'deem' is to make a subsequent power-laden statement that alters a situation, restoring it to entirety. As consciousness fragments by its experience of the dark, it is also able to heal itself. This happens when it can accept that it is part of a higher purpose, that it should have needed to fragment in the first place. When this is accomplished, not only deeper and more powerful self-knowledge ensues, but the healing gifts of the higher nature become active and present in the world, by being applied deliberately to the self. Then, revelation and teaching, rising from the shared voice of Isis and Osiris, unite in love to resonate through the world as a glorious message of **redemption.** All that has gone before is expressed anew, from a place of expanded consciousness and release.

OMNISCIENCE: THE WEDDING GIFT OF ISIS AND OSIRIS FROM THE BROW CHAKRA

From the brow chakra of the sacred marriage of Isis and Osiris, **intuition** aligns with **resurrection**. This is a cosmic connection which brings as its wedding gift the power of **omniscience.** All I can say about this most mystical of experiences is that it *is possible to be omniscient, if only in one moment, and only within the limitations of your own knowing.* As you rise to the married brow of Isis and Osiris, you may 'know everything' in that moment, but as a creature of human limitations, you will also know what you cannot stand 'knowing'. You will know the ineffable and the unknowable and you can both know and 'unknow' them.

OMNIPOTENCE AND OMNIPRESENCE: THE WEDDING GIFTS OF ISIS AND OSIRIS FROM THE CROWN CHAKRA

This is the highest level of attainment to which the great initiates and priest-Pharaohs of Egypt aspired. At the crown of the sacred marriage of Isis and Osiris, **wholeness** and **sovereignty** combine in love to link to the highest **omnipotence** and **omnipresence** of the Godhead. Again, as mortal beings, we can only aspire to a glimpse of this, or possibly an experience of it in a single moment of mystical union. This Wedding Gift, to be attained at the shared crown of Isis and Osiris, flows in perpetuity from the peak and pinnacle of their love. And as mere mortal beings, we can perhaps be allowed a sense of their omnipotence, in order to find and exercise with love and discretion the great and glorious gift of perfect judgment.

OSIRIS AND NEPHTHYS

At this point it is both valid and interesting to examine the shared qualities of the Adulterous Relationship of Osiris and Nephthys as they proceed through the chakras. Nephthys, who has shared one illicit night with her bright brother, stands integrated with her sister Isis behind the Throne of Osiris in Paradise, and clearly has an important role to play in the maintenance of the sacred marriage itself.

If we place the chakric qualities of the principles of Osiris and Nephthys together, we can perceive how, in human terms, the qualities of Nephthys as Shadow queen are employed or dissipated when conjoined to the forces of light.

The magical perfume blend for helping to realise the gifts of this relationship consists of one drop of essential oil of **lemon**, to one drop of **sandalwood,** to two drops of **lotus**. As mentioned above, if **lotus** is not available, **myrhh** or **spikenard** will serve instead.

GIFTS OF THE ADULTEROUS RELATIONSHIP OF NEPTHYS AND OSIRIS THROUGH THE CHAKRAS

NEPHTHYS	RELATIONSHIP	OSIRIS
Crown: Self-importance	*cannot co-exist*	Sovereignty
Brow: Illusion	*cannot co-exist*	Resurrection
Throat: Concealment	*cannot co-exist*	Teaching/Doctrine
Heart: Guilt	*Forgiveness*	Acceptance
Solar Plexus: Sorcery	*Charm*	Sacrifice
Sacrum: Imagination	*Idealism*	Service
Root: Concern	*Responsibility*	Trust

On the lower levels, in fact up to the heart chakra, we can see that the combined qualities of this relationship give rise to some very valuable gifts, whereas on the higher levels, the Adulterous Relationship can only give way to the marriage of Isis and Osiris for any creative input to occur. There is surely an essential truth in this dynamic regarding the power of commitment. From the first three chakras, the Adulterous Relationship of Nephthys and Osiris produces **responsibility, idealism** and **charm,** perhaps all 'canine' qualities we may associate with the fruit of their union, the dog god Anubis. From their shared heart however, springs the divine gift of **forgiveness**, which is perhaps the most important reason for their relationship. The dynamic between dark or unconscious feminine and bright masculine produces these helpful qualities to be embraced and integrated on the journey to 'perfect judgement'. But it has to be the tortuous travails of Isis, albeit supported and abetted by Nephthys and Anubis, and redressed by Horus, which bring about self-Rulership on all levels.

Anubis (as **responsibility, idealism, charm** and **forgiveness**) brings the initiate to the Shores of Paradise, to witness the weighing of the heart against the Feather of Maat (**truth**).

This being successful, he is greeted by Horus and led into the holy presence of the three sacred principles – Isis and Nephthys joined in love, behind the Throne of the fully re-membered and all-loving Osiris.

If you are, or have been, in a committed relationship, here is the perfect opportunity to look deeply at your part in it, to assess for yourself how 'light-in-heart' you are about it now. Let Anubis witness the Weighing for you, for he has brought you this far, and, as the progeny of the adulterous relationship of Osiris and Nephthys, he can be said to hold the gift of forgiveness in his own heart.

RITUAL PREPARATION FOR THE SACRED MARRIAGE OF ISIS AND OSIRIS AS A THIRD LEVEL INITIATION

Having prepared oneself, with contemplation on the virtues of the sacred marriage of Isis and Osiris, and those of the less sanctioned and sanctified relationship of Nepthys and Osiris, it is helpful to follow the ensuing 'mystical revelation'. As in the earlier 'revelations' of the sacred marriages, it is recommended that you receive it gently, as though you were reading or listening to a story or a poem, rather than a guided meditation or a Pathworking. Let its images just wash over and through your psychic system so that its emotional and spiritual message may flow easily and readily into your heart.

MYSTICAL REVELATION OF THE SACRED MARRIAGE OF ISIS AND OSIRIS

She is in a low boat, gliding through marshes thick with rushes and green papyrus reed... The birds are big and fat, rainbow fish gleam in the clear, still water. Everything sings to her in a sweet, low note of wetness, of fertility. She is punting easily through the tall reeds, finding her way. Heavily pregnant, her body feels rich and full; slow in the damp warmth of the dreaming day.

He is not waiting for her. She is not going to meet him. He is inside. There is a deep, slow- moving feeling of lush completion, the safe and steady fulfilment of purpose. She feels as though she can call upon him any time, anywhere, for he has given her everything. There is no excitement at going to meet him, only a sense of peaceful satisfaction at having employed him, and the inner knowing of his joy at having been employed.

Now she has come to a place of tangled weed. The gleaming green spires form a temple tent of dancing, dappled light. There are blue fish and thickly fleshed lotus blossom. She can reach down and take any one of them if she likes. The water is so clear. She lies down, cradled by the gently rocking boat, and lets the green-blue light and the scent of the lotus wash her soul with peace.

Now she stands, with her round arms dripping, she pushes the reeds aside. She is going to an island; she and the child. He lives on in the child. He has given both this rich and peaceful feeling. She gave all in her quest to find him; now she holds him within, in herself, in the child. She doesn't need him any more. For now he is always with her. He is her contentment with the green reeds and the water, and the child within. He was sacrificed for this. For her. And now that he is absorbed into her, she has a constant communication with all that he ever could be. This is the gift of Heaven for Earth, for Heaven does not contain Earth and can only sacrifice itself for it. But Earth contains Heaven. And he lives in the Divine Child, the lush wetness of the marshes, the emerging island. He has put spirit into the water, and into her womb and into everything. She knows she can never lose that. It will always be there. She knows she will find the island. There, she will give birth to the child he has given her. She will give it life, and she will give it nourishment, and when the time comes she will release it onto its own path towards the Light of its Father.

Self-Preparation and Planning

As you have done for your previous celebrations, it is best to plan for your third sacred marriage in seven stages. Each stage will represent a preparation for your attainment of each of the seven Wedding gifts of Isis and Osiris, where you can begin to combine their shared chakric qualities within yourself. Some suggestions follow.

Stage 1. Belonging:

Make a pilgrimage to a place from your past, where you felt truly safe. Allow your feelings of trust and sorrow to meet and marry within you.

Stage 2. Fertility:

Re-awaken a project or an idea that you have left aside, and actively vivify it. Get it moving by placing it in the service of humanity, and let it go.

Stage 3. Hope:

Focus on a troublesome relationship or situation in your immediate life. Visualise golden light and blessings around the people involved, and the most positive outcome for them.

Sanctify the situation, and sacrifice your personal feelings of doubt and mistrust.

Stage 4. Faith:

Spend time celebrating your beliefs. Make a commitment to yourself, such as investing in a course or workshop you have been hesitant about, or throwing a party, or giving a gift to a friend. Open your heart to your friends and loved ones. Say yes when your heart tells you to.

Stage 5. Redemption:

Write down all the positive things about yourself that you know to be true, and those that you know can be true. Go to an open space where you feel private and comfortable, and declaim them.

Stage 6. Omniscience:

Give yourself special meditational time and space in your temple. Place flowers on your altar, play soothing music, burn incense and candles. Experience the light of Isis and Osiris joining in your higher centres. Keep note of the inner visions you experience.

Stage 7. Omnipotence and Omnipresence:

Take a meditational exercise of welcoming all the seven gods and goddesses, and Nephthys into your space. One by one, ask them to place a special gift for you on your altar. Keep note of these gifts.

We may now proceed with the celebration of the marriage itself. This occasion is one of absolute commitment so it is best to allow yourself a whole day to complete it. The following requirements will support your celebration

Ritual Requirements

One new white garment

White flowers

One white and one violet candle, four tea lights

A white altar cloth

Representations of Isis and Osiris

Essential oil of violet or sandalwood, lotus or myrhh

Incense of sandalwood chips and myrhh

Ceremonial Site and Day

Choose a day that is special for you, an anniversary perhaps or one of the sacred festivals, such as a solstice or an equinox. If you have astrological knowledge, you could choose a day that has appropriate planetary significance for you. Your ceremonial site can be your own ritual working area, or temple, but it may be more special to celebrate your third and final sacred marriage in a venue that has extra symbolic resonance with the higher realms. I feel particularly blessed in that I can offer my own meditational space directly in front of the Pyramids to celebrants who have come this far. But any place in which you feel you can access the holy energy of creation will be right for you, as long as you do not inconvenience anyone else.

Wedding Dress

Prepare a new white garment. If you feel self-conscious wearing a robe in public, a new white shirt or dress will serve, for you must be comfortable and practical, but it is best if it at least feels that you are wearing a special garment to honour your wedding. If you want to provide yourself with a commemorative adornment, cleanse it in salt, water and incense smoke, then wrap it in a clean white cloth and put it aside for your ceremony.

Witnesses

If you want your ceremony to be witnessed by like-minded people whom you trust, all to the good, and if you have a wise and respected friend or teacher whom you can designate to officiate as priest or priestess, so much the better.

Purification, Altar Preparation, Anointment and Robing

On the day, bathe or shower in the morning, put on your new white garment, anointing yourself on your brow and crown chakras with a mixture of essential oils of violet or sandalwood with myrhh or lotus. After a light breakfast, devote some time to performing an act of love or healing which serves the higher good. This could be a simple charitable act of kindness, or, if you have the skills, a healing/treatment session given for free to someone who cannot afford to pay.

This act is offered up as a Wedding Gift to yourself, and blessed with universal light so that you might never yourself go cold, hungry, or uncared-for in the service of the Divine. If you prefer to deliver alms, then you can give some money to a needy person in the street. Do so with all your heart, with a silent acknowledgement to Isis and Osiris, the loving principles of light whom you are to unite this day within your own soul and consciousness.

Altar Preparation

When you are ready for the solemnisation of your ritual, set up your altar. If you are working out of doors, a simple white cloth spread on the ground in the Eastern direction will do. Adorn it with flowers (white lilies are perfect), representations of Isis and Osiris, and a white and a violet candle. Burn incense of sandalwood chips and myrhh.

Delineation of Sacred Space

Create your sacred space in the usual way. If others are present, include them within your Circle of Power. You or your officiating priest and/or priestess may light the candles and perform the invocations on the gods Isis and Osiris, given on pages 257, 298.

Then repeat aloud:

'I have entered into this sacred space to celebrate the Sacred Marriage of Isis and Osiris within myself.

I (name) do hereby commit my body, mind and power to the service of spirit,

in the desire that I might mingle my Essence with the Essence of the Divine.

I solemnly swear that I undertake this initiation in the name of Truth and Love,

for the good of the world,

from my highest purpose and my deepest desire,

to the best of my ability.'

Closing your eyes, surround yourself in a veil of violet light, and repeat out loud the Personal Affirmations of the goddess Isis. Then take yourself to the ante-room of the Isis Temple on the lake.

Lie down on the couch to undertake your chakra exercise on the gifts of Isis. Concentrating on your emotional body, try to experience each gift at your truest level of feeling. Chant the names of the gifts in a soft undertone, allowing your emotional memory to connect them to experiences and events in your past. Visualise yourself in the centre of these events, and re-experience the feelings. Although this is painful on the lower levels, as you rise it becomes an uplifting and healing exercise.

When you have integrated this part of the procedure, allow the veil of light to change into an aquamarine colour. Take yourself to the deserted shore that you visited in the Nephthys guided meditation. Repeat the exercise with the Personal Affirmations and the gifts of Nephthys through the chakras, this time with focus on the physical/sensation levels. For example, you can experience the physical sensations of 'concern' as restlessness in your body, a tightening of your muscles and so on. Allow your face and body to express the qualities as you work through them. This will help to release them. When you reach the crown, work your way back down again to the root, revisiting the qualities and acting them out with your body. When you feel that you have experienced all of these qualities with both your emotional and your physical body, you may return to your ordinary consciousness.

Reaffirm your commitment to the Sacred Marriage.

Visualise the presence of Osiris as a spiralling shaft of diamond light pouring into you at crown chakra, filling you with love.

Repeat the Personal Affirmations on the god Osiris, and undertake the exercise of remembering the chakric gifts of Osiris. Go very deep inside you this time.

Working from root to crown, acknowledge the Wedding Gifts of the sacred pair. If you have not chosen an officiating priest or priestess, repeat the responses yourself, changing the pronouns appropriately.

'With sorrow and with trust do I welcome the gift of Belonging.'
PRIESTESS: 'You have reached your home in Love of the Divine.'
'With search and with service do I welcome the gift of Fertility.'
PRIESTESS: 'You may bring forth all that is good in Love of the Divine.'
'With consecration and sacrifice do I welcome the gift of Hope.'
PRIESTESS: 'The Light of Hope will illuminate your Path in Love of the Divine.'
'With healing and acceptance do I welcome the gift of Faith.'
PRIESTESS: 'Divine Love is yours.'
'With revelation and with teaching do I welcome the gift of Redemption.'
PRIESTESS: 'And thus are you redeemed.'
'With intuition and resurrection do I welcome the gift of Omniscience.'
PRIESTESS: 'All things knowable are yours to know.'
'With wholeness and with sovereignty do I welcome the gift of Omnipotence.'
PRIESTESS: ' May you hold and deliver the power of Perfect Judgment.'

You may now be presented with your commemorative adornment.

The ceremony may now proceed in any way you feel appropriate. You can offer insight or guidance to those gathered to witness your celebration, or you can quietly commune with the newly integrated powers within you. You can do both if you wish.

When you are ready to close down, thank the god and goddess for their combined presence in your midst, bidding them

HAIL AND FAREWELL.

CHAPTER TWELVE

SET

SET: DARK STAR IN THE BRIGHTNESS

Since the dark lord, Set, has been mentioned so much in this volume, I feel it is only fair to include a chapter on the principle of the dark god. This work is very useful as a background to the principles of Osiris and/or Horus. After all, if you 'know your enemy' you are all the more likely to be able and ready to overcome him. Strictly speaking, the principle of Set can be said to reside in the solar plexus, but any lower chakra work can include him. As I have included correspondences and material dedicated to his wife, Nephthys, I have also presented the dynamics of the Unholy Alliance of Nephthys and Set as an effective working parallel, to gain deeper insight into the sacred marriage of Isis and Osiris.

As a guideline to understanding the energy of Set, I have provided ritual correspondences, chakric gifts, a guided meditation and a hymn.

I have not recommended a ritual procedure, nor provided an invocation, as I feel that the darkness within is difficult enough to deal with and needs no further encouragement, nor particular glorification.

SET

Set is the son of Nut and Geb, the brother of Osiris and Isis, and husband-brother to Nephthys. As the personification of darkness and chaos, who effected the dismemberment of Osiris from a sense of envy, he has earned a dubious reputation from Egyptologists, but there is more to him than this. The great Pharoah Sety 1, the father of Rameses, was a priest and devotee of Set, the cults of his worship flourishing during the 19th and 20th Dynasties when Egypt was often in a state of war. As a sky-god, he is actually closer to his mother, Nut, than to his father, Geb, who translates more readily into his gentler son, Osiris. In the same way that his later counterpart Lucifer, or Satan (from whom the name derives), was the angel closest to the Throne of God before his Fall from grace, so Set, who also personifies the darkest aspects of humanity, is closest in aspect to the light of God, as the beloved twin brother of the Bright Lord Osiris. As a primarily stellar, rather than a terrestrial entity, he is not as subject to the laws of dispersion and return as Osiris, but more the perpetuator of them. This explains the popularity of his cults when the arts of warfare were needful in society.

Rather than the cosmic wisdom and flow of stellar light exemplified by his mother Nut, he can be viewed more as the fierce fire and noxious gases of the geo-physical stars. His power is ruthless. In Egypt he was given rulership over the arid 'red lands' of the desert wastes, the opposite to his bright brother Osiris who ruled 'the black lands' and (like his father Geb) was concerned with the green growth of cultivation. Linking in power to his mother Nut, but without her feminine qualities of compassion and adoration, Set symbolized the cosmic plan by embodying the principles of chaos and destruction, which are required to keep order in the universe. It can be said that it is the consciousness of chaos that keeps nature in place.

Set is usually depicted with the body of a man, swishing tail and tall flat ears of an animal, and a long pig-like snout. One of his titles is 'Lord of the Flies'. This is the title of a book by William Golding, which powerfully evokes the energy of Set. At festival times in Egypt, a pig was brought to symbolize the presence of Set, and ritually beaten and driven from the area, in much the same way that the scapegoat was used by the Israelites. In Golding's novel, English public school boys find themselves marooned on a desert island, whereupon they revert to savagery, quickly symbolized one of their fellows whom they term 'The Pig', then beat him to death. The great success of this novel in the 1960s points to the presence of Set in the collective.

The Egyptians held that the principle of Set was present and powerful, but did not, like more recent dualistic theological doctrines, hold that he was equal in power to God. More, they viewed him as an unavoidable necessity, who acted out the fear, greed, envy, inertia and so on that arises in humanity from the actual process of being alive. As such he could be considered as Adversary and thus Redeemer, for to meet ones inner foe with courage and righteousness redeems any hitherto evil perpetrated on, by and to the self.

It is important to contemplate the myth of the dismemberment of Osiris and the subsequent avenging of this act by the son of Isis and Osiris, Horus, in order to understand the mystery of Set, and the important role he has to play in the realisation of self.

The myth itself is a clear portrayal of the laws of destruction and renewal. After the emergence of the children of Nut on the Epagonomenal Days, the gods decree that the rule of the Two Lands (or duality of manifest existence) shall be divided. To gentle Osiris is given the black fertile lands of the Delta (or the positive/creative) while his savage brother Set is given the barren 'red' deserts of Upper Egypt (or negative/destructive). Osiris and Isis set about inculcating the arts of agriculture and domesticity into the consciousness of their people, while Set, who is wild, predatory and bi-sexual, roams the wastelands with his seventy-two companions, hunting wild boar, drinking and brooding on rebellion and war. Eventually news reaches Set of Osiris' success in rulership, which inflames his envy and ambition to such an extent that he devises a plot to destroy Osiris and all that he stands for

As we have seen, the subsequent quest of Isis is a beautiful allegory of the soul's healing search to realise itself through Love. The Battle of Horus and Set symbolized the on-going struggle between darkness and light, on which material manifestation depends, and of which the light always emerges triumphant. It is interesting to consider at this point the subtle weapons of Set, which are so effective in the physical destruction of order, symbolized by Osiris. These are alcohol, lust for material possessions and a naïve assumption, which holds a certain arrogance at its core, that Goodness and Right prevail at all times. The message of Set here is to be aware of the dark power of the Shadow, which always lurks behind manifested brightness, and to be wary of the unconscious (or drunken) need to consort with it. Its gifts are, like the jeweled chest, rich and perfectly designed for oneself, but there is a need to be clear and careful in receipt or discovery of them. In psychological reference, Set is *The Shadow Animus*; the unacknowledged dark masculine principle within us, that is by nature greedy, jealous, unscrupulous, cruel, but thankfully sterile.

In terms that are more energetic, we can regard him as the key player in the conflictual drama of life, the celestial force that brings about the constant process of renewal and the mystery of redemption.

For Set is a lone star. His wife Nephthys is secretive, unfaithful and hidden and even she abandons him to his devices after the dismemberment of her brother. He has his seventy-two conspirators, but thieves always 'fall out'. Collusion invariably leads to betrayal. Set ultimately, as we all do in our journey through the valley of the Shadow, stands alone. Set Consciousness is neither an easy nor a good thing to share. It does however make for great efficacy in the world. Set is devious and ambitious, but he is effective. The principle of Set, which is the first and only negative active god-force we encounter on our quest to wholeness, leads us to meet and understand our darkness. Thus eventually, as Horus, we can continue the struggle to conquer the weaknesses and fear of life that our unconscious will constantly manifest for us to meet. Sometimes it is necessary to carry the Shadow, sometimes we must be the one to act it out; but it is always important to be aware of it. Set Consciousness teaches us the value of destruction in the higher cause of life. This does not make us popular, but it does bring about the possibility of growth towards expanded levels of consciousness in others and ourselves. Without Set we would not face the pain and learn the subsequent lessons of separation and death. We would, like the innocent Osiris, in our naïve imaginings that everything was always sweetness and light, fall into his power. It is necessary to understand and integrate the ruthless power of Set within ourselves to be effective. In this way dispersal becomes consciously chosen; without conscious dispersal and renewal we could never face the darkness of betrayal and loss in ourselves, and thus would never arrive at the integration of Heaven and Earth or the true sovereignty of our selves which is symbolized for us in the Egyptian Mysteries as the resurrected and Risen Osiris.

On embarking on any work dedicated to the god Set, ensure that you feel ready to face the darkness within, and be ruthless with yourself in aiming to transform the power that you encounter there for the highest good and in the service of Evolution.

RITUAL CORRESPONDENCES ON THE GOD SET

COLOUR:	*Black*
INCENSE:	*Cannabis*
PERFUME:	*Jasmine*
CHAKRA:	*Solar Plexus (Root)*
ANIMAL:	*Pig (Boar), Goat*
TAROT CARD:	'The Devil'

HYMN TO SET

Dark Star in the Brightness
Great Lord of Death!
Thy Truth is Delusion
Destruction thy Breath.
Thou seest through Light
To the meaning beyond
Holding all life in Time
Then releasing the bond.
The Covenant of Freedom
Is crushed in thy hand
By Will and by Purpose
Dost Thou understand.
Let me face then Thy power
O Lord of the Lie
To know Thee gives ever

The courage to die.

PERSONAL AFFIRMATIONS ON THE GOD SET
My fears and weaknesses show me my strength
I take responsibility for my own deeds
I am not afraid to be alone
Separation is a valuable part of Unity
As I walk in the Shadow I am blessed by the Light

Before attempting the following exercise, re-familiarise yourself with the chakric gifts of Osiris.

THE SHADOW ASPECTS OF THE GOD SET THROUGH THE CHAKRAS
CROWN:	*Tyranny*
BROW:	*Delusion*
THROAT:	*Coercion*
HEART:	*Rejection*
SOLAR PLEXUS:	*Strategy*
SACRUM:	*Ambition*
ROOT:	*Survival*

GUIDED MEDITATION ON THE SPHERE OF SET
You are enthroned in a vast chamber, in a Pyramid open to the stars. Your throne is placed on a dais of black basalt, high above the floor. It is magnificently wrought in precious metals and thickly encrusted with glittering gems. It is flanked on either side by animal-headed statues. You are wearing a head-dress with two upwardly pointing horns, like tall ears.

Your throne places you in direct alignment with the matrix of the Constellation known to us as 'The Bear'. This stellar pattern is inflexible. Its influence, flowing down from the open apex of the Pyramid into the two horns of your crown, is your only governance and guide.

Below you in the Precinct are prostrate human figures, lying in obeisance to your will.

They will await your command. Whatever you tell them to do, they must and will carry it out. Not to do so brings the penalty of death. However, here, in this place, you have no advisor, no counsel nor support, only the hard and direct influence of your link with the stars. Right and Might are one. Your own will reigns supreme. You are impassive as your glance meets the prostrate figures below you on the floor. They are merely instruments of your will, waiting for your command.

Time is your servant as you sit there. Life and Death your Generals. You experience them as two currents of force, flowing down into you, from the horns of your crown into your whole psychic system.

The Strategy of your Life appears before you. You begin to understand the meaning of its structure. You begin to see where you must prevail. You know that the waiting supplicants are projects in the great scheme of your existence. You accept total responsibility for their presence. You may grant them Life if they will serve your purpose, and you will order their extinction if they will not.

The flow of stellar light from your crown is intensifying your intelligence. You feel a diamond-like brilliance. This gives you direct access to the fluid possibility of your purpose. You consider your projects and how they are serving the whole strategy. You are quite calm. The Chamber glimmers in silence. Everything and everybody within waits for your decision and command. You become aware that there are two supplicants. One is a personal project of yours; through him you will adequately and efficiently fulfill the higher strategy of your being. The knowledge of how this may be affected is clear. You see with vision unclouded by sentiment or emotion how you may direct him. You issue an order. He rises. He backs out of the Chamber to expedite your command. You realise that the other does not serve your vision. You see this very clearly. To employ him further is a waste; he is incapable of meeting your requirements. You signal that you have no need of him. He is dispensed with. Your decision is final. You rise from the throne. You remove your Head-dress. You descend from the high platform, and pass through the Chamber without a glance.

You are clear, strong, and ready to resume your life.

QUALITIES OF THE SACRED MARRIAGE OF NEPHTHYS AND SET THROUGH THE CHAKRAS

The magical perfume blend for the Sacred Marriage of Set and Nephthys consists of two drops of **jasmine** to one drop of **lemon** and one drop of **sandalwood.** It is recommended that any work on this Marriage is conducted on the **lower two** Chakras only, and that it is always held in concert with the two lower chakras of the Sacred Marriage of Isis and Osiris. Thus, the magical perfume should include proportioning one drop of **violet** with one drop of **lotus.** If lotus is not available, **myrrh** or **spikenard** will be as efficacious, if not as fragrantly pleasing.

NEPHTHYS	MARRIAGE	SET
Crown: Self-importance	*Chaos*	Tyranny
Brow: Illusion	*Insanity*	Delusion
Throat: Concealment	*Deceit*	Coercion
Heart: Guilt	*Envy\ Hatred*	Rejection
Solar Plexus: Sorcery	*Corruption*	Strategy\Rationale
Sacrum: Imagination	*Worldly Success*	Ambition\Control
Root: Concern	*Ruthless Determination*	Survival

On contemplating the qualities of this Marriage through the chakras it is evident that it cannot survive on the higher levels. Without the guardianship of Isis and Osiris, the shared qualities of Set and Nephthys degenerate. Within their own marriage they are focused on actualising their desires through the Shadow or fear principle. This explains Nephthys abandonment of Set after Osiris is dismembered.

To illustrate the dynamics of this Marriage, it is necessary to return to the Mystical Revelation on the Sacred Marriage of Isis and Osiris on page

317. Follow the story from where it left off.

She knows she will find the island. There, she will give birth to the child which he has given her. She will give it life, and she will give it nourishment, and when the time comes she will release it onto its own path towards the Light of its Father.

CONTINUED AS A REVELATION ON THE SACRED MARRIAGE OF SET AND NEPHTHYS

She begins to feel concern for the safety of the child. There is a sudden urgent need to reach dry land, to get out of the uncertain rocking of the boat. She experiences a heavy, responsible feeling. The bottom of the boat seems slippery; she feels she should not have been subjecting her precious burden to the effort of punting and the dangers of falling. Aware now that her body is heavy and cumbersome, she begins to think about her movements, making them faster and more efficient in her need to find a way out. Now her sharp eyes see a clear space. Using her concern and responsibility as a focus, she concentrates all her intent upon pulling the boat through. It passes out into a clear expanse of daylight. Her purpose is fixed upon finding a dry slope to beach the boat safely. She must and she will get to it. She visualises the inlet to the island clearly, and effectively. She finds the channel. The boat speeds along it, propelled by her clean, effective movements. Now she sees the slipway she was making for. The shingles crunch as she moors the boat and ties it securely.

She must find somewhere to rest and deliver the child. She knows there is a fisherman's hut somewhere nearby. She saw the nets drying on the slipway. Employing all her inner focus, she wills what she requires and how to realise it, get it, and manage it. The fisherman's hut appears. She immediately transforms it into a palace, the fisherman and his family all displaced to make way for a prince. Her prince must have everything.

Her prince will control an empire. Restlessly she walks around her palace making sure that everything is in readiness before the tearing pains of birth diminish her power. She will cultivate the island and turn the marshland into a harbour. She will destroy the environment and she will create a fortress which will need to be defended from the covetous and the power-hungry. After a while, everybody else in the world will become a threat to her security and the birthright of her unborn child.

AFTERWORD

For further information on the Path of Love training, contact www.sacred-egypt.com. Regular residential courses and workshops are held at the Sacred Egypt Mystery School, Giza Pyramids, and at Tofte Manor, Bedfordshire Endland, www.toftelabyrinth.co.uk. For personal questions regarding the work or requests for supplies of the ritual oils, incenses and Egyptian statuary email KatyNoura@aol.com

BOOKS

O books

O is a symbol of the world, of oneness and unity. In different cultures it also means the "eye", symbolizing knowledge and insight, and in Old English it means "place of love or home". O books explores the many paths of understanding which different traditions have developed down the ages, particularly those today that express respect for the planet and all of life.

For more information on the full list of over 300 titles please visit our website
www.O-books.net

myspiritradio is an exciting web, internet, podcast and mobile phone global broadcast network for all those interested in teaching and learning in the fields of body, mind, spirit and self development. Listeners can hear the show online via computer or mobile phone, and even download their favourite shows to listen to on MP3 players whilst driving, working, or relaxing.

Feed your mind, change your life with O Books, The O Books radio programme carries interviews with most authors, sharing their wisdom on life, the universe and everything...e mail questions and co-create the show with O Books and myspiritradio.

Just visit **www.myspiritradio.com** for more information.

Torn Clouds

A time-slip novel of reincarnation and romance, threaded through with the myths and magic of ancient Egypt.

Judy Hall

This is a great novel. It has suspense, drama, coincidence, and an extra helping of intrigue. I would recommend this literary marvel to anyone drawn to the magic, mystery and exotic elegance known as Egypt.
Planet Starz
1903816807 400pp **£9.99 $14.95**

The Art of Being Psychic

The power to free the artist within

June Elleni-Laine

A brilliant book for anyone wishing to develop their intuition, creativity and psychic ability. It is truly wonderful, one of the best books on psychic development that I have read. I have no hesitation in recommending this book, a must for every bookshelf. **Suzanna McInerney**, former President, College of Psychic Studies
1905047541 160pp **£12.99 $24.95**

Journey Home

A true story of time and inter-dimensional travel

Tonika Rinar

2nd printing
A lifeline that has been tossed out from the universe to help tether those lost in the wake of recent world events. If you are willing to open your mind,

Tonika will take you on a journey home, to a place that shines bright within each of us...... all you have to do is reach for it. **Amazon**
1905047002 272pp **£11.99 $16.95**

Spirit Release
A practical handbook
Sue Allen

A comprehensive and definitive guide to psychic attack, curses, witchcraft, spirit attachment, possession, soul retrieval, haunting, soul rescue, deliverance and exorcism, and more. This book is the most comprehensive I have seen on the subject of spirit release. This book is a must for anyone working and dealing with people. **Becky Walsh**, presenter of The Psychic Show on LBC
1846940338 256pp **£11.99 $24.95**

Spiritwalking
Poppy Palin

Drawing together the wild craft of the shamanic practitioner and the wise counsel of the medium or psychic, Spiritwalking takes the reader through a practical course in becoming an effective, empathic spiritwalker. In an era blighted by professional mystics, Poppy Palin is the real thing. You can trust her - and what she writes - completely. **Alan Richardson**, author of *The Inner Guide to Egypt and others*
1846940311 320pp **£11.99 $24.95**

Back to the Truth
5,000 years of Advaita
Dennis Waite

A wonderful book. Encyclopedic in nature, and destined to become a classic. **James Braha**

Absolutely brilliant...an ease of writing with a water-tight argument outlining the great universal truths. This book will become a modern classic. A milestone in the history of Advaita. **Paula Marvelly**
1905047614 500pp **£19.95 $29.95**

Beyond Photography
Encounters with orbs, angels and mysterious light forms
Katie Hall and John Pickering

The authors invite you to join them on a fascinating quest; a voyage of discovery into the nature of a phenomenon, manifestations of which are shown as being historical and global as well as contemporary and intently personal.

At journey's end you may find yourself a believer, a doubter or simply an intrigued wonderer... Whatever the outcome, the process of journeying is likely prove provocative and stimulating and - as with the mysterious images fleetingly captured by the authors' cameras - inspiring and poten- tially enlightening. **Brian Sibley**, author and broadcaster.
1905047908 272pp 50 b/w photos +8pp colour insert **£12.99 $24.95**

Don't Get MAD Get Wise
Why no one ever makes you angry, ever!
Mike George

There is a journey we all need to make, from anger, to peace, to forgiveness. Anger always destroys, peace always restores, and forgiveness always heals. This explains the journey, the steps you can take to make it happen for you.
1905047827 160pp **£7.99 $14.95**

IF You Fall...
It's a new beginning
Karen Darke

Karen Darke's story is about the indomitability of spirit, from one of life's cruel vagaries of fortune to what is insight and inspiration. She has overcome the limitations of paralysis and discovered a life of challenge and adventure that many of us only dream about. It is all about the mind, the spirit and the desire that some of us find, but which all of us possess.
Joe Simpson, mountaineer and author of *Touching the Void*
1905047886 240pp **£9.99 $19.95**

Love, Healing and Happiness
Spiritual wisdom for a post-secular era
Larry Culliford

This will become a classic book on spirituality. It is immensely practical and grounded. It mirrors the author's compassion and lays the foundation for a higher understanding of human suffering and hope. **Reinhard Kowalski,** Consultant Clinical Psychologist
1905047916 304pp **£10.99 $19.95**

A Map to God
Awakening Spiritual Integrity
Susie Anthony

This describes an ancient hermetic pathway, representing a golden thread running through many traditions, which offers all we need to understand and do to actually become our best selves.
1846940443 260pp **£10.99 $21.95**

Punk Science
Inside the mind of God
Manjir Samanta-Laughton

Wow! Punk Science is an extraordinary journey from the microcosm of the atom to the macrocosm of the Universe and all stops in between. Manjir Samanta-Laughton's synthesis of cosmology and consciousness is sheer genius. It is elegant, simple and, as an added bonus, makes great reading.
Dr Bruce H. Lipton, author of *The Biology of Belief*
1905047932 320pp £12.95 $22.95

Rosslyn Revealed
A secret library in stone
Alan Butler

Rosslyn Revealed gets to the bottom of the mystery of the chapel featured in the Da Vinci Code. The results of a lifetime of careful research and study demonstrate that truth really is stranger than fiction; a library of philosophical ideas and mystery rites, that were heresy in their time, have been disguised in the extraordinarily elaborate stone carvings.
1905047924 260pp b/w + colour illustrations **£19.95 $29.95** cl

The Way of Thomas
Nine Insights for Enlightened Living from the Secret Sayings of Jesus
John R. Mabry

What is the real story of early Christianity? Can we find a Jesus that is relevant as a spiritual guide for people today?

These and many other questions are addressed in this popular presentation of the teachings of this mystical Christian text. Includes a reader-friendly version of the gospel.
1846940303 196pp **£10.99 $19.95**

The Way Things Are
A Living Approach to Buddhism
Lama Ole Nydahl

An up-to-date and revised edition of a seminal work in the Diamond Way Buddhist tradition (three times the original length), that makes the timeless wisdom of Buddhism accessible to western audiences. Lama Ole has established more than 450 centres in 43 countries.
1846940427 240pp **£9.99 $19.95**

The 7 Ahas! of Highly Enlightened Souls
How to free yourself from ALL forms of stress
Mike George

7th printing
A very profound, self empowering book. Each page bursting with wisdom and insight. One you will need to read and reread over and over again! Paradigm Shift. I totally love this book, a wonderful nugget of inspiration.
PlanetStarz
1903816319 128pp 190/135mm **£5.99 $11.95**

God Calling
A Devotional Diary
A. J. Russell

46th printing
"When supply seems to have failed, you must know that it has not done so. But you must look around to see what you can give away. Give away something." One of the best-selling devotional books of all time, with over 6 million copies sold.
1905047428 280pp 135/95mm **£7.99** cl.
US rights sold

The Goddess, the Grail and the Lodge
The Da Vinci code and the real origins of religion
Alan Butler

5th printing

This book rings through with the integrity of sharing time-honoured revelations. As a historical detective, following a golden thread from the great Megalithic cultures, Alan Butler vividly presents a compelling picture of the fight for life of a great secret and one that we simply can't afford to ignore.
Lynn Picknett & Clive Prince
1903816696 360pp 230/152mm **£12.99 $19.95**

The Heart of Tantric Sex
A unique guide to love and sexual fulfilment
Diana Richardson

3rd printing

The art of keeping love fresh and new long after the honeymoon is over. Tantra for modern Western lovers adapted in a practical, refreshing and sympathetic way.

One of the most revolutionary books on sexuality ever written. **Ruth Ostrow**, News Ltd.
1903816378 256pp **£9.99 $14.95**

I Am With You
The best-selling modern inspirational classic
John Woolley

14th printing hardback
Will bring peace and consolation to all who read it. **Cardinal Cormac Murphy-O'Connor**
0853053413 280pp 150x100mm **£9.99** cl 4th printing paperback

1903816998 280pp 150/100mm **£6.99 $12.95**

In the Light of Meditation
The art and practice of meditation in 10 lessons
Mike George

2nd printing

A classy book. A gentle yet satisfying pace and is beautifully illustrated. Complete with a CD or guided meditation commentaries, this is a true gem among meditation guides. **Brainwave**

  In-depth approach, accessible and clearly written, a convincing map of the overall territory and a practical path for the journey. **The Light**
1903816610 224pp 235/165mm full colour throughout +CD **£11.99 $19.95**

The Instant Astrologer
A revolutionary new book and software package for the astrological seeker
Lyn Birkbeck

2nd printing

The brilliant Lyn Birkbeck's new book and CD package, The Instant Astrologer, combines modern technology and the wisdom of the ancients, creating an invitation to enlightenment for the masses, just when we need it most! **Astrologer Jenny Lynch**, Host of NYC's StarPower Astrology Television Show
1903816491 628pp full colour throughout with CD ROM 240/180
£39 $69 cl

Is There An Afterlife?

A comprehensive overview of the evidence, from east and west

David Fontana

2nd printing

An extensive, authoritative and detailed survey of the best of the evidence supporting survival after death. It will surely become a classic not only of parapsychology literature in general but also of survival literature in particular. **Universalist**

1903816904 496pp 230/153mm **£14.99 $24.95**

The Reiki Sourcebook

Bronwen and Frans Stiene

5th printing

It captures everything a Reiki practitioner will ever need to know about the ancient art. This book is hailed by most Reiki professionals as the best guide to Reiki. For an average reader, it's also highly enjoyable and a good way to learn to understand Buddhism, therapy and healing. **Michelle Bakar**, Beauty magazine

1903816556 384pp **£12.99 $19.95**